Acting
Beautifully

SUNY series in Psychoanalysis and Culture

Henry Sussman, editor

Acting
Beautifully

Henry James and the
Ethical Aesthetic

Sigi Jöttkandt

State University of New York Press

Cover design by Bernd Uhlig

Uitgegeven met steun van de Universitaire Stichting van België

Published by
State University of New York Press, Albany

© 2005 State University of New York

All rights reserved

Printed in the United States of America

No part of this book may be used or reproduced in any manner whatsoever
without written permission. No part of this book may be stored in a retrieval system
or transmitted in any form or by any means including electronic, electrostatic,
magnetic tape, mechanical, photocopying, recording, or otherwise
without the prior permission in writing of the publisher.

For information, address State University of New York Press,
194 Washington Avenue, Suite 305, Albany, NY 12210-2384

Production by Michael Haggett
Marketing by Anne M. Valentine

Library of Congress Cataloging-in-Publication Data

Jottkandt, Sigi, 1965–
     Acting beautifully : Henry James and the ethical aesthetic / Sigi Jottkandt.
          p. cm. — (SUNY series in psychoanalysis and culture)
     Includes bibliographical references and index.
     ISBN 0-7914-6557-8 (hc : acid-free paper)
     1. James, Henry, 1843–1916—Criticism and interpretation. 2. Didactic fiction,
American—History and criticism. 3. James, Henry, 1843–1916—Aesthetics. 4. James,
Henry, 1843–1916—Ethics. 5. Conduct of life in literature. 6. Ethics in literature. I. Title.
II. Series.

PS2124.J87 2005
813'.4—dc22

                                                                2004060828

For my mothers

Contents

List of Tables   ix

Preface   xi

1   Portrait of an Act: Representation and Ethics in
The Portrait of a Lady   1

2   "A Poor Girl with Her Rent to Pay": *The Wings of the Dove*   43

3   Lighting a Candle to Infinity: "The Altar of the Dead"   99

Notes   147

Works Cited   165

Index   173

List of Tables

Table 1. Lacan's Formulas of Sexuation   135

Preface

It occurs to me that my title may seem a little misleading once one realizes that my subject implicitly deals at least as much with Lacan as it does with James. My decision to leave Lacan out, however, comes not so much out of a furtive desire to deceive the reader as from an intent to emphasize how the psychoanalytic concepts I will be dealing with here make their appearance primarily in and through the terms by which they appear in the novels and short stories of Henry James. The non-Lacanian reader can immediately breathe more easily, knowing that in what follows very little direct reference will be made to Lacanian psychoanalysis, with its notoriously difficult formulations, and such a reader may well be advised to skip this Preface altogether and begin with the James. However, given their deliberate "burial" within the main body of the text, I thought it might be worthwhile to outline briefly the psychoanalytic concepts explored in this discussion of three acts in Henry James.

First to be explained is the concept of the act in Lacan. In simplest terms, an act is an ethical action: an action made in accordance with the ethical demand placed on us by an encounter with what Lacan calls the Real. Here the act is to be distinguished from another Lacanian concept, the *passage à l'acte*, which occurs when the subject, confronted with a certain impasse within its fantasmatic structure, "jumps" out of its sustaining fantasy. Although, depending on its circumstances, the *passage à l'acte* may also on occasion constitute an ethical act, the act as I am using the term has a broader scope and, as we will see in what follows, can take a variety of different forms. What primarily differentiates the act from the *passage à l'acte* is the fundamental transformation of the subject's subjective structure that an act entails. Where the *passage à l'acte* remains tied to some extent to the fantasmatic scenario sustained by the Other's desire, the act occasions the total reorganization of the relation between the subject and the Other that Lacan calls traversing the fantasy.[1]

The ethical act, then, amounts to a creative solution to the problem of how to give phenomenal expression to something within our representational system that can have no phenomenal form known, in Lacanese, as the Real. Ethics, for Lacan, revolves around how we manage to remain faithful to this representational impossibility that lies at the heart of our experience, whether our fidelity is expressed through various Symbolic mediations, as I explore them in the first two chapters, or, as we will see in the final chapter, through a direct, that is, unmediated relation to the Real itself—as impossible and paradoxical as that may sound. The first option describes an ethics based around the desiring formations, representing primarily an ethics of the Symbolic as detailed in Lacan's seminar on *Ethics*, while the second represents an ethics established on the Real of the drives as elaborated in the later *Encore* Seminar of 1972–1973. But although this narrative trajectory might therefore imply a teleology to Lacan's ethical thought, as it is sometimes, and I think a little misleadingly, held—that is, as representing a positively valorized ethical shift from desire to drive—it is important to remember, as we will see in greater detail in the final chapter, that these two ethical modalities represent simply the two contrary yet commensurately ethical outcomes of the primordial, foundational choice that first delivered us into our subjective condition as sexed beings.[2]

The main intent of this work is to allow Henry James to *symptomatize*, that is, to give some form of body to these two aspects of Lacanian ethics. But in the process, as it should be clear from this formulation, what James additionally contributes to the psychoanalytic discussion is to confirm the inseparability of aesthetics from Lacanian ethics. Filtering the Lacanian concepts through James helps to bring to light a certain submerged aesthetic narrative present in the psychoanalytic invocation of the ethical act. My feeling is that this fundamentally *aesthetic* dimension of psychoanalytic ethical subjectivity is largely being overlooked in the recent drive to identify a Cartesian origin for the Lacanian subject as the subject of science.[3] This book is an attempt to rectify this. Here I identify and advance a specifically ethical role for the aesthetic as I see it indicated in psychoanalytic discourse.

Accordingly, in the following I present three acts by three heroines in James that I determine to be ethical in the Lacanian senses. Each of the three acts I outline has this one thing in common: they separately represent a singular expression of fidelity to the impossibility encountered in the realm of experience that fundamentally transforms not only the characters' own subjective constitutions but also that of the world in which they live. In every case, we will see how the James heroine explicitly calls on the aesthetic in order to perform her act. When, at the end of *The Portrait of a Lady*, Isabel chooses to return to Osmond; when similarly, in *The Wings of the Dove*, Milly sacrifices her life to prevent knowledge of Kate and Densher's engagement from getting out; and when, in the short story "The Altar of the Dead," James's unnamed woman first categorically insists on and then reverses her demand that Stransom light the missing candle for Hague, each performs an aesthetic feat that meets the conditions of the Lacanian ethical act. Let us look briefly at the material covered.

The first chapter addresses the foundational psychoanalytic narrative of subject-formation that Freud called the *Neurosenwahl*, the "choice of neurosis." This idea involves the paradoxical notion that as subjects we primordially chose the way we desire. Ethics, for both Freud and Lacan, revolves around the way this original choice is attested to in our lives: how we take responsibility for it and remain faithful to it. What makes this idea paradoxical of course is the fact that this first, original choice can never be represented within our spatial-temporal, or as Kant would say, phenomenal system. We can never point to any specific moment in time when we made this choice, but, as Kierkegaard observes in his discussion of a similar idea in *Either/Or*, the fact that we have the possibility of making any choices at all attests to the fact of this choice as having already been made. As Kierkegaard puts it: "the original choice is forever present in every succeeding choice."[4] What Kierkegaard makes clear with this remark is the way every ethical choice represents a simultaneous fidelity to the original choice through which all succeeding choices first became available to us. While Freud tropes this original decision in terms of *Ur-Verdrängung*, primary repression, in James's *The Portrait of a Lady* it takes the form of what Lacan calls a "forced choice."

Isabel's controversial decision to return to Osmond at the end of the novel has long vexed critics. But the specifically ethical dimensions of this choice become evident once we understand it as occurring within a very similar structure to that of the *Neurosenwahl*. While many critics continue to read the novel through the peripatetic narrative structure of the *Bildungsroman*, in my first chapter I show how the logic and ethics of Isabel's final decision begins to make sense only once we understand it through the psychoanalytic concept of repetition. When Isabel returns to Osmond, I submit, she acts not out of any of the pathological considerations variously proposed by critics of this novel but, rather, simply according to the moral law that for Kant gives us practical knowledge of our noumenal freedom. As such, her act entails the paradoxical attempt to phenomenalize something that is strictly speaking impossible to represent: the Idea of free causality. Because, as an Idea of reason, free causality cannot be represented—and because, I argue, James, like Kant, rejects the Schillerian aesthetic solution represented in the novel by Osmond and, more generally, in the narrative structure of the *Bildungsroman* itself—the only means available to Isabel for representing this impossibility is through the *aegis* of a repetition: the repetition through which, in choosing Osmond again, Isabel testifies and maintains her fidelity to the original freedom with which she first chose to choose.

Through a transposition of the psychoanalytic terminology into the philosophical dialectic of freedom and determination, James's novel helps us to see what is really at stake in the psychoanalytic narrative of ethical subjectivity, namely, the radical philosophical, ethical, and political potential of transcendental freedom. But, significantly, what James additionally draws attention to in the psychoanalytic narrative is the peculiarly *aesthetic* nature of the psychoanalytical ethical act. Returning to Osmond, Isabel's ethical choice is shown to be the practical expression—the putting into action—of her habitual mode of aesthetic perception, troped in the novel as synecdoche: Isabel's persistent error of taking the part for the whole. This is a mode of perception that bears striking similarities to how Kant describes the aesthetic or reflective judgment, which similarly manages to generate a conceptual whole out of a particular intuition. Hence what James helps us to identify in *The Portrait of a Lady* are certain formal parallels between the Lacanian ethical and Kantian aesthetic judgments, both of which originate from and defend the incompleteness of our knowledge, troped by psychoanalysis as the unconscious.

It will quickly become clear that the concept of the aesthetic I am elaborating here is markedly different from its traditional reconciliatory modulation, long critiqued by Paul De Man as a dubious and ethically suspect means for reconciling the two irreparably divided realms of nature and freedom (or, in De Man's terms, a phenomenal and a linguistic consciousness). In this account, the aesthetic serves rather a different function, namely, that of preventing such a synthesis from ever occurring. In the second chapter, on *The Wings of the Dove*, I develop this obstructive, inhibiting quality that I retrieve from Kant's account of beauty to argue that in this novel the aesthetic acts as a form of protection against the threat of total symbolic determination posed to Milly Theale by her apotheosis. Here, the earlier questions of freedom and determination become transposed into the linguistic and representational concerns that haunt the psychoanalytic discourse of hysteria. I suggest that by understanding Milly's illness as an hysterical episode, we are better placed to comprehend what I see as the specifically ethical dimension of her final, aesthetic death in Venice. James's contribution to the psychoanalytic perspective is thus not simply to highlight the aesthetic dimensions of hysteria but, more crucially, to help us to reappraise the centrality of beauty in the psychoanalytic ethics of desire. Freud of course gestures toward the aesthetic character of the hysterical neurosis in *Totem and Taboo* where he observes how hysteria might be thought of as "a caricature of a work of art," while in his famous account of the Sophocles' play, Lacan explicitly names Antigone's beauty as constituting a protective barrier against the destruction known in his later work as the Real.[5] It is James, however, who provides the most tangible presentation the aesthetic's ethical province.

My aims in this second chapter, then, are twofold. First, I show how Milly's hysterical solution represents an answer to the problem of representation, long noted by James critics as one of the central concerns of *The Wings of the Dove*. Somewhat differently from most clinical psychoanalytic perspectives perhaps, here I argue that hysteria *itself* constitutes an ethical stance with regard to the unrepresentable, with important implications for the way we understand Milly's final act and, ultimately, the ethical dimensions of this novel. But second, this chapter advances my central contention with respect to the ethical dimensions of beauty. I suggest that beauty is nothing less than the paradigmatic case of hysteria— hysteria's *Ur*-narrative—enabling us to appreciate how a primordial aesthetic experience lies at the heart of the psychoanalytic "ethics of desire."

The final chapter returns to the question of ethical choice and judgment, only to trope it this time through the permanently vexed question of sexual difference that some recent psychoanalytic critics, notably Joan Copjec, have begun to reassess under the terms of a universal, that is, nonhistoricizable, ethic. Returning to an hypothesized moment prior even to the primordial choice of neurosis discussed in chapter 1, here I suggest that the concept of a foundational sexual "choice" instrumental in the creation of both masculine and feminine subjective identities can be given further specificity and contemporary critical relevance by relating it to one of contemporary theory's interminable bugbears: the question of whether deconstruction, specifically here in its De Manian form, is an ethical discourse.

Accordingly, in this chapter I take up the De Manian critique of the aesthetic as it is represented by Andzrej Warminski whose reading of James's short story, "The Altar of the Dead," provides a tour de force in De Manian deconstructive reading. I demonstrate how, its trenchant critique of aesthetic ideology notwithstanding, deconstruction itself epitomizes an aesthetic discourse. As it should be clear from my previous chapters, this is far from being a negative charge and, in fact, I go on to show how an ethic of beauty much like what I described in the previous chapter characterizes the deconstructive project, at least as represented by De Man and his followers. I suggest that the repetition compulsion of deconstruction, manifested in its endless productions of extraordinarily beautiful and inventive but ultimately repetitive rhetorical readings, represents a structure of deferral very like what I identified as Milly's hysterical/aesthetic solution. Such an identification then makes it possible to diagnose the deconstructive project as a hysterical discourse, designed to maintain a certain sustaining distance from what Lacan calls the Real—the unrepresentable excessive horror/enjoyment that underpins the symbolic order but for which deconstruction inevitably, for very specific structural reasons that I outline, must fail to possess a concept.

But just as important, as I suggested, this analysis of deconstruction's neurotic structure finally helps us put to rest the enduring question of whether or not there is such a thing as an ethics of deconstruction. I show that indeed there is, but that this ethic is not where deconstruction imagines it to be. What my analysis enables us to see is the specificity of where the deconstructive ethic lies with regard to what Lacan, in his *Encore Seminar*, calls the structures of sexuation. As countless female graduate students have long intuited but without quite knowing why, deconstruction is a masculine discourse, and therefore possesses a masculine ethic; deconstruction inhabits the masculine side of the Lacanian formulas of sexuation. As such, its ethics are founded on (the repression of) precisely the kind of limit signifier on which it accuses psychoanalysis of being too overly cathected, namely, the phallus. I show how it is the primordial repression of this signifier, around which its entire hysterical, that is, desiring discursive structure is subsequently built, that represents deconstruction's fundamental fantasy, its primordial *ethical* choice.

A portion of chapter 1 first appeared in *The Henry James Review*. I thank the Johns Hopkins University Press for permission to reprint it. Let me also take this opportunity to thank several individuals whose careful reading and support was crucial in the early stages of this writing: Henry

Sussman, Joan Copjec, Rodolphe Gasché, and, more recently, J. Hillis
Miller, Gert Buelens, Ortwin de Graef, and Paul Armstrong. Peter Otto
deserves special mention as well. I thank James Peltz for his support of
this project and Laura Glenn for her help in preparing the manuscript.
David Odell knows what I cannot say, namely, how much I owe him for
innumerable things, including his tremendous help with the mathematical argument in the final chapter. My deepest debt is to David Ottina,
whose unwavering support continues to manifest itself in a vigilant, steadfast, *ethical* resistance to the truth of psychoanalysis.

SIGI JÖTTKANDT
GHENT, BELGIUM

1

Portrait of an Act

Representation and Ethics in
The Portrait of a Lady

Few of James's novels have generated as much reader frustration as *The Portrait of a Lady*. While Isabel's final decision to return to Osmond famously had such supportive contemporary readers as Grace Norton confessing to having thrown the book across the room in vexation, our collective irritation today at what seems like James's distinctly perverse refusal to allow us a satisfying narrative ending manifests itself only slightly less hysterically in the growing plethora of competing critical interpretations seeking to explain—and thereby in part to mitigate—Isabel's controversial decision. Leaving aside for the moment certain formal similarities that will be discussed later on, my suggestion will be that it is not so much perversion on James's part but, rather, his attempt to represent an ethical act that leads him to resolve the novel in this contentious way.

Granted, a concern with the ethical dimension of Isabel's story is nothing new. We find this expressed both thematically—few other James characters, after all, are as fascinated with the unfolding of their ethical development as Isabel Archer,—and in its encircling critical interpretations where the novel has been understood for the most part in terms of a narrative of aesthetic/ethical education: as a female *Bildungsroman*. For a significant number of critics, Isabel's final decision to return to Osmond is best comprehended as the result of an ethical widening of perspective produced by her experience of suffering that finally enables her to integrate herself more fully into the communal body and take up a socially responsible role as Pansy's mother. But even when critics trope Isabel's return rather more negatively on the ethical spectrum—Dorothea Krook, for example, for whom Isabel's return is discovered to result from her sexual fear of Goodwood—the prevailing tendency in the reception of *The Portrait of a Lady* has been to try to produce a convincing *reason* for the interminably vexed question of why it is that Isabel returns to the "house of suffocation."[1]

Given our ongoing failure to achieve critical consensus through such an approach, I propose that it is time now to head in the opposite direction. Rather than advocating yet another empirical or, as Kant would say, pathological reason for Isabel's decision, I will suggest that it is only by understanding her choice as intentionally empty—that is, made deliberately without reference to empirical considerations—that we can begin to approach the specifically ethical dimension of her act.

Before exploring the ethical implications of her act, however, let us simply note the extent to which the question of ethics has reasserted itself in the past couple of decades. As Lawrence Buell puts it in his introduction to a special *PMLA* issue on Ethics and Literary Study, ethics is rapidly becoming "the paradigm-defining concept [of the 1990s] that textuality was for the 1970s and historicism for the 1980s."[2] The origins of this "revival of ethics" are many, of course, but we can identify some of the major moments marking this shift that can be loosely grouped as follows: the continuing interrogation of the political and ethical implications of deconstruction, as witnessed by Jacques Derrida's recent works addressing more overtly "political" concerns, as well as his dialogues on ethics with Emmanuel Levinas; the critical legacy of Michel Foucault, whose examination of the discursive constructions of subjectivity has been invaluable in reorienting criticism toward the critiques of ideology and the construction of the "other" that the studies of gender, class, and race have adopted as their mandate; the politicizing of psychoanalytic concepts by the so-called new Lacanians, such as Slavoj Žižek and Joan Copjec, and their concomitant focus of attention on Lacan's *Ethics* and *Encore* Seminars in formulating a concept of an "ethics of psychoanalysis."[3] What is common to each of these diverse critical practices is that they are all in one way or another concerned with critiquing what has come to be called the "metaphysics of presence," whose founding principle is the philosophical concept of identity. Thus Levinas's philosophical concern to found an ethics of alterity on the Other shares with more deliberately "politically" oriented theory an interest in finding ways of relating to otherness that do not involve the violent subsumption of difference to identity.

It is just such a concern that drives one of the more interesting recent readings of *The Portrait of a Lady*. For Jonathan Freedman, the novel tells the story of Isabel's aesthetic education, in the course of which she is led to reject what he calls Osmond's reifying "aesthetic vision" and to embrace a more "ethical" mode of "seeing" at the end of the novel.[4] Through recognizing the common nature of suffering, Freedman argues, Isabel asserts her own aesthetic vision, which grants her an "embeddedness in historical process, her own participation in the human community" (Freedman, 162). I want to briefly examine this essay because I believe it explicitly presents what is often only implicit in many of the critical responses that trace the novel's trajectory in terms of the narrative of ethical progress or *Bildung*. This is the notion that the aesthetic possesses a specifically ethical function insofar as it is empowered to reconcile social and epistemological antagonisms. The teleological narrative of *Bildung* is unthinkable without the help of a recuperative aesthetic capable of redeeming bad or damaged experience for a wider social gain.

Let us take a brief look at Freedman's argument in order to identify the features of the reconciling or "redemptive" aesthetic. Freedman divides the aestheticism in the novel between what he calls the bad "Osmondian" reifying aesthetic, characterized by a violent objectification of other people into works of art, and Isabel's "higher" form of aestheticism in chapter 42 where, in a state of heightened perception, she discovers the truth about her relationship with Osmond. This heightened state of perception, Freedman argues, is homologous with Walter Pater's conception of aesthesis whereby "a 'quickened, multiplied consciousness' comes into powerful visionary being" (Freedman 160).

Accordingly, for Freedman, Isabel's vision in this chapter represents a form of perception that is "structurally different" from the Osmondian perceptual paradigm, which seeks to force the objects of the world to serve as objects for "detached contemplation" (160). For here Isabel achieves a moment of vision "experienced in, of and for itself"—a vision which, while detaching her from the world of objects, nevertheless allows her to "understand the nature of that world" (160). Yet even this form of aesthetic vision is still implicated for Freedman in a negative, because potentially alienated, aestheticism. Such a vision, he argues, is open to the criticism that the transcendence achieved by consciousness alone effectively removes the self from the world, from contact with others, "from any possibility of action, indeed from history itself" (161). In its place, Freedman offers a third version of aestheticism that he says sidesteps this critique: riding on the Campagna a few chapters later, Isabel is struck by the "splendid sadness of the scene," which seems to reflect her own "personal sadness" (*PL* 431). Recognizing the ruins of Rome as a place of human suffering, Isabel comes to an understanding of her own share in that suffering. As Freedman puts it, "Isabel achieves at this moment a humanizing vision in which her individual 'sadness' and the sadness of the scene connect to form an image of commonality and community, not one of alienation and superiority" (Freedman 162). And such an aesthetic vision, Freedman asserts, possesses a certain ethical dimension to the extent that, through the uniting power of sympathy in suffering, it allows an encounter with others that respects their fundamental difference.

Perhaps now is the time to put my cards on the table and admit that I sympathize with Freedman's desire to rescue the aesthetic from the powerful critiques mounted against its oppressive mechanisms, not to mention its implication in the totalizations of systematic thought, discovered most tellingly in post-Kantian idealist philosophies and literary Romanticism. However, by answering Osmond's "malevolent" aestheticism with a vision of community and the commonality of human suffering, Freedman unwittingly participates in the very tropes of the totalizing aesthetic he seeks to circumvent. To permit Isabel to find a reflection of her own suffering in nature is to call on the most powerful master trope of the aestheticizing vision, the metaphor that enables the reconciliation of two irreparably severed worlds. It is to subscribe to the idea that a specular relation exists between the sensible and supersensible realms of nature and of mind (or Spirit). Metaphorizing the external world as a reflection of her own consciousness, Isabel is able to bridge Kant's "immeasurable gulf" between the laws of nature and human freedom. But in order to do so, she must succumb to the violence of a reflective paradigm that, enabling one to see likeness in and through the fractures of difference, implicitly subsumes otherness beneath an imperial Identity. In Freedman's revised aesthetic, Isabel achieves her vision but only at the cost of the very ethical stance it was intended to promote (the respect for otherness). Tellingly, then, Freedman ends his essay with a gesture that confirms his allegiance to the traditional "aesthetic of redemption."[5] Offering James's style as a paradigmatic example of the redeemed, or "ethicized" aesthetic, Freedman understands the novel's refusal of closure—the unanswered question of why Isabel returns to Osmond—as the author's attempt to allow his characters a measure of their own autonomy without being "enmeshed" by the author's controlling vision. But when he argues that

the effect of reading the novel is to give us the vaguely disquieting experience of seeing a "painted picture move" (Freedman 163), Freedman
resorts to what is perhaps the most grandiose (and ethically suspect) of all
of the aesthetic fictions that purport to bridge the distance between the
world and art, namely, Pygmalion's gesture of bringing the aesthetic
object to life.

Freedman's argument is interesting mainly because I find it emblematic of this recent "ethical" trend in literary criticism that turns on the
philosophical problem of intersubjectivity, that is, on the question of how
to relate to otherness in a nontotalizing way.[6] What is useful about it is
the way it highlights what may often otherwise be obscured in many of
these attempts to conceive of a nonviolent relation toward the other,
namely, an unacknowledged dependence on aesthetic tropes such as
reflection and recuperation which, if left unexamined, may work against
the ethical solutions being sought after. I believe Freedman is right to ori-
ent the question of ethics toward the aesthetic realm. James's novel, however, provides a cautionary tale against the dangers of mistaking aesthetics for ethics.

I

For James, as for many of his contemporaries, the problem of ethics begins
with the question of representation. Since at least as far back as the Kantian revolution, ethics has seen itself relegated to the realm of the noumenal, remaining with the other Ideas of reason (God, the thing in-itself)
strictly unrepresentable. And while we have no evidence of the same level
of direct interest in speculative philosophy as his brother William, James
nevertheless cannot fail to have been at least mildly familiar with these
basic tenets of Kantian thought as they came to him filtered through the
intellectual tradition of mid-nineteenth-century thought and letters.[7] The
question of how an ethical act can be represented must thus form the
nucleus of this discussion of Jamesian ethics, as indeed it correspondingly
also makes up one of the central thematic concerns not only of *The Portrait of a Lady* but also, as we will see, of *The Wings of the Dove* and "The
Altar of Dead." In Isabel's case, however, the question is not so much how
to make these representations, but rather how to *read* the preexisting ones
in which she already finds herself. Let us begin, then, with this question as
it first confronts our heroine on her arrival in Europe. Discovered moping

after her father's death in Albany, Isabel is brought to Europe by her Aunt Lydia to see what might be made of her. Arriving at her uncle's ancient English seat of Gardencourt—whose name already denotes the uneasy marriage of nature and culture that we will investigate as being forged by representational language—Isabel, the "free keen girl," must now learn to navigate her way through a society far more richly layered with signification than she has been accustomed to in America. The question confronting Isabel, as many critics have already pointed out, is the question of how she should interpret these new representational complexes.

How, then, does Isabel read? It is now a critical commonplace to assert that Isabel's problem lies in her inability to distinguish between people's appearances and the reality behind them: that she is a naive reader of representations. After all, her terrible mistake in choosing Osmond results from her inability to see beyond the mask of his self-presentation. Reading synecdochically, Isabel finds herself unable to project beyond the part he shows her to a vision of the whole man. As Isabel later discovers,

> she had seen only half his nature then, as one saw the disk of the moon when it was partly masked by the shadow of the earth. She saw the full moon now—she saw the whole man. She had kept still, as it were, so that he should have a free field, and yet in spite of this she had mistaken a part for the whole. (*PL* 357)

But whether, in so doing, Isabel is guilty merely of a simple perceptual blindness or, more damningly, of what Moody calls her "grave moral blindness" resulting from her deliberate and willful refusal to see anything other than what she wants to see, there appears to be a fundamental disjunction between representation and reality that Isabel is, at least initially, unable or unwilling to perceive.[8]

At first sight, it seems that Isabel's problem is simply a naive confidence in the coincidence of signs and their meanings. Isabel's assertion that "she would be what she appeared, and she would appear what she was" (*PL* 54) lends credence to this picture of Isabel as an unsophisticated reader of representations who is unable to distinguish the difference between an inside and an outside; so much so, in fact, that she fancies she can judge books by their frontispieces, and people by the image that they project. Indeed as Elizabeth Sabiston points out, the novel colludes with this mode of seeing through a persistent metaphorical linkage between people and their houses, that is, with their visible social (and economic) representations.[9] Thus despite Isabel's protest to Madame Merle that it will not be for his house that she chooses a husband (*PL* 175), she refuses Warburton because she perceives that life at Lockleigh would imprison her in a social, territorial, political system in the same way that the house "locks up" its women, the Misses Molyneux. Caspar Goodwood is similarly incarcerating, as Osmond perceives with exquisite irony when he asks Isabel why she refused his suit: "It would have been an excellent thing" he muses, "like living under some tall belfry which would strike all the hours and make a queer vibration in the upper air" (*PL* 412). Similarly, Isabel's impaired view of Osmond is reflected in James's description of the Florentine villa house, which was a "rather blank-looking structure" (*PL* 195), wearing "more or less of that air of undervalued merit" that characterizes Osmond himself. It has a face like a mask, a "somewhat incommunicative character" with "heavy lids but no eyes; the house in reality looked another way" (*PL* 195).

Significantly, the power of these architectural metaphors derives from the way they work in the service of a mimetic representational paradigm that maintains that a visible, motivated connection exists between a person's inside essence and their outward appearance. Had Isabel only been better able to perceive this connection, this reading would argue—had she, that is, been able to read more subtly or "skeptically"—she would have refused Osmond on the same basis that she refuses Warburton and Goodwood. For she would have seen through his external guise and into the "whole man"; she would have understood that, like his house, he was looking at her "awry."

In either case, whether she reads naively or skeptically, both strategies share a founding assumption about the role of representation. This is the idea that the function of representation is to attempt to reflect (imitate on the basis of a visual resemblance) an already existing reality (Osmond's "true" nature). Hence mimesis contains certain inherent epistemological assumptions. It implicitly asserts the prior existence of a reality "out there," independent of the observer and the intentions of consciousness. Reading "mimetically" then, is to peel away the layers of representation in order to discover the truth behind it, to match the representation to the reality on the basis of a reflective relation. Signs may or may not be truthful, but the fundamental assumption is that their purpose is to represent a prior reality.

From this perspective, it is hard not follow those critics who fault Isabel's reading strategy, for hers seems only a particularly naive version

of the seemingly more "critical" stance that Isabel's detractors uphold as
a preferable mode of reading. For if Isabel could only read or "see" more
critically, they suggest—that is, beyond the "false" appearances or facades
of things—she would apprehend the truth of her situation, of the world,
of relations between people, and ultimately, the truth of representation
as an inherently untrustworthy mode. She must learn to see the reality of
things and of people, to penetrate the veil of representation in order to
see the essence behind appearances. Hence reading, for these critics,
becomes a process of *aletheia*, the discovery or, better, the unveiling of
prior truth.

The problem with such an epistemology of reading with regard to
Henry James, of course, is that truth is never a simple concept for this
writer whose narratives are typically much more concerned with the
unfolding dramas of a character's "seeing" and knowing than with the
peripeteias of plot (or, better, the plot's reversals are precisely moments of
vision rather than of action). Truth is never static in James but requires
the active, albeit subjective, participation of his characters to "fill out" its
reality. The very difficulty of delimiting some prior truth is extensively
thematized in his novels and short fiction, forming the narrative's central
problematic in texts such as *The Golden Bowl*, *What Maisie Knew*, "The
Beast in the Jungle," and "The Turn of the Screw" to name only a few of
his best-known fictions. So we should at least be alert to the dangers here
of oversimplifying James's dialectical understanding of the relation
between representation and reality.

In case this seems like an unnecessary, external philosophical problem
I am imposing on the novel, let us look again at the much-cited discussion between Isabel and Madame Merle where they quite deliberately
speculate on such "metaphysical" matters. At first sight, Merle appears to
advocate the naive perspective critics accuse Isabel of holding when she
asserts the existence of a seemingly necessary continuity between the self
and its representations. Merle lectures Isabel:

> "When you've lived as long as I you'll see that every human being has
> his shell and that you must take the shell into account. By the shell I
> mean the whole envelope of circumstances. There's no such thing as an
> isolated man or woman; we're each of us made up of some cluster of
> appurtenances. What shall we call our 'self'? Where does it begin?
> where does it end? It overflows into everything that belongs to us—and
> then it flows back again. I know a large part of myself is in the clothes
> I choose to wear. I've a great respect for *things*! One's self—for other

people—is one's expression of one's self; and one's house, one's furniture, one's garment, the books one reads, the company one keeps—these things are all expressive." (*PL* 175)

A closer look, however, shows that Merle's sense of self is no fixed or prior entity that finds expression in the representations of her famous "things." Rather, it is Isabel who clings to a concept of essential identity, and it is the representations that fail to represent her that she objects to. Isabel replies:

"I don't agree with you. I think just the other way. I don't know whether I succeed in expressing myself but I know that nothing else expresses me. Nothing that belongs to me is any measure of me; everything's on the contrary a limit, a barrier, and a perfectly arbitrary one. Certainly the clothes which, as you say, I choose to wear, don't express me; and heaven forbid they should! . . . My clothes may express the dressmaker, but they don't express me. To begin with, it's not my own choice that I wear them; they're imposed upon me by society." (*PL* 175)

Here we have not only two very different conceptions of self, but also different understandings of the way representation functions. For Isabel, one's self-representations in the form of one's clothes, houses, friends, and so on are unable to reflect what she holds to be her essential identity; indeed they inhibit her self's expression. She conceives of her self as a self-contained entity, existing prior to the structures of representation that she inhabits. Rejecting the "cluster of appurtenances" as arbitrary, for Isabel an adequate concept of representation would claim an essential relation between the self and its representational expression. It must represent the self in a nonarbitrary manner, reflecting her innermost self in a necessary relation.

Serena Merle, on the other hand, proposes a different view of the self and its relation to representation. For Merle, the self is a fluid concept, constituted by the very signifying representations that Isabel rejects as contingent. Accepting the arbitrary nature of signs, Merle puts them to work for herself, and understands their power for creating meanings. Where Isabel rebels against the limits of representation, seeking a more profound presentation of herself (although she is unable to say what this would be), Merle finds possibilities in those very limitations. Understanding the self as a product of representational structures, Merle is free to choose and select the meanings she finds useful. Thus Ralph is more astute than he realizes when he calls Madame Merle the "great round world herself" (*PL* 216). Not confined by a concept of essential selfhood, Merle can use the structures of representation to create her self and her world. If the result is a trifle artificial, this is because the self understood as a product of its representations has no need of the fantasy of spontaneity and naturalness that typifies the interiorized concept of subjecthood that Isabel favors: "If for Isabel [Madame Merle] had a fault it was that she was not natural [. . .] her nature had been too much overlaid by custom and her angles too much rubbed away. She had become too flexible, too useful, was too ripe and too final. She was in a word too perfectly the social animal that man and woman are supposed to have been intended to be" (*PL* 167).

I don't wish to place too much emphasis on this conversation, since of course the irony is that Serena Merle's position is merely one more stance she adopts in order to shield her "real" self from the scrutiny of others, that is, the fact that she is Pansy's mother. By the same token, despite Isabel's insistence on a stable, interiorized self, she undergoes the greatest transformation of all the characters in the novel. Nevertheless, this exchange is useful for articulating the two competing concepts of representation and their implicit epistemological positions at work in the novel. For here James presents *in nuce* the debate between two philosophical positions on representation which, as John Smith suggests, effectively comprise the history of philosophy.[10] The first is the idea that things-in-themselves can be known "in a universal, abstract and internal form which is independent of observer and context." The second is the idea that the truth "exists only in some mode of appearance, or representation-for-a-mind, whereby knowledge can consist only of myriad, necessarily incomplete, particular perspectives" (Smith 31). At issue in both of these positions is the question of determination, that is, where the ground of knowledge is to be situated. The first holds the ground in the object world. Here, the stakes of representation hinge on the success (or failure) of representation to accurately depict or reflect what is already given in nature. The second position asserts the priority of the structures of representation. This position has two facets; either it must authorize a concept of (auto-constituting) subjectivity as the grounding agent (where the structures of representation are understood as the structures of the perceiving consciousness). Or, like Merle, it abandons any concept of an autonomous subject in favor of a grounding in the nonintentional determinations of linguistic structures.

To assume, then, that Isabel's problem with reading entails a simple failure to match people's representations accurately with their underlying truth is thus to implicitly endorse a mimetic concept of representation whose philosophical implications are wide-ranging. As indicated, mimetic representation aims to accurately portray the object world but its paradox is that it has difficulty giving a "measure of commensurability" against which the representation can be gauged for accuracy (Smith 31). Furthermore, as Smith explains, this engages a vicious circle whereby every attempt to measure the accuracy of the representation would also have to be represented and therefore measured against another gauge, and so on to infinite regress (Smith 31). Mimetic representation must fail to depict the "truth" of its object, must always fall short, because like Isabel we can never be sure that the process of representing has adequately matched things as they are.

Here, then, is the paradox of mimetic representation: even while it attempts to reflect the reality of things as they are, mimesis forces us to confront the mediated nature of all representation. For as soon as we try to re-present an object, we are obliged to realize that there is no guarantee that the relation between the thing and its representation will match. There is no outside position, no neutral observation that can tell us whether we are successful. Epistemologically, this realization mirrors the dilemma of the Kantian subject confronted with an object world that is inherently unknowable as it is in-itself. What we see are "representations" of a world whose reality is forever inaccessible to our cognition. Ethically, this plants the subject firmly within the laws of the phenomenal world: construed as an "appearance" even to itself (as Isabel discovers when she flounders looking for an adequate "expression" of herself) the phenomenal subject finds itself determined by the empirical laws of nature. Actions performed by the (phenomenal) subject therefore take place according to nature's law of causality, which states that any action that takes place at a certain point in time is a necessary result of what existed in preceding time. And since the subject is unable to change what occurred in the past—as Kant puts it, "time past is no longer in my power"[11]—it follows that the subject's acts are acts of necessity—the results of prior causes—and not of freedom. They are acts, that is to say, determined by grounds not within the subject's power.

In James's time, the trope of irony seemed to offer a way out of this impasse of freedom and necessity that sentences the subject to a fatal determinism by its phenomenal nature.[12] Irony, after all, purports to take the subject out of time, or at least out of the temporality of mimetic representation by splitting the self, enabling it to see itself in two different places at the same time. As Hayden White observes, irony is essentially a trope of negation where "entities can be characterized by way of negating on the figurative level what is positively affirmed on the literal level."[13] In irony, the split opened by mimesis between subject and world becomes internalized as the split between two selves, empirical and linguistic. Irony's "subversive mimesis," in Alan Singer's words, appropriates the epistemological divide as an aspect of itself. Thus irony steps in where mimetic representation flounders, that is, by founding representation's "measure of commensurability" within its own reflective processes.

But by grounding knowledge in representational structures, irony presents its own epistemological and ethical dilemmas. For it either must assert a thoroughgoing idealism, where all representations are conceived as the product of a subject's self-activity; or, it is obliged to do away with the notion of a unified self altogether and with it, any concept of intentional subjective agency. This is because of irony's well-known tendency to reproduce, or to ironize itself in what Paul De Man calls "irony to the second power."[14] De Man explains how, while the temptation of irony is to construe the function of the reflected or "linguistic" self as one of assistance to the original or empirical self, in fact the structure of irony is such that it makes any return to the empirical world impossible. Irony's tendency to "gain momentum," to ironize itself, effectively severs the world of fiction from the empirical, foreclosing any return to the original self (Rhetoric 218). De Man explains,

> When we speak [. . .] of irony originating at the cost of the empirical self, the statement has to be taken seriously enough to be carried to the extreme: absolute irony is a consciousness of madness, itself the end of all consciousness; it is a consciousness of a non-consciousness, a reflection on madness from the inside of madness itself. (Rhetoric 216)

Wresting the subject from the determinations of nature, irony purports to free the subject from causal necessity by internalizing the gap between subject and world. But the resulting freedom is the freedom of utter lawlessness, since any ground on which to base an action is immediately annulled by the ironic gesture. Hence in the thoroughgoing freedom of the ironic consciousness we have no way of returning to a concept of subjective agency that requires at least a minimal ground in order to act. For in irony, each position is progressively negated in the madness of irony's self-annihilation.

The discourse of aesthetics was born precisely to address this seemingly intractable problem of the division in our being. As rational subjects, we can transcend the laws of nature and inhabit a world of intellectual freedom, but in order to act we must submit to the laws of the sensible world. Aesthetics surmises that there must be a way of mediating these two aspects of ourselves: either there is a rational basis to the sensible that will correspond to our rational nature, or there may be a sensible aspect to reason itself, a way of apprehending rationality directly through the senses. For Isabel, it is this second approach that initially seems to provide the ideal solution to her philosophical problem.

II

Let us begin by considering Dorothy Berkson's simple but incisive question: Why does Isabel marry Osmond?[15] Indeed, why does she marry at all, given the high value she places on her freedom? Critics have long noted how at the beginning of the novel, Isabel's freedom is largely conceived in negative terms. Isabel's peculiar vision of happiness—"A swift carriage, of a dark night, rattling with four horses over roads one cannot see" (*PL* 146)—gives body to this ideal of freedom as an ongoing, open horizon of as-yet unseen possibilites. Central to this ideal is the concept of choice. As Isabel tells her aunt, she wants to be free "so as to choose" (*PL* 67). But, as Donatella Izzo points out, because any one choice would close off future choices, her ideal of freedom seems essentially to be the freedom *not* to have to choose.[16] Despite Isabel's prodigious enthusiasm for "life" there is a strange passivity or inertia in this concept of freedom, a trait that leads some critics to argue that her much touted "independence" actually masks an overriding fear of the world.[17] Ralph makes a similar observation when he gently chides Isabel in his often quoted statement, "You want to see but not to feel" (*PL* 134).

Nevertheless, Isabel's decision to marry is heavily predicated on her understanding this decision as an act of freely willed choice. Indeed, this "single sacred act" (*PL* 386) of her life, the choice of mate, is so frequently couched in devotional terms that we understand her choice to have almost religious significance for her. Why should choice be so significant for her? It is because choice is the means by which Isabel believes she actualizes her freedom. Tellingly, then, when Isabel refuses Warburton's suit, she justifies it to herself on the grounds that he had offered her no opportunity to consciously choose:

> What she felt was not a great responsibility, a great difficulty of choice;
> it appeared to her there had been no choice in the question. She could-
> n't marry Lord Warburton; the idea failed to support any enlightened
> prejudice in favour of the free exploration of life that she had hitherto
> entertained or was now capable of entertaining. (*PL* 101)

Similarly, the deprivation of freedom Isabel famously feels in Goodwood's company can be equated with the inhibition of her continuing
right and ability to choose. Hence despite his protestations that he wants
to marry her in order to make her free—"It's to make you independent
that I want to marry you" (*PL* 142)—the kind of freedom he propounds
is precisely the opposite of what Isabel means. Goodwood imagines that
a woman's independence is to be found in marriage that can provide freedom from the social and economic constraints facing a young, unmarried
Victorian woman in society: "An unmarried woman—a girl of your age—
isn't independent. There are all sorts of things she can't do. She's ham-
pered at every step" (*PL* 143). Dorothy Berkson points out how for
Goodwood, freedom is assumed to be a "gift which he can bestow."[18] For
Isabel, however, the issue is not pragmatic but transcendental. It involves
an absolute freedom to judge and to choose her destiny, a freedom of
mind that she finds all too restricted in Goodwood's company: "it was
part of the influence that he had upon her that he seemed to deprive her
of the sense of freedom. There was a disagreeably strong push, a kind of
hardness of presence, in his way of rising before her" (*PL* 104–5). She
finds him unyielding in the pressure he exerts on her, pressing his suit like
a creditor assuring an economic obligation as Isabel's frequent metaphors
of debt imply: "there was something in having thus got rid of him that
was like the payment, for a stamped receipt, of some debt too long on her
mind" (*PL* 144). His presence, "the stubbornest fact she knew," only
serves to enforce her resolve "to avail herself of the things that helped her
to resist such an obligation" (*PL* 105). Simply put, he deprives her of her
freedom to choose.

Much of Osmond's appeal, in contrast, is in the way he personifies
the act of choice for Isabel. When, after her first visit to the Val d'Arno,
Isabel takes away the image of Osmond strolling on the terrace with
Pansy, the image appeals not just for its aesthetic value—for the Romantic "lowness of tone" and the "atmosphere of summer twilight" (*PL* 237)
that Freedman points out in his critique of Isabel's early aestheticizing
vision—but also, more importantly, because it presents Isabel with a tan-

gible image of a life dedicated to the continual act of selecting and choosing: the life of the connoisseur. Meditating on the image, Isabel recognizes how it "spoke of the kind of personal issue that touched her most nearly; of the choice between objects, subjects, contacts—what might she call them?—of a thin and those of a rich association" (*PL* 237). Isabel imagines that life with Osmond will be liberating rather than confining precisely because, epitomizing choice itself, he impresses her with a sense of expansion and possibility. Their life together would be a walk in the "open air of the world, indifferent to small considerations, caring only for truth and knowledge and believing that two intelligent people ought to look for them together and, whether they found them or not, find at least some happiness in the search" (*PL* 359).

At the beginning of the novel, then, Isabel's love of independence and liberty is characterized by what Paul Armstrong perspicaciously notes is an "essentially futural" notion of freedom.[19] Freedom, for Isabel, means inhabiting the state of possibility. This is a negative rather than positive concept of freedom, understood as an absence of limitation. Isabel believes she is free as long as there is nothing impinging on her continuing ability to choose, and her new inheritance comes to symbolize this concept of freedom. James tells us that, "[her] fortune [. . .] became to her mind a part of her better self; it gave her importance, gave her even, to her own imagination, a certain ideal beauty" (*PL* 193). Her fortune incarnates the ideal of choice: "She had never had a keener sense of freedom, of the absolute boldness and wantonness of liberty. [. . .] The world lay before her—she could do whatever she chose" (*PL* 272–73).

However, Isabel quickly comes to realize what Kierkegaard would consider the "spiritual sickness" attending her understanding of freedom conceived as boundless possibilities. For after the first deep thrill of inheriting the means for doing anything she wants wears off, Isabel takes to her traveling plans with almost a sense of desperation. Reflecting that having money gives her the means for "doing," she finds she has no idea what she wants to do, and chapter 31 finds her roaming restlessly around the Mediterranean basin. James has Madame Merle dryly observe how "even among the most classic sites, the scenes most calculated to suggest repose and reflection, a certain incoherence prevailed in her. Isabel travelled rapidly and recklessly; she was like a thirsty person draining cup after cup" (*PL* 274). After several months of such aimless movement, Isabel returns to Rome with a new sense of the value of limitation. James explains how, "[t]he desire for unlimited expansion had been succeeded in her soul by the sense that life was vacant without some private duty that might gather one's energies to a point" (*PL* 297). It is at this point that she decides to marry, a decision that Isabel believes will "[simplify] the situation at a stroke" (*PL* 297). For Isabel now believes she understands what Armstrong calls the paradox of freedom, namely, that one requires some limitation in order to be truly free. Freedom without boundaries, she discovers, is no freedom at all but rather a wearisome slavery to her immediate whims. By marrying Osmond, Isabel imagines she will expand rather than contract her freedom—duty will give her a vehicle through which to articulate her freedom.

In fact, Isabel has simply now learned the lesson Madame Merle was trying to impart earlier. As she rejected what she considered the arbitrary "conventions" of representational structures, Isabel nevertheless found herself unable to articulate what she imagines is her "essential" self: "I don't know whether I succeed in expressing myself but I know that nothing else expresses me" (*PL* 175). In a similar way, Isabel's much-touted "freedom" remains meaningless without some kind of stabilizing ground or duty that will contract one's "energies," impose some limitation on her as yet formless freedom. Otherwise, her freedom remains a purely abstract idea, without any actualization in the world. Discovering that she must accept representational structures in order to gain expression for her self, Isabel now also realizes that the promise of unbounded possibilities will remain unfulfilled as long as she refuses to make a choice. Isabel had wanted to be free in order to "see life" but she realizes "that one cannot do anything so general": "One must choose a corner and cultivate that" she explains to Ralph (*PL* 288), "one must marry a particular individual" (*PL* 293).

Isabel's choice of Osmond astonishes everyone except herself (and of course the two involved in the deception). But her choice makes perfect sense to Isabel for whom Osmond seems to embody precisely the perfect balance between necessity and freedom she seeks. Osmond, like Merle before him, strikes Isabel as succeeding in the delicate task of managing to retain "one's independence" in the face of the demands of social convention. They do so, not by rejecting necessity out of hand, but by embracing it. In their easy submission to the "language" of manners, Osmond and Merle appear to Isabel to expand the possibilities of self-expression: "To be so cultivated and civilised, so wise and so easy, and still make so light of it—that was really to be a great lady, especially when one so carried and presented one's self" (*PL* 166), a trait Isabel resolves to try to emulate when she finds herself secretly exclaiming "I should like awfully to be *so*" (*PL* 165). Isabel finds Osmond the perfect counterpart to Merle's "greatness." His very fastidiousness in observing social conventions appears to put him beyond them, enabling him to achieve the appearance of exquisite naturalness: "Everything he did was *pose—pose* so subtly considered that if one were not on the lookout one mistook it for impulse" (*PL* 331). What makes Osmond so attractive to Isabel is that he appears to have found the solution to her philosophical dilemma. Rather than rejecting the limitations of (linguistic, social) structures, Osmond *identifies* with them, confiding to Isabel, "I'm not conventional: I'm convention itself" (*PL* 265). But in this way, through the paradoxical embrace of limitation, he appears to carve out a space of originality and freedom within the social network he inhabits. And, as Paul Armstrong points out, this is precisely the promise that the aesthetic holds out. Art, he explains, especially in the formal rigors of poetry, is a unique example of how the free adoption of limitation has the paradoxical effect of opening up the possibilities of expression (Armstrong 114).

In her portentous conversation with Ralph in chapter 34, Isabel lists her various reasons for choosing Osmond. Where Ralph sees only a "small," "narrow," "selfish," "sterile dilettante" (*PL* 291–92), Isabel finds Osmond's "being so independent, so individual" as a sign of his "noble nature" (*PL* 290). Deliberately misunderstanding Ralph's point about Osmond's "smallness," Isabel finds that quality to speak of his humility and indifference to the adulation of the world. Listing his qualities negatively, Isabel finds Osmond to have "no property, no title, no honours, no houses, nor lands, nor position, nor reputation, nor brilliant belongings of any sort" (*PL* 293). But despite the "smallness" of his possessions and position in the world, Isabel sees him inhabiting a far larger, richer, freer world than anyone she has yet met. What is it that gives Isabel this impression? It is because she makes the error of conflating his superior aesthetic sense with a superior morality. Why does she make this mistake?

As a fervent reader of German philosophy prior to her arrival in Europe, Isabel may well have had at least a passing acquaintance with the works of Friedrich Schiller whose popularization of Kant in his *Letters on the Aesthetic Education of Man* finds in beauty a means for reconciling humankind's conflicting sensuous and spiritual impulses. Extending the Königsberg philosopher's claim that beauty is a symbol of the morally good, Schiller's contribution to aesthetic theory is to permit Kant's unrepresentable or noumenal Idea of freedom to acquire phenomenal form in the shape of an ethical community founded on an appreciation of beauty.

Through acquiring a taste for beauty, Schiller surmises, one is led from
the state of nature to the state of freedom that for both philosophers is
possible only through morality. Yet for Schiller such morality is realized
not through the harsh imposition of strict laws but, more gently and effi-
ciently (or, as we might say now, "ideologically"), through desire. Seeing
nature in the free but lawful state that is beauty, we *want* to shed our natural mode as primarily sensuous creatures and similarly enter into the
bound condition of morality.

It is worth noting that this is precisely the promise of the concept of
Bildung which, as Lacoue-Labarthe and Nancy have shown in their mon-
umental study *The Literary Absolute,* is similarly implicated in bridging
two irreconcilable realms.[20] Through the process of *Bildung* or self-formation, the individual merges with universal humanity by becoming an
exemplary person, a tutelary figure whose singular narrative of coming-
to-self nonetheless provides a model for all other individuals. Despite her
disingenuous comment to Ralph, "if you look for grand examples of anything from me I shall disappoint you" (*PL* 133), Isabel's impassioned
interest in her own self-development indicates the extent to which she has
internalized the teleological narrative of *Bildung* in order to see her life in
terms of a progression toward an ethical end. Recall how, at the beginning
of the novel, Isabel "was always planning out her development, desiring
her perfection, observing her progress" (*PL* 56). Now, however, using the
Schillerian logic she has imbibed through Merle, Isabel discovers that an
ethical condition may be reached not through the application of prohibiting laws as she previously thought ("It was wrong to be mean, to be
jealous, to be false, to be cruel," *PL* 54), but with Osmond as her tutor,
through following the dictates of her own desire. As the telos of *Bildung*'s
activity of self-formation, a man whose life is dedicated to cultivating
himself, Osmond appears to Isabel as an ideal figure to emulate whose
exquisite taste is simply the visible, outward reflection of his equally
exquisite morals. It is this, more than anything, that convinces her of the
rightness of her choice: "You might know a gentleman when you see one,"
Isabel chastizes Ralph, "you might know a fine mind. Mr Osmond makes
no mistakes! He knows everything, he understands everything, he has the
kindest, gentlest, *highest* spirit" (*PL* 293) [my emphasis].

Armstrong argues that pride and idealism are responsible for Isabel's
choice; her decision is the result of her basic self-deception. Believing she
has understood freedom's lesson—the paradox of the "servile will"—
Isabel imagines she is freely accepting limitation, but rather, in marrying

Osmond, she is in fact "attempting to defy limitation in the guise of accepting it" (Armstrong 112). Armstrong cites Ralph's suspicion that Isabel has chosen Osmond as a result of a "fine theory" she has invented about him but, as Armstrong puts it, the problem is "it is too much a theory, and it is simply too perfect" (113). He explains, "[a]lthough she is binding her will by devoting herself to Osmond, Isabel's pride in accepting restraints blocks any sense that she is actually going to be limited. Romantically imaginative still, she senses only the possibilities of which she will avail herself" (113). Armstrong is right, I believe, to pinpoint Isabel's choice as the result of a "fine theory," but this stems less from her pride than from her mystified idea of the relation between ethics and aesthetics. Believing she is making an ethical choice, Isabel marries on the aesthetic's "fictitious theory," namely, that a motivated relationship pertains between moral and sensuous realms whose apotheosis is found in the man of taste, or the "beautiful soul." Whereas Goodwood represents (among other things) the demands of sensuous impulse, while Warburton, despite his liberal tendencies, personifies the claustrophobic constraints of preexisting social and moral systems, Osmond presents himself as the perfect combination of both. As Ralph observes, he is "the incarnation of taste" (*PL* 291): he is what Hegel would call the "living concept" of aesthetic ideology, of beauty's ideal synthesis of both sensible and supersensible realms.

Driven as she is by such aesthetic concerns, it is not surprising that Isabel should choose Osmond over her other suitors. Osmond will show Isabel how to reconcile her ideal of freedom within the constraints of necessity. The problem of course, which James presents with such exquisite irony in his portrayal of Osmond, is that such an aesthetic solution is accomplished only by disguising the violence through which this synthesis is ultimately forged. The violence with which Osmond inflicts his will on everything in his sight is in fact no arbitrary or capricious facility but the underlying truth of what De Man calls "aesthetic ideology" that succeeds in yoking together two irreconcilable realms and whose primary trope, as we saw with regard to Freedman earlier, is metaphorical identity (i.e., metaphor in its "symbolic" modulation).[21] James's Osmond ironizes the hidden truth of *Bildung*'s metaphorical ideal, namely, the violence of a will that assimilates everything under its purview.

Of course, as a parody of some of the worst excesses of late Victorian aestheticism, Osmond simply represents James's satiric commentary on contemporary aesthetic concerns. However, as with all parodies, it only works to the extent that it contains a grain of truth. The deep insight that James has us discern through Osmond is the way the fantasy of aesthetic reconciliation remains just that, a fantasy that purports seamlessly to integrate the realms of nature and freedom on the basis of a perceived identity while at the same time veiling the underlying violence by which this apparent synthesis is achieved.

But just as important concerning our tendency to read *The Portrait of a Lady* in terms of a novel of development is the way James's Osmond simultaneously directs a revitalized attention to the mechanisms by which the *Bildungsroman* itself secures its reconciliatory narrative goals. For to the extent that he embodies the telos of the *Bildungsroman*'s ideal of *Bildung* (as the beautiful soul), Osmond's obscene will to power obliges us to confront a similar will expressed structurally in the *Bildungsroman*'s drive toward narrative closure which, as Martin Swales observes in his influential study, characteristically follows a certain established pattern. Swales explains how the *Bildungsroman* "operates with a tension between concern for the sheer complexity of individual potentiality on the one hand, and a recognition on the other that the practical reality—marriage, family, career—is a necessary dimension of the hero's self-realization, albeit one that by definition implies a delimitation, indeed, a constriction, of the self."[22] Following Marc Redfield, it is what we might now call the "aesthetic ideology" of the *Bildungsroman* that permits Isabel to suddenly perceive during her aimless travels how, what had appeared to be a constriction of the self, is nothing but the actuality, that is, the practical realization, of her freedom which will finally be able to reach temporal and phenomenal expression through the public ritual of marriage. Incorporating the individual into the social body, the beauty of marriage—the ultimate telos of the *Bildungsroman*—for Isabel and other heroines of nineteenth-century fiction lies in the way it promises to realize the ideal synthesis of freedom and necessity, uniting under one term both individual desire (sensuous impulses) and the larger social Good (an ethical or moral community). In marriage, the individual's desire coincides with society's law, transforming what is essentially (as Osmond knows very well) an economic transaction into an expression of personal freedom. Like Schiller's beauty, the marriage contract elicits *voluntary* consent to society's limitations on the individual's erotic freedom by revealing how, what appeared initially to be opposed (individual desire and duty), are really one and the same thing. But we need not wait for twentieth-century critics such as Adorno to point out how such an apparently ideal synthesis is nevertheless founded on a systematic suppression of individuality or "otherness." When Osmond conceives of Isabel as a prize specimen for his collection, anticipating how her imagination was to "ring" like a silver bell with the single tap of his knuckle, he performs a metaphorization that, in subsuming Isabel's difference under the sign of his own taste, reduces the "free keen girl" to a mere thing—a "representation," as Ralph discovers to his horror, of her husband. But does not a similar subsumption also occur in the aesthetic synthesis that enables the *Bildungsroman* to generate narrative closure in marriage? When the protagonist leaves home and embarks on a series of painful adventures, only to emerge from those experiences with a greater sense of self and ethical destiny—when, that is, the teleology of the *Bildungsroman* teaches the individual to sacrifice her presumptuous individuality and voluntarily submit to the greater Good of an ethical destiny within the larger social group by troping it as the realization and expression of her singular desire—the very same aesthetic ideology is in play that makes us blind to the potentially very real violence that may be inflicted in the name of that social Good. As De Man has repeatedly shown, it is on this violence that all such idealizing tropes as metaphorical resemblance, synecdoche, and symbol, not to mention sublime narratives of sacrifice and recuperation, and even, as I indicated earlier with regard to Freedman's argument, the virtue of sympathy itself as a metaphorical transfer of affect, depend.

As a satire of aestheticism, then, James presents Osmond as the grotesque end-product of the aesthetic's fundamental promise to reunite the sensible and supersensible realms kept rigorously apart by Kant. But insofar as the man of taste embodies the telos of *Bildung*, even as a caricature James's Osmond simultaneously alerts us to the implicit violence through which the *Bildungsroman* attains its narrative goals. For if, as Freedman cogently points out, Osmond's virulent aesthetic vision brutally reifies people into objects, transforming them into works of art for the collector, so too, does the apparently gentler (Schillerian) aesthetic of the *Bildungsroman* implicitly reify the individual's experience into an educative mission, recovering and transforming the singularity of Isabel's suffering into a universal moral lesson. It is for this reason, I submit, that readings of the novel that give a thematic reason for the mystery of Isabel's final return to Rome must fail from a (Kantian) ethical perspective. Reading her narrative through the teleological trajectory of the *Bildungsroman*, critics inevitably "pathologize" her decision, that is, give it some form of empirical content or "body" that provides the ground not only for her final choice, but also the yardstick against which our critical judgment of her ethical transformation is measured. It is this that then enables us either to celebrate or castigate her according to the pedagogical lesson she is seen to embody. From the narrative perspective of the *Bildungsroman*, in other words, Isabel's decision can only be approached in terms of the final *anagnorisis*, the belated recognition of a previously unseen identity that enables her finally to integrate her individual pathos into the wider social body, regardless of how it is troped (as sexual fear, social responsibility, love of renunciation, etc.). But as Osmond ought to caution us, whether explicitly or implicitly such recognition of identity in the narrative resolution is accomplished only by inflicting (and disguising) a certain violence or will to power onto the conditions of the narrative itself.[23] As Osmond directs us to see, at its ideological worst the "spiral return" of the *Bildungsroman* is driven by an ethically suspect, pragmatic utilitarianism masquerading under an aesthetic fantasy of self-affirming free will.

III

If the various, contested reasons given for Isabel's final return to Osmond have one thing in common, it is that each attempts to give her decision an empirical or as Kant would say, pathological content on which our own critical evaluation (and, by implication, imitation) of Isabel's ethical development is subsequently to be based. Thus while critics may individually disagree about the precise motivation for Isabel's return, most are at least agreed on the novel's basic picaresque structure that unfolds along a developmental pattern of away/home, and welcome Isabel's final decision as the collapse of an unrealistic idealism in favor of a more ethical reintegration with a wider social Good.[24]

As I have shown, this narrative implies a certain structure of sacrifice and recuperation facilitated by the aesthetic mediation of opposites that permits two irreconcilable realms to be brought together in a relation of identity. It was such an aesthetic mediation that not only enabled Isabel to find in Osmond the perfect synthesis of nature and freedom, but marriage itself (especially to him) could then be perceived to be, according to this aesthetic principle, the full realization of her individual desire, seamlessly (i.e., synecdochally) inserting her into a wider, law-based community. To this extent we might say that the reconciliation brought about by aesthetic mediation takes place within what we might call an economy of "equivalent exchange." The aesthetic reconciles oppositions by revealing a hidden identity between competing poles but, as the figure of Osmond makes explicit, this discovery comes at a price: the systematic suppression of one side of the opposition in favor of the other, according to a logic of deferred gain. The relevance to James's novel of this exchange economy underlying both the aesthetic resolution and its narratological expression in the reconciliatory devices of the *Bildungsroman* is nowhere more in evidence than in the subplot of the novel, in Osmond's and Merle's attempts to exchange Pansy in marriage to the suitor with the highest bid. Here the novel effectively thematizes the *Bildungsroman*'s driving ideology—and in the process reveals that ideology in its unadorned truth—as a system of exchange that transforms people into reified commodities.

The question is whether we can ever step out of this closed economy in which everything is already accounted for, where freedom is merely aestheticized necessity, and where consciousness is doomed to a fateful overpowering subjectivism that imprisons otherness within its dark "house of suffocation." Clearly James does in fact offer an alternative economic paradigm through which the novel should be read, otherwise *The Portrait of a Lady* would simply end according to the traditional narrative telos of the domestic novel, with Isabel's aesthetic resolution and marriage. The fact that James extends *The Portrait of a Lady* well beyond the Victorian novel's traditional completion in marriage quite clearly points to the necessity of reading it as a critique of the *Bildungsroman*'s reconciliatory aesthetic, as much as it situates the novel beyond the Victorianism of its day to suggest an early foreshadowing of James's later representational and ethical concerns in his proto-modernist novels of consciousness.[25] Isabel's story, in other words, should indeed be read as the ethical portrait its title suggests, but as a portrait that contests the utilitarian ethics of the *Bildungsroman*'s aesthetics of self-development.[26] The logic and, as I will argue, ethics of Isabel's decision cannot adequately be accounted for in the conventional sacrificial/recuperative terms of the novel of development whose linear trajectory circles around a decisive thematic (i.e., pathological) moment. For me, the vexed question of Isabel's return is resolved only by understanding her decision as the act of a transcendentally free subject acting solely in accordance with the moral law, that is, a strictly ethical act in Kantian terms.

To explain this, let us turn to the moment where Isabel finally discovers the truth of her relationship with Osmond and Merle. The turning point occurs in chapter 42 where, musing on the arrested image of

Osmond and Merle in a stance of greater than expected familiarity, Isabel
begins to realize the truth of her situation. The chapter is famous for the
increasing subjectification of the narrative voice, and the paths it traces
toward Isabel's growing self-awareness and recognition of Osmond's and
her mutual deceptions. But the full realization of the extent to which she
has been a pawn in other people's plays comes in chapter 49 where Merle's
pressure on Isabel to marry Pansy to Warburton finally yields a moment
of illumination: "'Who are you—what are you?' Isabel murmured. [. . .]
'What have you to do with me?' Isabel went on. Madame Merle slowly
got up, stroking her muff, but not removing her eyes from Isabel's face.
'Everything!' she answered" (*PL* 430). For Isabel, of course, the horror of
this moment mirrors the horror of the Kantian subject faced with the discovery of the immense gulf separating phenomenal and noumenal realms.
Like a De Quincey quivering before the Kantian concept of causation,
Isabel recoils at the discovery that what she believed had been her free
choice was really determined by forces outside her knowledge and control.[27] What she had taken for freedom was really determination, what she
believed essence was mere appearance. Imagining herself as an active
agent, she discovers she has been a passive, "applied, handled hung up
tool" (*PL* 459).

One might think, then, that this discovery of the way her choice had
been determined might offer Isabel relief, that is, it might absolve her of
responsibility for her unhappiness, and provide her with an excellent reason for getting out of her disastrous marriage. This is, in fact, what both
Henrietta and Caspar Goodwood urge. After all, if she was not responsible for her choice, then surely she has no further duty toward her marriage and her husband, and should be free to go. Arguing that society has
no right to legislate over questions of personal morality, Goodwood urges
Isabel to leave Osmond:

> Why should you go back—why should you go through that ghastly
> form? [. . .] Why shouldn't we be happy—when it's here before us,
> when it's so easy? [. . .] We can do absolutely as we please; to whom
> under the sun do we owe anything? What is it that holds us, what is it
> that has the smallest right to interfere in such a question as this? Such a
> question is between ourselves—and to say that is to settle it! Were we
> born to rot in our misery—were we born to be afraid? (*PL* 488–89)

But it is precisely from Caspar's libertarian ideal, with its Emersonian pos-
sessive individualism and philosophy of self-reliance, that Isabel so res-

olutely turns away and beats her "very straight path" back to Rome. How are we to understand this?

The most striking thing about James's novel is the way it presents what is essentially the same act twice: Isabel's choice of Osmond. The novel, in other words, develops not so much according to the Aristotelian tragic narrative pattern of *peripetea* and *anagnorisis*, but around the structure of a Kierkegaardian repetition.[28] I suggested that Isabel's first choice of Osmond made the error of mistaking aesthetics for ethics. Her second choice, however, marks her shift into an ethical mode. To clarify this, let us look again at the final chapters of the novel. With her discovery that Merle has married her, Isabel suddenly finds herself thrown into a world of determination. Everything she believed was an act of volition is discovered to have been the result of causes beyond her control. Her choice had been forced, her will the puppet of others far stronger than her own, her knowledge incomplete. The second turning point, however, comes after her momentous talk with Osmond's sister, the Countess Gemini, who reveals the truth of Madame Merle's relationship with Osmond and Pansy. With this knowledge in hand, Isabel decides to leave for England to see Ralph one last time before his death, but before she leaves she pays a visit to Pansy who has been banished to the convent by Osmond after his failed attempt to marry her to Warburton. While at the convent, she encounters Merle, also visiting Pansy. If the first moment, Isabel's discovery of Merle's hand in her marriage, thrusts Isabel into a world of determination where all actions are revealed as being the result of other causes, this second moment, the encounter with Merle, marks the point when what she perceived as the totality of determination begins to break down.

Merle first approaches Isabel with the muted gravity of a woman "more than ever playing a part" (*PL* 457). Following her old script, she first apologizes to Isabel for her presumption in visiting Pansy without Isabel's consent, and then launches into her usual "brilliant" discourse. Suddenly she falters, though, perceiving a difference in her interlocutor. James writes how, "She had not proceeded very far before Isabel noted a sudden break in her voice, a lapse in her continuity, which was in itself a complete drama. This subtle modulation marked a momentous discovery—the perception of an entirely new attitude on the part of her listener. [. . .] The person who stood there was not the same one she had seen hitherto, but was a very different person—a person who knew her secret (*PL* 458). In this split-second break, this momentary "lapse" in Merle's continuity, Isabel sees for the first time behind the mask of Merle's

self-representations; what she finds there is a question mark, a query from
the other woman as to what she knows. Although the question is immediately answered by Merle herself—"Merle had guessed in the space of an
instant that everything was at end between them, and in the space of
another instant she had guessed the reason why" (*PL* 458)—nevertheless
the posing of the question, implying a lack in Merle's knowledge, has the
effect of immediately changing Isabel's status. From being the dupe of
appearances, Isabel is transformed into "a person who knew her secret."

   This scene is important, I think, not just for the moment of revenge
it potentially offers Isabel (who nevertheless subsequently rejects the
"moment of triumph" it might have afforded her, and is content to
remain silent throughout the encounter). For what it does, as I suggested,
is begin the transformation of Isabel from a causal, determined subject
into her own free or "intelligible" cause. Yet this occurs not through some
mystified, because aestheticized, reconciliation of freedom and necessity,
but through what I am calling the free *choice* of her determined status. Let
us look at the steps through which this takes place. Believing she freely
enters the world of necessity by choosing Osmond, Isabel comes to a
belated recognition that her choice was in effect "forced"—it was a determined choice. She had been used like any other object, the product of
forces not her own: "She saw, in the crude light of that revelation which
had already become a part of experience and to which the very frailty of
the vessel in which it had been offered only gave an intrinsic price, the dry
staring fact that she had been an applied handled hung-up tool, as senseless and convenient as mere shaped wood and iron" (*PL* 459). However,
in Merle's "momentary lapse" Isabel recognizes that the world of determination in which she finds herself remains incomplete—there is a gap in
the apparently seamless flow of representations emanating from the "great
lady." This recognition collapses the totality of the world of determination, leaving open a space for freedom. But the effect of this discovery is
not to throw Isabel back into the absolute freedom of her previous existence—the freedom of the subject without any ground. This time the
freedom Isabel realizes is ethical, rather than aesthetic. What is different
this time?

   When Isabel leaves Rome after her encounter with Merle, she begins
the process of extricating herself from the economic calculations that,
whether overtly or implicitly, have driven her decisions so far. James
describes Isabel's detachment from the scenes surrounding her, which previously elicited such eager interest: Isabel "performed this journey with

sightless eyes and took little pleasure in the countries she traversed" (*PL* 464). Now, for Isabel "[a]ll purpose, all intention, was suspended; all desire too save the single desire to reach her much-embracing refuge" (*PL* 465). Negativity characterizes Isabel's journey homeward: Isabel "envied Ralph his dying. [. . .] To cease utterly, to give it all up and not know anything more—this idea was as sweet as the vision of a cool bath in a marble tank, in a darkened chamber, in a hot land" (*PL* 465). But although in her journey from Rome, Isabel "had moments indeed . . . which were almost as good as being dead," it is important to distinguish this negativity from its sacrificial modality (and its concomitant recuperation) in the aesthetic narrative. In the narrative teleology of the *Bildungsroman*, this episode should mark the depths of Isabel's defeat before the "upward spiral" of recuperation begins once again and cements her within a narrative economy of exchange. However, a number of elements work against this model. In a traditional *Bildungsroman*, Isabel's return to Gardencourt should symbolize the heroine's triumphant "return" home after the pain and suffering her presumptuous actions have caused her. But, as we know, it is back to Rome that Isabel finally returns after her vigil in England with Ralph; thus there are too many "returns," complicating the teleological narrative pattern much in the way James's metaphor of death as a series of successive enclosures work against a strict binary dichotomy of hot and cold, life and death (a cool bath, a marble tank, a darkened chamber, a hot land). Similarly, the projected moment of *anagnorisis*, the recuperation of suffering through self-discovery is also somewhat delayed: instead of a flash of sudden insight, of self-knowledge, Isabel only has a deep sense "that life would be her business for a long time to come" (*PL* 466). Isabel's new "knowledge" is more a prescience of her capacity for endurance, for perseverance, rather than an empowering new "awareness"—of self, or of social responsibility. Instead, we must see Isabel's journey as marking the shift toward a different narrative economy, distinct from the series of positives and negatives that have structured the narrative's exchange until now.

What are the characteristics of this other economy? Isabel's all-embracing identification with Ralph's death gives us the terms of this economy as one of pure negativity, as Isabel discovers when she finds everyone surrounding her in Gardencourt appearing either dead or dying: she finds Mrs. Touchett becoming an "old woman without memories," while news of Warburton's impending marriage gives Isabel the feeling "as if she had heard of Lord Warburton's death" (*PL* 474). Ralph's death seems to have inflected everything around her, giving a strange ghostly kind of vitality to inanimate objects, while seeming to suck the life from the living. Waiting for Mrs. Touchett, Isabel grows nervous and scared, "as scared as if the objects about her had begun to show for conscious things, watching her trouble with grotesque grimaces" (*PL* 471). Ralph himself is already the "figure and pattern of death" (*PL* 476), but as Isabel watches over him in her silent vigil, she finds herself staring into the vistas of "immeasurable space" in his eyes (*PL* 476). Death seems to have reversed all of the ordinary temporal and spatial orders, leaving Isabel and Ralph finally together looking jointly at "the truth": "'he married me for the money' she said" (*PL* 478). With this admission, Isabel gives up the final pretense and with it the last vestiges of the aestheticism that has driven her decisions all along. The admission shatters the aesthetic fiction, revealing the "ideological" (in Adorno's sense) system of rewards and exchanges that underpin the fantasy of aesthetic reconciliation. Along with this admission, Isabel gives up her position in society, her wealth, her relationship with Pansy, even what little feeling she has remaining toward her husband. She gives it up precisely for "nothing," namely, for the truth that Ralph's death has revealed to her: her own destiny in death, her essential negativity.

The question is how negativity can serve in any practical sense as a positive grounding for an ethical subjectivity? When Isabel turns from Goodwood's kiss and runs back toward the house, she finds in front of her a "very straight path" (*PL* 490). She knows, now, what it is she must do. She knows she must return to Rome—not because of her promise to Pansy, or because she idealizes renunciation, or for any of the other reasons given for her return. Isabel's decision has none of the vacillations of pathological reasons. She returns simply because she must, because, as she tells Ralph, she will do what is "right" (*PL* 479). But in returning to Osmond, Isabel is not returning out of any conventional idea of a woman's duty toward her husband. Rather, Isabel acts out of duty toward the moral law itself, which for Kant is the only way through which our transcendental freedom can be realized.

To explain this we need to make a brief detour into Kantian moral philosophy. Recall how for Kant, as for Schiller, the moral law gives us access to our state as free (or noumenal) beings, but where for Schiller freedom gains phenomenal expression in the form of the aesthetic state, for Kant freedom, as an Idea of Reason, remains strictly unphenomenalizable. Nevertheless Kant does allow that we can experience freedom "practically" through the moral law that tells us how we should act. But rather than a set of prohibiting laws or positive injunctions, the Kantian categorical imperative simply gives us a principle according to which we might act and live ethically. The Kantian categorical imperative states: act in such a way that the principle of your actions could at the same time hold good as a universal law. Now, at the end of his *Critique of Practical Reason* Kant makes a peculiar gesture where he praises the "Wise Adaptation of Man's Cognitive Faculties to His Practical Destination." Kant remarks how, should we have direct, sensible presentations of our moral nature, we would indeed avoid all transgressions of the law. And yet, confronted with the "awful majesty" of God and eternity perpetually before our eyes, our moral acts would not be motivated from duty alone but from hope and fear. Kant writes, "As long as the nature of man remains what it is, his conduct would thus be changed into mere mechanism, in which, as in a puppet show, everything would *gesticulate* well, but there would be *no life* in the figures" (*CPrR* 176). Here Kant seems to be cautioning against the consequences of the Schillerian aesthetic solution. Presciently, Kant foresees the dangers (which we would do well still to heed) of pathologizing, that is, of giving *body* to the ethical. Instead, with his comment, Kant reaffirms the fundamentally *approximate* nature of all ethical acts which, however much we test them against the Kantian imperative, nevertheless retain something unknowable about them, namely, whether or not our acts have been entirely emptied of pathological content. But it is precisely because of this, because we cannot know whether we have succeeded in evacuating all empirical considerations from our acts that, Kant tells us, "there is room for true moral disposition, immediately devoted to the law" (*CPrR* 176).

The moral law in Kant, then, is the guarantee against the dangers of a Schillerian aestheticization of ethics that purports to give us a physical embodiment of the moral law. For Kant, rather, the moral law is the custodian of the eternal gap separating the realms of freedom and determination, a sort of positivation of the negativity that Isabel finds at the heart of her experience. And it is out of respect for this negativity expressed as the moral law, rather than for any empirical reason, that Isabel makes her momentous decision at the end of the novel. She returns neither for Pansy, nor from fear, nor love of renunciation or a wish to pursue life "motionlessly seeing."[29] She returns simply because she must—she must obey the moral law that obliges her unconditionally. The immediately following question is why the moral law requires Isabel to return to

Osmond. Why couldn't the moral law instead allow her to break her marriage contract, set off for America with Caspar, remain in England, or even set up shop with Henrietta? But for Isabel, as we know, the most important thing in her life is her freedom. It is for the sake of freedom that Isabel interprets the moral law as dictating her return to Osmond.

If, as Isabel now discovers, her first choice had been unfree, her decision to choose the same choice again might be conceived as a *remaking* of that first choice. As Irene Ramalho Santos puts it in her penetrating reading of the novel, "There is only one gesture left for Isabel: to invest with freedom, retrospectively, her initially determined, conditioned choice."[30] But where for Santos this gesture is merely a symbolic one, indicating James's equivocation about the nature of such a willed freedom that points to his "subtle problematization of late-nineteenth-century values" (Santos 125), I suggest that Isabel's second choice in fact goes deeper to represent something more paradoxical, namely, the phenomenal expression of the original free choice by which she first *chose* her determination. Now this sounds rather bizarre. Surely either we are determined subjects—phenomenal beings subject to the laws of causality—or we are free: noumenal subjects inhabiting a world of rational freedom but from which we cannot perform any actions in the world because this would subject us to the natural laws of space and time. How, then, can we freely *choose* our determination?

Psychoanalysis can help us to navigate these strange temporal paradoxes whereby the normal relations of cause and effect are inverted such that an effect can, in psychoanalytic terminology, become its own cause. The clearest example of such a temporal inversion in psychoanalysis is found in the way trauma comes about retroactively, that is, *after* the (traumatic) event has been inserted into a symbolic system of meaning, which then causes that first event subsequently to be "traumatic." But insofar as it relates to our concern with choice here, let us take for another example the case of fetishism where the subject can never objectively identify a moment in time when he or she said to him- or herself, "This object is what I will desire." Nevertheless, the subject can also never say, "This fetish object was imposed on me from without, I had no choice in the matter," since the fetishist nevertheless remains fixated on an object that he or she refuses to give up—the object, in other words, was in a sense *chosen by the subject*. Although the original choice to freely choose this or that object can never be phenomenalized, it nevertheless must be presupposed, otherwise the object would have no more meaning for the fetishist than it does for any other desiring, nonfetishistic subject. The fetishist's refusal to give up the fetish object is, in a sense, the act of remaining faithful to that original choice to desire it, even though that choice can never have actually taken place "in time."

It is something of this paradoxical nature that Isabel undergoes when she decides to return to Osmond. Although, as she and we both know by now, her first choice was "forced" (i.e., we can never know the totality of the situation and hence make an absolutely calculating choice by which all choices are available to us), her decision to return to Osmond carries the burden of remaining faithful to an act of free choice that can never actually have taken place in time. Her second choice, in effect, *causes* the first as a free rather than determined act precisely because, like the fetishist, she remains faithful to it. Had she given it up and followed Caspar back to America, her first choice would indeed be revealed as determined. But Isabel's decision to remain faithful to that choice retroactively confirms it as free. To use a paradoxical formulation familiar to us from psychoanalysis, Isabel's second choice causes the first *to have been free*. Hence Isabel's return to Osmond must be seen as the phenomenal expression of a strictly unphenomenalizable but necessarily presupposed act by which she originally "chose to choose," as Kierkegaard would say.[31] Her return is the repetition or *reduplicatio* in the phenomenal world of something that is strictly impossible, namely, free causality. It is in this sense that I say that Isabel's second choice retroactively confirms her original (free) choice of determination. Although we can never have phenomenal knowledge of that original free act, by repeating that choice in time, Isabel remains faithful to it in the only way possible for her: by acting in accordance with the moral law and returning to Osmond.

Does this simply mean that in a futile or merely symbolic gesture we voluntarily submit to the deterministic natural laws that inevitably direct all our actions? By choosing Osmond a second time, doesn't Isabel simply assume the conditions of her determination in a sort of pragmatic resignation that says, well, this is how things are and the best bet we have for freedom is to voluntarily assent to what is otherwise imposed by necessity? No. When Isabel returns to Osmond, she extricates herself from such an aesthetic economy and performs what is, within the terms of the narrative, an *impossible* act. By choosing again, she bears testimony to something—a freedom—beyond our determined realm of space and time that momentarily suspends the laws of nature. But because, of course, this is impossible (and because James, like Kant, rejects the aesthetic solution of

a Schiller or an Osmond), this freedom can be attested to only in a paradoxical and retroactive way: in the form of a repetition whose sole function is to bear witness and remain faithful to that first, original, impossible choice.

Hence where the aim of aesthetics (at least in its form as "aesthetic
ideology") was to heal the split between phenomenal and noumenal
realms, we now see how Jamesian (Kantian) ethics insists that our only
possibility of freedom is found in maintaining that gap that splits the subject from itself. And where the aesthetic's promise of unification was
founded on what transpired as Osmond's violent will to identity that we
saw as powering the metaphorically driven exchange economy of the *Bildungsroman*'s aesthetic ideology, ethics requires the subject to step out of
the economy of equivalency altogether and act, not for the sake of any
pathological reasons, but from pure duty alone, which Kant calls the
respect *(Achtung)* for the law. In so doing, the subject has no guarantee
that his or her actions will have been ethical, that is, removed from any
traces of pathological desires. The subject cannot know in advance what
the moral status of any act will be—Kantian ethics can have no basis in
calculus—but she must act anyway. In this respect, Kantian ethics recalls
the dilemma of representation with which I began this discussion. Just as
the representing subject can occupy no outside position (there is no "measure of commensurability" by which to judge whether her representations
match the reality of things in themselves), so the Kantian ethical subject
has no way of stepping outside the system of appearances to assure herself
of the ethical nature of any act. But again, for Kant, it is precisely this
impasse that provides the solution to the problem. Precisely because there
is no guarantee that our actions will be ethical, because we can never step
outside our phenomenal nature and see things as they are in themselves,
an ethically grounded community can be formed.

When Isabel discerns the gap in Madame Merle's knowledge, she
recognizes it as correlative to the gap in her own. It is around this gap,
which Adorno would call "non-identity," that the possibility of an ethical society forms. To the extent that we are all barred from knowledge of
the totality, because of the fact that none of us are wholly within the system of representation, nor wholly outside it, we can form a community
that is ethical. This community therefore is not founded on some essential commonality, or injunction to reach consensus. Rather it forms
around a collective impossibility: the collective inability to know what
the other knows, or is thinking. Just as we cannot guarantee that our acts

are free of pathological desire, but must act anyway as if they were, so in representative political life we cannot know what the other wants, what his or her "good" is, but must judge in his or her place anyway. We do so through reference to a universal. But the universal involved in the formation of an ethical community differs significantly from that found and critiqued already as an aestheticization of the relations of particular and universal (or part and whole) (where the universal designates some kind of prior, naturalized, exterior standard against which various particulars are measured). Where an aesthetic concept of community—the driving ideology of the marriage plot—requires the subsumption of particulars beneath the concept of a universal (in the process reducing and reifying those particulars through an ethically questionable economy of sacrifice and recuperation), an ethical community rearticulates this relation. How does it do so?

According to the formulation of ethics I have outlined, the Kantian ethical obligation has no content but is binding on the subject to act. The ethical subject, in other words, is not held to some idealized standard of conduct—the moral law is not founded on any concept of the good. Because it is an empty yet binding principle, the moral law obliges the subject to take full responsibility for realizing the categorical imperative in a particular, empirical context, transforming a purely formal law into a concrete ethical obligation. It is, therefore, not a question of applying some external universal to a particular content—not a subsumption of a particular under the universal—but a matter of creating or "inventing" a universal from a particular. In this respect, as several commentators have noted,[32] the structure of the Kantian ethical judgment parallels what happens in Kant's formulation of aesthetic (or "reflective") judgment: both begin with a consideration of the particular and, through reflection on an *a priori* principle, as Kant puts it "ascend [. . .] to the universal" (*CJ* 16). In both cases, in Alan Singer's words, we confront the "necessity of fitting our knowledge to experience without abstractly presupposing the standard of fitness by which we judge" (Singer 226). The relation between the universal and the particular is thus quite different in what we must now call the ethical reflective judgment (or "aethical" judgment). Rather than subsuming particulars beneath a universal, with all of the violent reduction associated with this process in what I've been calling the "metaphoric" representational mode, the structure of the ethical reflective judgment requires us to fit the universal to the particular—to invent a universal from a concrete particular.

We must be careful to distinguish this from the position of those critics who, in their "ethical" concern to rescue particularity (or difference)
from the tyranny of the universal (or identity), are in danger of an unwar-
ranted idealization. The difficulty with some recent multicultural critiques of identity is that, by founding ethics on alterity, they risk ontolo-
gizing difference[33]—granting it some kind of absolute foundational
status—whereas, as Adorno has shown to great effect, difference (or in his
terms "non-identity") can only be thought in a dialectical relation with
identity.[34] So when a critic like Freedman, defending particularity against
the violence of Osmond's universalizing gaze, champions Isabel's aesthetic
vision in terms of an ethical respect toward otherness, he has so far dis-
pensed with any concept of the universal that he foregoes any possibility
of ethics in the Kantian sense. Among the multiple, dispersed particular
individuals, Freedman can find a common relation only through the
empirical, "pathological" feeling of sympathy in suffering. And, as Kant
points out, in sympathy we do not put ourselves in the Idea, but in the
place of others as empirical beings, rather than humanity in general. Thus
sympathy cannot act as the foundation of a truly ethical intersubjectivity.

In contrast, what makes the community founded on reflective judgment ethical is that it retains a concept of universality. But, as I said, the
universality implied in reflective judgment is not found in some external
substantive content. For Kant, reflective or aesthetic judgment is universally communicable not because we all agree that objects with certain
characteristics such as harmony, proportion, symmetry, and so on are
beautiful. Rather, the Kantian "Copernican revolution" in aesthetics, as
with ethics, requires us to turn to the experience of the perceiving subject. For Kant, the pleasure we feel in perceiving a beautiful object
derives not from the object but rather from ourselves, from the feeling of
pleasure we get from the play of the faculties in their freedom, a pleasure
that is necessary and universally communicable. Kant's term for this
communicability is the *sensus communis* that obtains when the subject
abstracts from the content of judgment and reflects on the formal features of our "presentational state," that is, on the conditions under which
such judgment arises. What is universal is thus not the content of the
judgment (i.e., certain qualities in the object being judged) but the *form*
of the judgment itself which, because we all share the same cognitive
powers put into play, must also be assumed to be the same in everyone.
In this way the subject steps out of his or her particular set of circumstances and speaks with what Kant calls the "universal voice," making

possible a sense of shared community and of morality. In Kant's words, aesthetic judgment implies a power to judge "which in its reflection, takes account *(a priori)* of the mode of representation of all other men in thought, in order, as it were, to compare its judgment with the collective reason of humanity" (*CJ* 136).

Critiques of Kant therefore miss the point when they argue that the universality of Kantian aesthetic judgment is an ethically suspect concept that occupies a privileged neutral ground abstracted from all sensible content (the "subject without properties") and against which all other subjects, cultures and races (implicitly subjects with properties) may be judged.[35] The "universal voice" of Kantian reflective judgment can never be divorced from the particular set of circumstances through which it is derived—it can never be fully divested of its particularity but remains grounded in the subjective even while it claims universal assent. The Kantian universal of reflective judgment is neither the imposition of some external concept, but nor is it to be conceived of as a kind of "inflated particular," in Naomi Schor's phrase.[36] How, then, are we to conceive of it?

I find that Ernesto Laclau's formulation of the universal as an "empty place" helps to illuminate the particular/universal relation as I understand it functioning in reflective judgment. In his book, *Emancipation(s)*,[37] Laclau develops his concept of the universal implicit in democratic political formations. Yet despite the fact that his concern here is with the relation of universal and particular specific to the political sphere, his formulation of how these are articulated derives from a clearly philosophical tradition. His formulations, therefore, are appropriate for helping to explicate our problem. In developing his concept of the universal as an "empty place," Laclau wishes to resist the implicit binarism extant in the couple particular/universal. Because neither one of the couples can be thought without the other, for Laclau, the relation is not one of exclusion, but rather of mutual "contamination." Opposed to the idea of the universal as a "pure" universality, a totality that incorporates (and transcends) all particularity, for Laclau, the universal itself "was once a particular" but one which has been divested of its particularity yet, and this is crucial, *not wholly*. Laclau maintains that there can be no universal without some remainder of particularity. The universal, rather, is an empty place, a placeholder that can be occupied by particulars insofar as they represent or incarnate what Laclau calls the "empty signifier."

To explain this, we need to look at Laclau's concept of the empty signifier as something that represents the limit of a signifying system. Laclau argues that, in order for a signifying system to produce meaning, something must remain outside the differential series of signifiers. That is to say, without some kind of absolute or "exclusive" limit against which all signifiers are equally negated, a signifying system, understood in Saussure's terms as a system of differences, would be unable to function. For without such a limit, a system cannot form a totality, with the result that meaning would be endlessly deferred. This limit can never be represented (otherwise it would not constitute the limit of the representing system) but must be marked in some way within the system. This is where the concept of the empty signifier comes in. The empty signifier is a signifier that has been shorn of its particular content and "assume[s] the role of representing the pure being of the system—or, rather, the system as pure Being" (Laclau 39). What enables it to do so is what Laclau calls the unit of signification's "constitutive split" whereby each unit is both different from all the others, and yet equivalent to all of them in relation to the exclusionary limit. For a particular signifier to occupy the role of the "empty signifier," it must divest itself of its "differential" nature, and "privilege the dimension of equivalence" (Laclau 39) (i.e., its relation to what is "beyond" the limit). Insofar as every unit of signification has the same equivalent relation of negation to the beyond of the signifying system, any one particular can theoretically occupy the position of the empty signifier—any particular can empty itself of its unique content and "universalize" itself in order to mark the limit of the system. But, as Laclau points out, "the being or systematicity of the system which is represented through the empty signifiers is not a being which has not been *actually* realized, but one which is constitutively unreachable" (Laclau 39). Each empty signifier that assumes the role of representing the totality, therefore, "will always be constitutively inadequate." In other words, it is not a question of a signifier having any specific "universal" qualities that enables it to empty itself and assume the function of the empty signifier. As Laclau puts it, "nothing predetermines that one particular body should be the one predestined to incarnate negation as such" (Laclau 41). The fact that a single particular at any one historical moment comes to perform that function is purely the result of what Laclau calls "hegemony," or, "the unevenness of the social" (Laclau 43). Hegemony, as Linda Zerilli explains, "means that the relation between universal and particular entails not the realization of a shared essence or the final overcoming of all differences but an ongoing and conflict-ridden process of mediation through which antagonistic struggles articulate common social objective and political strategies."[38]

Here we have a universal (the "system") represented by a particular but not in such a way that the particular must be subsumed under a pre-existing concept of universality. This is no metaphorically induced synec-dochic relationship of part and whole, where the part comes to embody the totality through the expression of some ideal unifying content. Instead, Laclau's formulation helps us to conceive of a universal articu-lated *through* a particular, insofar as the particular shares with all other particulars a common distance to an absolute negation. The universality of the particular occupying the place of the "empty signifier" is thus derived not from some common essence but from a shared relation to the exclusionary limit, a universalism that signifies simply the impossibility of ever achieving full identity. Now we are in a position to see how a com-munity may be founded on an absolute negation without giving up the notion of an ethically grounded freedom. An ethical community is not one that founds itself on some shared essence, or common experience (of suffering, or sympathy, etc.). Rather it is formed around a central impos-sibility in relation to which every individual is equally distant. Although no one individual is able to know the totality, nevertheless anyone may occupy the place that marks the lack in our knowledge. We can thus say that an ethical community is one dedicated to maintaining the limit that prevents us from making an unwarrantable totalization, by marking the place of impossibility within the system.

IV

Finally, I want to return to the question with which this discussion began, namely, the question of how Isabel reads. Recall how critics defined Isabel's problem as an inability to read properly, that is, an inability to see beyond appearances into the truth of people and things. With Osmond, Isabel failed to see the "whole man"; her problem was that "she had seen only half his nature then, as one saw the disk of the moon when it was partly masked by the shadow of the earth. [. . .] She had mistaken a part for the whole" (*PL* 357). This criticism is aimed at Isabel's inability or, in Moody's terms, her willful "refusal" to synthesize the disparate parts into a totality—in hermeneutic terms, to "project" beyond the part to the whole. But, in the light of our discussion, perhaps instead of expressing a naive understanding of the relation of part and whole, a naïveté which must be corrected through suffering (the teleology of the *Bildungsroman*),

Isabel's reading should be conceived differently. Isabel's failure to see the whole, her refusal to see through surface appearances to the universal truth lying behind them, gives us a concrete example of the rearticulated relation of part and whole that obtains in the reflective ethical judgment.

As we saw, by taking the part for the whole, Isabel reads through the trope of synecdoche. But in this case, the synecdoche is not operating in the service of a symbolic or metaphorical concept of language, where the part is subsumed under the whole through an affirmation of an underlying unity that obtains between them. It was just such a synecdochic relationship that was seen to underpin the relation of individual and universal in the aesthetic reconciliation of marriage—a synecdoche driven by metaphor's protocol of identity. But, as Paul De Man notes, synecdoche as a "borderline figure" can have another figurative affiliation, with metonymy, and it is this metonymically driven synecdoche that seems more appropriate to describe the way Isabel reads.[39]

On a number of occasions, we notice Isabel's predilection for concentrating on the relation between the parts rather than what they add up to. Both Goodwood and Warburton, for example, appear to Isabel not so much as complete, united personalities, but as collections of multiple particulars. Thus for Isabel, "Lord Warburton loomed up before her, largely and brightly, as a collection of attributes and powers" (*PL* 95), while Caspar Goodwood appears as so many fitted segments of a suit of armor: "She saw the different fitted parts of him as she had seen in museums and portraits, the different fitted parts of armoured warriors—in plates of steel handsomely inlaid with gold" (*PL* 107). Rather than combining the various parts into a synthetic whole, this analytical mode of seeing remains concentrated on the relations of the particulars (a trait shared oddly enough by Madame Merle who retains a minute memory of certain particulars in the famous works of art found in the museums of Florence: "she recalled the right-hand corner of the large Perugino and the position of the hands of the Saint Elizabeth in the picture next to it" [*PL* 211]).

But this mode of seeing is most in evidence in the passages where James describes Isabel's reactions to art. On Isabel's first visit to Gardencourt, she asks Ralph to show her the portrait gallery. Although it is late, Ralph acquiesces to her request. James describes how,

> The lamps were on brackets, at intervals, and if the light was imperfect
> it was genial. It fell upon the vague squares of rich colour and on the
> faded gilding of heavy frames; it made a sheen on the polished floor of

the gallery. Ralph took a candlestick and moved about, pointing out the things he liked; Isabel, inclining to one picture after another, indulged in little exclamations and murmurs. She was evidently a judge; she had a natural taste; he was struck with that. She took a candlestick herself and held it slowly here and there; she lifted it high, and as she did so he found himself pausing in the middle of the place and bending his eyes much less upon the pictures than on her presence. (*PL* 50)

Instead of subsuming particulars beneath an all-embracing concept of the whole, Isabel's way of perceiving has a curiously decomposing ability that turns objects into a multitude of different parts, into "collections" of attributes and features. Here, as Isabel moves from picture to picture, she breaks up the whole into its component elements, allowing her candle to light up first one and then another section of the paintings. Her disarticulating vision seems to mimic the play of the "imperfect" light that reorganizes the complete portraits into the small squares of shape and color that are given new and unexpected prominence in the flickering light.

When, back in Albany after her first meeting with her aunt, Isabel reflects on moments of her previous life, what appears to her mind is a succession of individual scenes and figures jostling each other for her attention. James tells us how "Forgotten things came back to her; many others, which she had lately thought of great moment dropped out of sight. The result was kaleidoscopic" (*PL* 42). This figure of the kaleidoscope seems aptly to characterize Isabel's "ethical" or "reflective" mode of seeing. The kaleidoscope is the device that allows one to create (invent) a geometric image using only parts but which, literally through reflection, constitute a whole—a kaleidoscopic totality that nevertheless has no other "being" than its part.

In fact, Isabel's "kaleidoscopic" form of vision recalls nothing so much as the experience of the imagination in the Kantian sublime. As is well known, in sublime experiences the imagination is confronted with a sensible manifold for which it can obtain no "presentation." Faced with objects that are immensely large (the mathematical sublime), or with those eliciting terror or amazement (the dynamical sublime), the imagination expands its power of presentation in an attempt to perform a comprehension that surpasses its ability to encompass the progressive apprehension in a whole of intuition. This is the famous moment of the subject's "bafflement" or sense of self-annihilation before reason steps in to provide an Idea of the totality (e.g., freedom, one's supersensible nature, etc.)—the moment, that is, when the imagination extends itself beyond its ordinary role of providing concepts to intuitions. Trying to present the unpresentable, the imagination is brought up against the limits of phenomenal comprehension, but before it collapses, and performs its "identification with reason," it has *expanded* its powers of presentation in its attempt to progressively apprehend the whole.

So when James tells us that Isabel's habitual way of perceiving the world is identified with her faculty of imagination, we must be careful to distinguish between the imagination's role in making determinant judgments (where, as the predominant faculty of synthesis, it subsumes the manifold under concepts of the understanding), and its role in aesthetic judgment, especially in experiences of the sublime. James describes how

> [Isabel's] imagination was by habit ridiculously active; when the door was not open, it jumped out of the window. She was not accustomed indeed to keep it behind bolts; and at important moments, when she would have been thankful to make use of her judgment alone, she paid the penalty of having given undue encouragement to the faculty of seeing without judging. (*PL* 39)

Isabel's habitual mode of "seeing without judging" is surely a description of the faculty of the imagination in aesthetic experience. Although James's formulation seems to imply the voiding of all judgment, this way of seeing in fact describes the imagination under the condition of reflective (rather than determinant) judgment. Thus Ralph's wish to see Isabel's life fit the "requirements of her imagination" takes on a different meaning than what might initially be supposed. Rather than an idealizing movement that obliges "life" (understood as accidentality, particularity, contingency) to fit the categories of representational consciousness, Isabel's "imaginative" or reflective way of seeing would require that the totality somehow get "bigger," to expand itself like the imagination does in experiences of the sublime. It requires that the totality enlarge itself, to make room for those particulars that have not traditionally been included in it, a demand, as Alan Singer puts it, "for a greater number of discursive places of recognition" (Singer 234).

In this sense, Isabel's perceptual, or reading strategy might be considered analogous to James's own representational style. James's formal predilection for the successive accumulation of subclauses in his sentences—his famous "interruptive" style—seems to express his conviction that the whole of something can never be told but that we must endeavor to mark the place of the absent totality within our linguistic and representational systems nonetheless. Recall James's March 16, 1879 notebook entry where he observes, "The obvious criticism of course will be it *[The Portrait of a Lady]* is not finished—that I have not seen the heroine to the end of her situation—that I have left her *en l'air*. This is both true and false. The whole of something is never told; you can only take what groups together. . . ."[40] Similarly, the formal patterns of Jamesian sentences, with their endlessly delayed predicates, their parenthetical asides, their anaphoric qualifications which, as Singer notes, have a tendency to reverse the "predicative polarity" of the sentence (Singer 165), combine to give the appearance of language circling around a centralized absence that is marked in relief, as it were, by the effusion of proliferating clauses. Just as the windows in James's metaphorical House of Fiction in the Preface each look out onto the same view—"life"—but the authors standing behind them perceive the scene slightly differently, so his characters in search of truth and knowledge each refine their individual or particular vision. However, in James this is accomplished not through "High Romantic" moments of proleptic or totalizing vision but rather in the successive, accumulative, but necessarily incomplete, singular viewpoints through which each come to perceive the world. No single viewpoint, James seems to be saying, can comprehend the whole, but each must successively attempt to circle around it. In the process, a whole is articulated *negatively*, in the collective impossibility of our being able to say it all.

2

"A Poor Girl with Her Rent to Pay"

The Wings of the Dove

"... a case of hysteria is a caricature of a work of art."
—Sigmund Freud, *Totem and Taboo*

In his landmark study of *The Wings of the Dove*,[1] Peter Brooks sets the terms for what has subsequently become one of the major thrusts in the novel's critical reception.[2] For Brooks, the novel has as its central concern the question of representation and its limit, or as he puts it, the "abyss of meaning," a question that for him possesses a uniquely ethical urgency. Situated as it is within James's "major phase" of the 1890s to the early 1900s, Brooks argues that this novel properly belongs to that group of James's work involved with exploring the void, the hidden yet determining absence that retroactively confers order and structure on the lives of James's characters. Brooks cites numerous examples from James's tales from this period to demonstrate James's preoccupation with this "abyss of meaning," from the epistemological uncertainties of "The Beast in the Jungle"—where John Marcher's futile wait for the meaning-conferring event of his life is finally revealed as the great event itself—to the onto-logical dilemmas raised by what the governess saw in "The Turn of the Screw." With *The Wings of the Dove*, Brooks asserts, James presents a sustained investigation of the void that lies at the heart of representation which, because its final reference points for Brooks are the Manichean struggle between good and evil, ultimately reveals itself as a uniquely "moral occult" (Brooks 178).

Brooks is not alone in his assertion. Laurence Holland also finds the novel interrogating the limits of the sayable, but for this critic the emphasis is put on the way the failure of language is given thematic and formal expression. Accordingly, James's stylistic technique is found to "perform" the "passion" of sacrifice and betrayal that constitutes the novel's main thematic content, Milly's betrayal and sacrifice by her false friends. Hence, in James's signature style of withdrawal and approach, Holland finds an ambiguous "tribute" to the unrepresentable: art, like Milly's friends, must inevitably "betray" what it seeks to represent insofar as it always, ultimately, "falls short of the full communion it nonetheless manages to imitate and celebrate." In a famous passage Holland writes,

> [T]he novel tacitly acknowledges that it cannot completely or directly embrace the ultimate reality—neither the ultimate horror nor the ultimate beauty, neither the pulsing actuality of life beyond art, nor the completely imagined vision which was the novel's origin or muse. [. . .] But the novel is not content to acknowledge this by saying it. Instead it acts as if its vision lay within the presence but beyond the reach of language: as if its horrors were unspeakable horrors and its beauties too beautiful for words, the novel intimately acknowledges the fact in the contortions of expressive movement, the rhythm of approach and withdrawal as a tribute of devotion to what it leaves behind. As [. . .] an act of devotion it reveals by betraying the life and sacred presence it adores.[3]

Because language cannot "completely or directly embrace the ultimate reality," the response, Holland argues, can only be the ambiguous tribute to the unspeakable bestowed by art that ultimately "betrays" what it seeks to memorialize. The question pursued in this chapter is whether the "aesthetic" response outlined by Holland must inevitably be understood as a tragic narrative of betrayal in the face of representation's limits. Here I ask whether the novel in fact presents another reading of the aesthetic gesture of "betrayal," one which, continuing the concerns of the previous chapter, can be properly described as "ethical."

Let me say at once that I share Brooks and Holland's conviction that the novel is preoccupied with the question of the limit of representation. After all, the plot of the novel, insofar as it is Kate's "plot" to persuade her fiancé Densher to make love to the wealthy but mortally stricken heiress, Milly, depends for its effectiveness on their joint refusal to "name names," that is, to say aloud what for most critics is a sordid and villainous plot against the innocent "dove" Milly. Similarly, in allowing herself to be taken in by Densher's overtures, Milly demands in return a reciprocal refusal to acknowledge her illness in words, resulting in the elaborate dissimulation of the characters as they circle around this forbidden topic. Milly's illness, like Kate's plot, and Lionel Croy's original mysterious "crime" with which the novel begins by alluding to, thus takes on the status of what Tzvetan Todorov, in a move akin to that of Brooks and Holland, designates the "absent cause"—the unarticulated but motivating source of the action. In his celebrated structuralist account of James's short fiction, Todorov observes how "the secret of James's tales is [. . .] precisely this existence of an essential secret, of something which is not named, of an absent, overwhelming force which puts the whole present machinery of the narrative into motion."[4] Further, Todorov makes the same observation as the previous critics as to how James's late style enacts or, in his words, "translates," the same general pattern of the "absent cause" into formal terms. Published in 1902 as the first of James's three "major phase" masterpieces (although actually written after *The Ambassadors*), *The Wings of the Dove* further refines and perfects James's "indirect style" to such an extent that many of its contemporary readers wished, like William James, that James would simply "say it out and have done with it!"[5] But, as the novel shows all too clearly, such bald statements of the facts in some cases can kill. Both thematically and formally, *The Wings of the Dove* poses itself the question: What is the ethical response to the unrepresentable? Simply saying it out, as William urges, finds Milly dead at the end of the novel from Lord Mark's violent outburst, but complying with Milly's prohibition on speech puts us uncomfortably in Densher's shoes, resulting in an unsatisfactory quietism.

This question moreover takes on a greater urgency when we realize that it bears directly on the problem of the psychoanalytic cure. For psychoanalysis poses itself the same question in treating the traumatic neuroses, namely, the relationship of language to the unspeakable trauma or, as Freud later revised his theory, the unspeakable desire *(Wunsch)* that resulted in the hysteria or obsessive compulsion. Anna O's invention of the "talking cure" was originally an attempt to "say out" the unconscious desires obliquely articulated in her hysterical symptoms, resulting in Freud's and Breuer's early belief that hysteria could be cured by the successful representation of the traumatic and unspeakable event whose repression had originally led to the hysteria. However, as they soon realized, simply saying it out was not enough if it was unaccompanied by "affect," that is, by an emotional reliving of the events in the person's life

resulting in the *Durcharbeiten,* the "working through." In their "Prelimi-
nary Communication" to *Studies on Hysteria* Freud and Breuer write,
"Recollection without affect almost invariably produces no result. The
psychical process which originally took place must be repeated as vividly
as possible; it must be brought back to its status nascendi and then given
verbal utterance."[6]

Milly's usual diagnosis by critics is the one that takes its cue from
James in the Preface where he associates Milly with his consumptive
cousin Minny Temple. However, as my reference to Freud implies, I
believe there is good reason to suggest a psychological rather than physiological basis for her illness. Kate herself tells Densher, "it's not lungs," a
statement that I have no reason to suspect, as Matthiessen apparently
does, is duplicitous.[7] Milly's doctor, Sir Luke Strett, seems to concur that
the matter with Milly is not the obvious diagnosis of tuberculosis when,
after examining Milly, he finds it not to be the case she had imagined.
Susan reports to Aunt Maud:

> "He says it isn't a case. [. . .] It isn't, at least" Mrs. Stringham explained
> "the case she believed it to be. [. . .] She went because there was some-
> thing she was afraid of, and he examined her thoroughly—he has made
> sure. She's wrong—she hasn't what she thought." (*WD* 245)

Still, the closest James comes to suggesting a hysterical basis for her
illness occurs when, on her second visit to Sir Luke Strett, Milly asks, "So
you don't think I'm out of my mind?" he smiles and replies, "Perhaps that
is [. . .] all that's the matter" (*WD* 151), (a suggestion Milly immediately
rejects as "too good").

Of course, one of the dangers of approaching a text like *The Wings
of the Dove* is the same one confronting Milly's friends: simply by trying
to "name" the matter with Milly, one risks doing the same kind of violence to the text as was done to Milly by Lord Mark—one risks "killing"
the text's subtleties.[8] Nevertheless, a diagnosis of hysteria makes a certain
amount of sense for Milly. We know that she has symptoms but that
these are without an obvious organic cause. We also know that, as Kate
puts it, she won't "smell of medicine"—her illness is not something that
will necessarily respond to medical attentions. If she survives at all, it will
be, as Sir Luke Strett advises, a question of mind. Furthermore, a diagnosis of hysteria would clarify some of the central issues of the novel
raised already by Brooks and Holland regarding the problem of representation (and further, might help to illuminate Sir Luke Strett's ambigu-

ous medical advice to Milly, that she "could live if she would"). For, if Milly's illness is rather a hysterical manifestation, it foregrounds the problem of the unspeakable in a particularly apposite way, since hysteria is precisely the illness that derives from the failure of language, from the trauma of the unrepresentable.

Such a diagnosis would seem to gain some support from another member of the James family who could serve just as well as Minny Temple as the model for James's heroine, namely, his sister Alice to whom he was closely attached in the decades preceding the appearance of *The Wings of the Dove*. Alice's final death by cancer in 1892 followed many years of undiagnosable symptoms. Recognized by their mother as a case of hysteria as early as 1868, the James family long seemed to accept that Alice's mysterious collapse and protracted illness had as much psychological as physiological origin.[9] Further support for identifying Milly's illness as a case of hysteria comes from a consideration of what we know about her immediate past, which appears to have much in common with the patients then being treated by Freud and Breuer in the 1890s. Recall that Freud notes how sick-nursing plays a significant part in the prehistory of cases of hysteria and goes on to observe how,

> if [the sick person] dies, and the period of mourning sets in, during which the only things that seem to have value are those that relate to the person who has died, these impressions that have not yet been dealt with come into the picture as well; and after a short interval of exhaustion the hysteria, whose seeds were sown during the time of nursing, break out. (Freud 232)

Although our knowledge of Milly begins only after the expiration of her entire immediate family, "on a scale and with a sweep that had required the greater stage" (*WD* 77), leaving Milly the last of her family, the "potential heiress of all the ages" (*WD* 79) with a "mass of money so piled on the girl's back" (*WD* 77), the trauma of all these deaths in close succession clearly shows itself in Milly's habitual appearance in mourning:

> [Milly's] American references, with their bewildering immensities, [. . .] their record of used-up relatives, parents, clever eager fair slim brothers—these the most loved—all engaged, as well as successive superseded guardians, in a high extravagance of speculation and dissipation that had left this exquisite being her black dress, her white face and her vivid hair as the mere last broken link. (*WD* 113)

However, my point here is not so much to "psychoanalyze" Milly, that is, to try to pinpoint the specific traumas that resulted in her hysteria, as simply to suggest the possibility that her illness might not have organic origins—to indicate that there is as much in the novel to plausibly suggest a psychosomatic diagnosis as a somatic one.[10] But if one grants that the matter with Milly is in fact a case of hysteria, it begins to clarify some of the issues that I find so far unsatisfactorily addressed in the critical tradition. It helps to elucidate, for example, as I will go on to argue, a feature of the novel that initially seems somewhat puzzling, namely, the propensity for each of the main characters to change places with one another. It also serves to illuminate the oddly mimetic relationship between Kate and Milly, which otherwise tends to become obscured in many readings of the novel that traditionally pit the two women against each other in a moral drama of redemption. Finally, as I suggested above, it serves most appositely to foreground the question of the limits of representation and its accompanying dilemma—the ethical approach to the unspeakable—since hysteria is itself a reaction to a certain deadlock or failure of representation.

I

The opening chapter introduces us to the novel's geometry. The novel begins with James's famous description of Kate at her father's house, waiting for him to come in so that she can make her offer to "go with him" (*WD* 25), that is, to stick by him in the face of his public scandal. This scene is often referred to by critics who wish to exculpate Kate by emphasizing the way she is herself a victim of her family's demands. James describes how Kate conceives herself in relation to them as a "trembling kid" being led to the slaughter, or "chalk-marked by fate like a 'lot' at a common auction" (*WD* 21). She is both her sister's and her father's last hope for dragging them out of their misery and poverty, as well as for rescuing the family name, and it is for this that she is to be "sacrificed," to go and live with Aunt Maud in the hope that, by satisfying her with a "great" marriage, Kate will eventually become her aunt's heir.

The ostensible choice confronting Kate in this scene is a version of the traditional dilemma of Victorian fiction, "love or money," the same choice that ultimately drives the narrative through to its conclusion in a parallel scene at the end of the novel, where Kate is once again faced with the dilemma of choosing between Densher without Milly's money, or the money without Densher. In this first choice, Kate's situation seems relatively simple. Kate wants to marry Merton Densher but Aunt Maud opposes the marriage, implicitly promising Kate a vast inheritance if she will abide by all of her aunt's wishes, one of which is that Kate must give up all relation with her abject family. Kate's offer to live with her father is thus implicitly also a way of avoiding Maud Lowder's clutches and marrying Densher, albeit by living in dire poverty. The choice seems to be in favor of love.

But, as it transpires, Kate's choice is not really a choice at all. Not only does her father reject her offer—and for some critics, like Mitchell, Kate knew before making it he never would accept (Mitchell 187)—but living without money amounts to no life at all for Kate, whose realization of the way "things" speak to her is one of the key moments of Kate's self-discovery in the novel:

> She saw as she had never seen before how material things spoke to her. She saw, and she blushed to see, that if in contrast with some of its old aspects life now affected her as a dress successfully "done up," this was exactly by reason of the trimmings and lace, was a matter of ribbons and silk and velvet. She had a dire accessibility to pleasure from such sources. She liked the charming quarters her aunt had assigned her— liked them literally more than she had in all her other days liked anything. (*WD* 35–36)

Within the terms of the novel as they are given to us, the couple "love or money" is seen as a false opposition that rapidly gives way to the new couple "desire or duty." Kate couches her offer to go live with him within the ostensibly ethical terms of her family responsibility but, as Lionel Croy astutely gleans, her supposed "generosity" masks her own desire, and he meets her ethical sleight of hand when he characteristically turns the tables on her and represents that her duty really lies in renouncing him in favor of Maud's cash. Kate's filial duty, she is told effectually, is to prostitute herself for her family, a proposition implicitly endorsed later by Kate's sister Marion who knows all too well the consequences of having married for love (five undernourished children and an abject flat in Chelsea). To Kate's initial offer, Croy presents a counteroffer which, in its absurd reversal of her own "ethical" position, is enough to make Kate wince: "You must do me the justice to see that I don't do things, that I've never done them, by halves—that if I offer you to efface myself it's for the final fatal sponge I ask, well saturated and well applied" (*WD* 31). Kate's offer to "sacrifice" herself for her family is thus effectively parodied in her father's extreme language of effacement, reversing the positions between the two so that Kate finds herself finally, as it were, in her father's "place." With the total "effacement" of her father, it is Kate who is left to try to redeem the Croy name, "the precious name she so liked and that, in spite of the harm her wretched father had done it, wasn't yet past praying for" (*WD* 22).

More reversals abound throughout this scene. Kate is struck again by her father's arts for turning a situation around: "He gave you absurd feelings, he had indescribable arts, that quite turned the tables" with the result that "[f]or a minute after he came in it was as if the place were her own and he the visitor with susceptibilities" (*WD* 24). In a particularly preposterous exchange Croy even goes so far as to invert the meaning of his scandal, arguing that he can be a valuable asset to his daughter and exhorting her that "your duty as well as your chance, if you're capable of seeing it, is to use me. Show family feeling by seeing what I'm good for" (*WD* 29). These chiasmic inversions are further reflected in James's use of parallel constructions such as when he describes how Kate "tried to be sad so as not to be angry, but it made her angry that she couldn't be sad" (*WD* 21).

The relations of synecdoche and analogy introduced into this scene also come to work in the service of reversibility. Kate is struck by the misery of her father's quarters, which gains in pathos to the extent that it replicates in miniature the rest of the street:

> The vulgar little street, in this view, offered scant relief from the vulgar little room; its main office was to suggest to her that the narrow blackhouse fronts, adjusted to a standard that would have been low even for backs, constituted quite the publicity implied by such privacies. One felt them in the room exactly as one felt the room—the hundred like it or worse—in the street. (*WD* 21)

Intended for privacy, the narrow house fronts have the opposite effect of projecting their interiors into Lionel Croy's room, which in turn projects itself, and the contents of all the rest of the houses' misery, into the street. What ought to be a firm distinction between public and private, room and street, instead becomes the means by which the inside changes places with the outside with the ironic result that the very attempt at privacy (Kate's father's secreting himself from the world) only serves to increase the publicity of his act.

In addition to foregrounding Kate's sense of the world as being unfixed by stable ethical or epistemological categories, the abiding effect of these reversals is to introduce an overwhelming sense of stasis that we will come to see as dominating the lives of James's characters at this stage in the novel. For, in spite of its ostensible movement, the logic of reversibility ensures that the polarities of the opposition remain intact. Kate's false choice between love or money describes this logic perfectly: Kate is told she must choose one or the other, but the outcome remains the same no matter what she chooses. This experience of stasis is nowhere better encapsulated than in the much-discussed first sentence of the novel where James's delay in mentioning Kate's name enacts, linguistically, her sense of being suspended in tension between two wills. Sandwiched between the conflicting demands of individual desire and duty to her family, Kate's ethical dilemma is presented in neatly formal terms:

> She waited, Kate Croy, for her father to come in, but he kept her unconscionably, and there were moments at which she showed herself, in the glass over the mantel, a face positively pale with the irritation that had brought her to the point of going away without sight of him. It was at this point, however, that she remained. (*WD* 21)

For Holland, this opening sentence epitomizes the novel's larger rhythm of tension between approach and withdrawal from its subject. What is striking, however, is the way this suspension is represented in spatial terms to capture Kate and her mirror reflection. With this image James externalizes Kate's conflicting desires to stay or to go, and introduces the pervasive "specularity" of Kate's London as a polarized world in which battles of wills have become locked into stalemate positions. This polar structure is even replicated in Kate's relationship with Densher. Kate and Densher are described in terms of each other's opposites, so that the "value" of having Kate for a wife, Densher muses, "would be in her differences"; while Kate, "though without having quite so philosophised, had quickly recognised in the young man a precious unlikeness" (*WD* 47). Kate's imaginative conception of their first meeting confirms this sense of their antithetical complementarity:

> She had observed a ladder against a garden-wall and had trusted herself so to climb it as to be able to see over into the probable garden on the other side. On reaching the top she had found herself face to face with a gentleman engaged in a like calculation at the same moment, and the two enquirers had remained confronted on their ladders. (*WD* 49)

Their second meeting continues this theme when Densher, seating himself on a train, finds himself opposite Kate Croy. But even between Kate and Densher a sense of stagnation obtrudes. Not only are they locked against Aunt Maud's resistance to their marriage, but within the relationship itself there is a sense of stasis. James hints at the lack of progress when he suggests that a passerby would recognize them as parties to a "long engagement" (*WD* 52).

> It was indeed for each, already, as if they were older friends; and though the succession of their meetings might, between them, have been straightened out, they only had a confused sense of a good many, very much alike, and a confused intention of a good many more, as little different as possible. (*WD* 52)

As in *The Portrait of a Lady*, the underlying principle driving these relationships is one of exchange. Both Lord Mark and, later, Kate explain the system to Milly in terms of an economic wager, where each party is attempting to strike "bargains" with the other: "The working and the worked were [. . .] the parties to every relation [. . .] everyone who had anything to give [. . .] made the sharpest possible bargain for it, got at least its value in return. [. . .] The worker in one connexion was the worked in another; it was as broad as it was long—with the wheels of the system, as might be seen, wonderfully oiled" (*WD* 116). The problem at this stage of the novel, however, is that the system has stagnated; everyone is too evenly matched. No one can move forward, because nobody is willing to give way. James's metaphor of a medieval siege captures this deadlock when he describes Kate's perceptions of her new life at Lancaster Gate: "It was in fact as a besieger, we have hinted, that our young lady, in the provisioned citadel, had for the present most to think of [Aunt Maud]" (*WD* 37). To break this stranglehold it will take the addition of a third factor, and such is the function of Milly's arrival on the scene. Milly and Susan's sudden appearance in London rearranges the oppositional geometry of the relationships. With the addition of these two characters, the previously deadlocked oppositions find themselves dissolving into triangular relationships whose effects are to break up the circles of mutual reflection and antagonism and to set them in motion.

While the prevailing critical tendency has been to pit Kate and Milly against one another in a Manichean struggle of good and evil, once we observe how many similarities inhere between the two young women this simple opposition becomes untenable: both are in recent mourning for their families, each are paired with an older woman, both suffer the attentions of Lord Mark and are in love with Densher. Moreover, key scenes in the novel recur between them. For example, the famous scene at Matcham when Lord Mark shows Milly her "likeness" in the Bronzino painting contains echoes of the novel's opening scene where Kate gazes at a specular double of herself in the mirror. Similarly, Kate's offer to "go with" her father, to sacrifice herself for her family has shades of Milly's final gesture when in the closing section of the novel she "turns her face to the wall" and, in dying, gives up Densher to Kate. Some apologists for Kate even suggest that she is just as much a victim of circumstance as Milly, citing the novel's opening sentence as demonstrating Kate's "entrapment" by her family, which has parallels with the "entrapment" of Milly by Kate and Densher (and by James himself who memorably describes his approach to Milly in composing the novel in such predatory terms, that is, by beginning "with the outer ring, approaching the centre thus by narrowing circumvallations" [*WD* 7]).

Most important, both young women are equally possessed with an unspeakable "secret." For Kate, as we know, this secret (that she keeps entirely from Milly) is her father's disgrace, while Milly's is the less well-kept truth about her condition. But these secrets come to intersect one another around the point of the question of the other's relationship with Densher. It is through Densher that Kate hopes to be able to redeem her family (by prostituting him to Milly), while for Milly, Densher's love is to be the means through which she can survive. As the point of intersection between each woman's "secret," therefore, Densher himself initially comes to serve as the "absent presence," the unspeakable in the relationship between Kate and Milly.

But before I go on to discuss this central triangular relationship, I first want to point out several of the other pairings among the characters of the novel. The obvious pairs are the doubled relationship between the younger and older women, Kate and Maud, and Susan and Milly. But Kate and Milly, as the two "trembling kids" of sacrifice, also pair up against Maud and Susan who are coupled as equally complicitous in the "plot" against Milly, albeit for quite different reasons. The duo of Kate and Densher is subsequently doubled in the Densher/Milly pair, who then both figure as Kate's unwitting "victims," such as when Densher asks of Milly early in the plot, and before he finally comprehends Kate's motives, "She's just such another victim?" and Kate replies "Just such another. You're a pair" (*WD* 221). Conversely, Susan and Milly redouble the Kate and Densher pair, insofar as, like the young lovers, the two women initially strike each other as "opposed curiosities" (*WD* 78). On the male side we find Lord Mark and Densher paired in Eugenio's eyes late in the novel as equal adventurers seeking Milly's millions, as Densher belatedly and ruefully comes to realize: "There recurred moments when, in spite of everything, he felt no straighter than another man" (*WD* 330).

On closer inspection, however, stranger couplings also begin to suggest themselves. It is hard not to see in Lionel Croy's offer to Kate to "efface" himself, for example, an ironic commentary on Milly's own supreme gesture of effacement—turning "her face to the wall"—at the end of the novel. Croy is to some extent a kind of debased version or double of Milly herself insofar as he, too, inhabits the ambiguous realm of the "unspeakable." James writes how "it was one of the marks of what they called the 'unspeakable' in him—to walk a little more on his toes [. . .] under the touch of offence" (*WD* 28). Some of the key terms to describe Milly, moreover, are foreshadowed in descriptions of Lionel, hence, although we never learn what it is he has done, we find it couched in the identical terms that surround Milly. While Milly famously wonders to Susie after her meditation on the Brünig whether she in fact has "everything," Kate replies to Densher's question of "'what has he done, if no one can name it?' 'He has done everything'" (*WD* 57). Both Lionel and Milly, moreover, are surrounded by the same violent recoil on the part of their comrades to "know" anything about what they have or have done. Susie's exclamation "God keep me from knowing" (*WD* 246) the full diagnosis of Milly's illness recalls Kate's milder comment regarding Croy's crime, "It's known—only, thank God, not to us" (*WD* 57), which further recalls James's expostulation in the Preface that "heaven forbid we should 'know' anything more of our ravaged sister than what Densher darkly pieces together, or than what Kate Croy pays, heroically, it must be owned, at the hour of her visit alone to Densher's lodging [. . .]" (*WD* 12). The effect of such a pairing of Milly and Lionel distinctly problematizes any tendency to see Milly as unambiguously good to Kate's evil. Lionel's ironic doubling of Milly's ambiguous gesture of "generosity"[11] makes it difficult to interpret Milly's final act in the predominant terms of redemption and forgiveness that have come to typify the novel's reception.

An entire study could be made of the pairs discovered by a close reading of the novel, but let it suffice simply to indicate the main directions such an analysis suggested by the novel's metaphors could take:

1. The maritime metaphors of the novel that align Milly with Maud, when Milly's *Titanic*-like "great steamer," drawing an "inordinate number of 'feet of water'" (*WD* 81) toward its and everyone else's doom, tragically comments on Kate's Ruskinian reference to Maud as the "Britannia of the marketplace" (Britannia being, among other things, the name of the Prince of Wales's famous yacht, which won a record number of first places during its second season in 1894).

2. The military metaphors that continue to align Milly with Kate but where Kate is habitually described in terms of the siege mentality of medieval warfare ("she was always, for her beneficent dragon, under arms," *WD* 204), Milly is the victim of modern revolutionary violence. James notes in his notebook, "She is like a creature dragged shrieking to the guillotine—to the shambles,"[12] a metaphor that eventually finds its way into the novel in Milly's first visit to the doctor: "when pity held up its telltale face like a head on a pike, in a French revolution, bobbing before a window, what was the inference but that the patient was bad?" (*WD* 148).

3. The class metaphors of the princess and the bourgeoisie. To Milly's and Lord Mark's "aristocracy" (Lord Mark "hover[ed] before her as a potentially insolent noble" [*WD* 101]), Kate is conceived by Mrs. Stringham in the role of "the chosen daughter of the burgesses," "the worthiest maiden" waiting on the princess "at the city gate" (*WD* 111).[13]

In addition to prompting unexpected alignments among the characters, thereby belying the attempt to forge a simple opposition between Kate and Milly, London and America, James's metaphors introduce us to three different legal, economic, and political systems, all of which come to bear on the main plot of the novel. While the much-discussed animal imagery of the novel references the rule of natural law according to which Milly, as dove, is helpless against the laws of nature that dictate the strongest will survive (Maud's eagle and Kate's panther), the equally prevalent maritime imagery introduces the more arbitrary law of the market and of trade, as well as ushering in the even less calculable effects of what the increased mobility and communications of the early twentieth century might do to established economic and political systems. Finally, in the metaphor of the princess James harnesses the rhetorical power of the French revolution to color Milly's encounter with her English friends in terms of the Terror following the collapse of ancient rules and justifications of law, before their replacement by democratic rule. James's irony in substituting a representative of the New World for the aristocratic victim of revolutionary violence only underscores the continuing disruption of the conventional oppositions between Kate's England and Milly's America. In James's new world, the traditional alliances and oppositions depart radically from their habitual places, ushering in a world closely modeled on the democratic political formation wherein the rule of law is guaranteed no longer by God but by the declarative power of language itself.[14] This, then, is the background against which Milly's drama occurs—the political, economic, and legal backdrop that reflects her own drama, the emergence of the subject of desire.

II

What we have established so far is a novelistic world dominated by a persistent dualism. James presents Kate's London as an oppositional world characterized by sets of alliances and antagonisms, all of which have finally reached a stalemate. Milly's arrival on the scene in London, however, changes this dynamic. Milly's presence breaks up the static circles of reflection and antagonism, opening up a space in which the repetitive, stultifying pattern of reciprocal inversion can finally move out of itself and into new formations. Since it is in the relationship between Kate and Milly that this change-inducing function occurs, it is to these two women we must now turn.

When she first encounters Kate at dinner at Lancaster Gate Milly is immediately struck by the "handsome girl" (*WD* 98). She wonders whether she and Kate are destined to pick up where Maud and Susan had left off years before, whether, that is, they will form a double of the older pair: "Were they, Miss Croy and she, to take up the tale where their two elders had left it off so many years before—were they to find they liked each other and to try for themselves whether a scheme of constancy on more modern lines could be worked?" (*WD* 99). Milly rapidly finds their relationship indeed quickly blossoming, although even early on she discovers a certain opacity in her new friend. Comparing the niece with her aunt, Milly discovers that, although each represent to her a "great reality," she senses that a "tour" of Kate's mind would be considerably harder to complete: "[Milly] felt Mrs. Lowder as a person of whom the mind might in two or three days roughly make the circuit. She would sit there massive at least while one attempted it; whereas Miss Croy, the handsome girl, would indulge in incalculable movements that might interfere with one's tour" (*WD* 99). What inhibits the easy formation of a pair between them—whether of antagonism or of alliance—is Kate's impenetrability. Milly muses to herself that "she should never know how Kate truly felt about anything such a one as Milly Theale should give her to feel" (*WD* 122). Reflecting on Kate, Milly suddenly feels herself "on the edge of a great darkness" (*WD* 122).

The form given to this darkness is of course the question of Kate's relationship with Densher. The moment Milly discovers through Susie that Kate and Densher know one another, the "handsome girl" begins to acquire a new luster for Milly, a strange otherness that presents Kate in terms of the "not wholly calculable" (*WD* 122):

> Kate had for her new friend's eyes the extraordinary and attaching property of appearing at a given moment to show as a beautiful stranger, to cut her connexions and lose her identity [. . .]—make her merely a person striking from afar, more and more pleasing as one watched, but who was above all a subject for curiosity. (*WD* 132)

Their mutual avoidance of Densher's name becomes a secret thrill for Milly whose excitement James describes as "containing measurably a small element of anxiety. [. . .] Twice over thus, for two or three hours together, Milly found herself seeing Kate, quite fixing her, in the light of the knowledge that it was a face on which Densher's eyes had more or less familiarly rested and which, by the same token, had looked, rather more beautifully than less into his own" (*WD* 121–22). What makes Kate so different all of a sudden is that Milly finds herself looking at Kate as if through Densher's eyes: "[S]he stood there suddenly, irrelevantly, in the light of her other identity, the identity she would have for Mr. Densher. This was always, from one instant to another, an incalculable light, which, though it might go off faster than it came on, necessarily disturbed" (*WD* 144).

Milly's odd behavior toward Kate's knowing Densher is not merely the awkwardness of a young, inexperienced, infatuated girl toward an older, more sophisticated couple. It marks the beginning of a more complex relationship than that of opposition. The terms of this relationship are introduced in the scene in the National Gallery when Milly, having left Susan to meet with the doctor Sir Luke in her absence, comes upon Kate and Densher in a secret rendezvous. Turning to look at what she expects to be a painting in the "English style" remarked on by the American group on whom she is eavesdropping, Milly discovers Densher looking abstractedly at works of art. But, before long, Milly is aware that, like Densher, she has also been the unwitting subject of a gaze, Kate's, who has taken them both in unawares. Initially, the direction of the gazes is unidirectional: Kate watches Milly watching Densher. But once she discovers Kate watching her in turn, Milly suddenly begins to see herself from the place where Kate sees her; her position shifts from an immediate relation to a mediated one, from seeing to being seen seeing:

> She was unable to think afterwards how long she had looked at him before knowing herself as otherwise looked at; all she was coherently to put together was that she had had a second recognition without his having noticed her. The source of this latter shock was nobody less than Kate Croy—Kate Croy who was suddenly also in the line of vision and whose eyes met her eyes at their next movement. (*WD* 177)

Here the pattern of recognition shifts from one of a simple reciprocity to the "shock" of discovering that one is seen from outside; there is a place from which I am seen by another who is not in my reciprocal line of vision. Although depicted here in temporal terms ("she had had a second recognition"), the effect is in fact to introduce a new spatial point into the novel's geometry. Becoming aware of Kate watching her, Milly finds herself split between identification with Densher—like him, she finds herself the unwitting object of a look—and identification with Kate as the seeing subject. Part of the "shock" that Milly experiences, then, is the shock of seeing oneself through someone else's eyes, seeing oneself, that is, from the outside or even, paradoxically, from the back of one's own head. The effects of such a perspectival shift, however, are immense, for with this addition of a third space from where one sees oneself from the point of view of a nonreciprocal other, the static pattern of dyadic identifications is breached, enabling the formation of new relations.

In fact, the scene in the National Gallery simply translates into visual and thematic terms the structural change that has already occurred on the economic level with Milly's arrival in London. Into Maud's world of fixed exchange, where every party's value is known in relation to everyone else, Milly introduces a rupture precisely because she doesn't know what her value is (Do people want her for herself or for her money?).[15] Extending Julie Rivkin's point when she argues that Milly introduces a radically unamortizable figure into the restricted economy of Kate's and Maud's

London, one might explain the change in terms of the difference between a barter or, more specifically, as James's many references to Maud's "gilded beak and claws" suggest, a gold-based versus a paper, or credit economy.[16] Literally, of course, London is just as much a mercantile capitalist society as Milly's United States. However, as James's medieval imagery of Kate's London implies, their metaphorical economy—and the economy by which people are literally "exchanged"—remains decidedly feudal.

The difference between the two economies lies in the immediacy of the relation between money and its objects of purchase. A gold-based economy assumes a direct one-to-one correspondence between the object and payment, that is to say, the payment has its own guaranteed value against which objects can be compared and priced. A gold-based economy is therefore scarcely removed from a barter system where goods with intrinsic value are directly exchanged for one another. With paper money, however, this direct correspondence is mediated. Instead of receiving the equivalent value in gold for an object, sellers receive merely a "promise to pay." These originally took various forms such as "promissory notes," bills of exchange, receipts, IOUs, notes of indemnity, and so forth that were issued either by banks or by individuals naming a particular merchant. Eventually, however, such "bills" or bank notes ended up simply naming the anonymous "bearer" as entitled to an equivalent amount of specie. What enabled this anonymization of the bearer, which became the defining moment for the widespread adoption of paper money in the West, was a change in late seventeenth-century English law that allowed a debt to be transferred to another person without the debtor's sanction.[17] With this legal right, paper money became divorced from any particular historical individual or transaction and was able to enter into the circulation of goods as a commodity in its own right, hence able to be bought, sold, and speculated on as to its future value.

The difference that paper money makes, and on whose principle capitalism is founded, is the temporal delay inaugurated between the issue of a note and its subsequent redemption in specie. This delay makes it possible for banks and individuals to lend the "value" of a specified amount of gold (or silver, tobacco, beaver pelts, cattle, whatever it is that serves a society as real value) many times over, at least within keeping of the range of possibility of redeeming the note should its bearer so demand. But as banks happily discovered, in the meantime, profiting on the interest gained by the loan, their capital increases so that, barring any unusual "run" on the bank for specie, redeeming any individual request was usually not a problem. Money really did seem to be made (almost) from nothing. With this discovery (which Braudel has shown was not confined to the West but occurred at various historical periods all over the world), what we know as modern banking was born.[18]

It is worth noting how in the mid-nineteenth century, presumably during the period when Milly's father and uncles were making their vast fortunes (possibly in currency speculation themselves[19]), America was engaged in a fierce political debate over the question of paper versus coined money. Paper money was viewed with hostility and suspicion by many precisely because of its ability to create wealth seemingly from nowhere, particularly when, as happened between 1862 and 1879, during and after the American Civil War, paper money became no longer redeemable for specie but, as the "greenback," was made to guarantee itself. Such self-guaranteeing paper money then becomes a kind of confidence game that lasts only as long as people continue to believe that there is some "real" value for which it can be traded in at the last moment. Such was the role played historically by the Bank of England throughout the past three centuries: as the "lender of last resort," it became the final guarantor of all the private and public banks of England and its colonies, as well as of government notes. But the history of money is dotted with the boom and bust cycle of this confidence game, from the scandal of the famous Royale Banque of France under the direction of the Scot John Law and his Louisiana gold bubble in the seventeenth century, its contemporary equivalents in England and the Netherlands in the South Seas and Tulip Bubbles, to the wild speculation in railroads, land, gold, and currency that went on in the United States during James's early childhood. As the financial disasters of the various bubbles confirm, if paper money is not at least perceived to be grounded in some "real" value, it is constantly in danger of flying wildly out of control, in the form of hyperinflation. If, as was always all too tempting for governments under pressures from war, too much money was printed (financing in this way both the American and French revolutions), its very excess in the marketplace makes it worth less. Prices begin to rise dramatically, people's wages are unable to keep up, and depression takes over, shrinking the economy, increasing unemployment and, at worst, collapsing the entire currency system.

The important point to be observed in all of this is the way that paper money, as Slavoj Žižek has pointed out, introduces a new dimension into the previously one-to-one exchange of the gold economy.[20] Paper money's anonymous "bearer" mediates the transaction between the buyer and the seller; the bearer of the bank note is now, as Brian Rotman explains, a "variable subject" by which he means "a subject in meta-lingual relation to any particular named and dated individual (the temporary owner of the note at a particular time) able to instantiate it."[21] As such, the bearer inhabits a paradoxical or contradictory space: it is simultaneously a sign within the system, and a marker for the system itself, comparable, Rotman argues, to the number zero, or to the empty set of set theory. This is because, once money has been divorced from any guarantee as to its intrinsic value in the real world, its ultimate guarantee comes to lie solely in the collective belief of the bearing subjects (a belief that can just as easily collapse, as in the case of hyperinflation). Hence the bearer occupies a unique place: as the particular, contingent owner of the note, it inhabits the temporal system of exchange. But as final "guarantor" of the exchange, it steps out of the temporal series to become the principle of the exchange itself.

Just as Kate's redoubled gaze of Milly watching Densher resulted in the advent of a third viewing position—the strange perception of seeing oneself from the point of view of the (nonreciprocal) other—so, too, paper money creates an intermediary subject whose function is identical: it forces a change in the symmetrical or binary logic of exchange by introducing a position that is neither completely inside nor outside the system proper, but rather traces a structural paradox: the case of being at one and the same time both part of the differential formal structure (the play of positives and negatives of the oppositional economy), *and* its founding or guaranteeing principle itself. In each case, a fundamentally nonreciprocal relation to an other is forged. With this creation of a third (reflexive) discursive space, the cycle of reciprocal inversion is broken to make way for new compositional patterns.

III

If until now the action has been dominated by oppositional pairs engaged in what might be considered a Hegelian life-or-death power struggle (for recognition, power etc.), the addition of this third discursive space has the ability to change these relations. The way this is formalized in the novel is through a peculiar propensity of the characters to exchange places with one another.[22] But it is important to note the difference between this movement and the previous pattern of inversion. Where inversion was defined by reciprocity—the endless seesawing movement between two oppositional poles—exchanging places implies a relation to a third person or position whose ability is to reconfigure the relation of pairs. Previously the only positions available were in the reversal of oppositions. Now, however, relations are possible that can fundamentally change the configuration of the characters. This change is reflected in the novel's metaphorical economy. If until now the dominant metaphors were military, of alliances and antagonisms, in the second volume we enter the more ambiguous realm of art.

In fact, this shift is already heralded in the famous scene at Matcham in the first volume where Milly confronts the Bronzino painting whose likeness to herself is marked by all the guests. This scene gives us (and Kate) the first intimation about the state of Milly's health, and it is in contrast to the possibilities of Milly's famous social "success" among the London social elite that Milly's confrontation with her own mortality gains its sharpest relief. In the midst of the "brilliant life" (*WD* 131) of the party, Lord Mark detaches Milly from the rest and invites her to come and see a painting by Bronzino that is thought to resemble her. As is frequently the case in James, the invitation to view works of art becomes a pretext for a more intimate exchange between characters, which Milly understands as Lord Mark's asking her to "let a fellow who isn't a fool take care of you a little" (*WD* 137). This unspoken request—James observes how "it was as if the thing had practically been said by the moment they came in sight of the picture"—is perhaps Milly's first marriage proposal, and it comes over her as if "it was a sort of magnificent maximum, the pink dawn of an apotheosis coming so curiously soon" (*WD* 137). Overcome, Milly collapses into tears and, as she realizes later, "it was Lord Mark who said nothing in particular, it was she herself who said all. She couldn't help that—it came; and the reason it came was that she found herself, for the first moment, looking at the mysterious portrait through tears":

> Perhaps it was her tears that made it just then so strange and fair—as wonderful as he had said: the face of a young woman, all splendidly drawn, down to the hands, and splendidly dressed; a face almost livid in hue, yet handsome in sadness and crowned with a mass of hair, rolled back and high, that must, before fading with time, have had a family resemblance to her own. The lady in question, at all events, with her slightly Michael-angelesque squareness, her eyes of other days, her full lips, her long neck, her recorded jewels, her brocaded and wasted reds, was a very great personage—only unaccompanied by a joy. And she was dead, dead, dead. (*WD* 137)

Milly's experience of viewing the Bronzino has often been taken as a moment of specular identification comparable, for Lee Clark Mitchell, to the earliest scene in the novel when Kate appears to herself in the mirror.[23] Both Nicola Bradbury and Marcia Ian, for example, assert that this moment is dominated by the "fusion" of subject and object. Milly and the woman in the painting—assumed to be the portrait of sixteenth-century Lucrezia Panciatichi—are found to merge with one another's identities so that when, minutes later, Lord and Lady Aldershaw arrive with Kate and interrupt her viewing, "Lady Aldershaw [. . .] looked at Milly quite as if Milly had been the Bronzino and the Bronzino only Milly" (WD 139). For Ian, this "fusion" of two young women, one alive, one "dead, dead, dead," creates a moment of self-transparency when Milly's fears about herself and others' beliefs about her (that she is doomed) coincide. Such a moment of "penetrated identity [. . .] moves Milly to tears of happiness" because "her deepest sense of herself [. . .] has been gently exposed and acknowledged [. . .] to be identical to and indistinguishable from the way others see her."[24]

I find it hard to see how she comes to this conclusion. Not only does Milly, minutes later, claim to fail to see the resemblance, but her tears, as I will elaborate, hardly seem the result of an excess of happiness. Milly does, nevertheless, recognize something in the portrait: "Milly recognised her exactly in words that had nothing to do with her. 'I shall never be better than this'" (WD 137). What does Milly mean with this statement? Lord Mark interprets her as comparing herself negatively to the woman in the painting. But as James tells us, "He hadn't understood." What Milly sees in the painting, as many critics have already observed, is an image of her mortality. What she recognizes, therefore, is not a mimetic likeness—"I wish I could see the resemblance" (WD 138) she tells Lord Mark—but as Reinhard argues, an allegorical one.[25] It is her own death she sees in the face of the "lady in question" who looks back at Milly from beyond the grave.

As her earlier discussion with Susan about whether she will have "everything" suggests, Milly's life until now has been largely directed toward the future. Now, however, with the image of her death before her, she has an existential understanding of the essential equivalence of all moments in the face of inevitable annihilation: "I shall never be better than this." Therefore, to interpret Milly's statement as Ian does as the expression of penultimate happiness and self-transparency completely misunderstands the meaning of Milly's apotheosis. An apotheosis is not only a supreme moment, or quintessential example of a thing. It is also the elevation to divine status whose concomitant implication is that one is already dead.[26] Milly's "magnificent maximum," occurring at the moment of her traumatic discovery of her temporality, is far from the expression of a moment of absolute happiness. Her tears express rather the horrifying realization of the absolute senselessness of comparing time with the end of time: "It was probably as good a moment as she should ever have with him. It was perhaps as good a moment as she should have with any one, or have in any connexion whatever" (*WD* 137). Instead of comparing moments and finding one superlative, Milly's discovery that the meaning of life is death turns all temporal hierarchies into bitter irony, since everyone, no matter how long they live, will eventually die. Death equalizes everyone and everything, making a mockery of the dead woman's "full lips, her long neck, her recorded jewels, her brocaded and wasted reds."

Coming as it does on the heels of Lord Mark's proposal, Milly's traumatic encounter with her memento mori helps to cement the connection she already dimly feels between love and death. Accepting Lord Mark would seem to amount to nothing less than her surrender to the people with the "kind eyes" whose pity shines out ghoulishly as a decapitated head on a pike bobbing before the window. Lord Mark's proposal and, with it, the intimation of death has come as an "apotheosis" much too soon.

The next day Milly and Kate go to see the doctor, Sir Luke Strett, who immediately impresses Milly with his interest, which she takes as a sign that there must be something seriously wrong with her. His interest, she feels, goes beyond a normal patient/doctor relation; it makes her feel she has mysteriously moved him to compassion, and he is trying to "let her down" gently, much in the way women do "when they deprecated the addresses of gentlemen they couldn't more intimately go on with" (*WD* 154). He seemed to be "'up to' [. . .] some disguised intention of standing by her as a friend" (*WD* 154). She reports back to Kate, almost gaily, "He knows all about me, and I like it. I don't hate it a bit" (*WD* 143). On her second visit to the doctor, Milly is again struck by the doctor's knowledge: "It was exactly as if, in the forty-eight hours that had passed, her acquaintance with him had somehow increased and his own knowledge in particular had received some mysterious additions" (*WD* 145). Sir Luke's knowledge is derived, however, from no crass action of "finding out" about her: "there was no source of information to his hand, and he had really needed none: he had found out simply by his genius—and found out, she meant, literally everything" (*WD* 145). This, Milly realizes, "was truly what she had come for, and that for the time at least it would give her something firm to stand on" (*WD* 146).

But although Milly has approached the doctor in order to gain knowledge about her condition, she finds afterward that he "had beautifully got out of it" (*WD* 154). He refuses to name what is wrong with her, contenting himself with merely advising Milly that she should "take the trouble" to live: "What indeed she was really confronted with was the consciousness that he hadn't after all pronounced her anything" (*WD* 154). The effect of her visit to the doctor is to turn the tables on Milly. She had come wanting something "firm" to stand on; she leaves instead with a heightened sense of the "grey immensity" of life, of the loss of life's foundations. As she walks back through Regent's Park, Milly finds that "Grey immensity had somehow of a sudden become her element" (*WD* 152). Arriving with her demand for the doctor to tell her what is wrong with her, Milly leaves with the new question of what it is to "live": "grey immensity was what her distinguished friend had, for the moment, furnished her world with and what the question of 'living,' as he put it to her, living by option, by volition, inevitably took on for its immediate face" (*WD* 152). At the same time that this question gives Milly a new and invigorating sense of a "great adventure, a big dim experiment or struggle in which she might more responsibly than ever take a hand," she is also aware of the loss of her old way of life: "the beauty of the bloom had gone from the small old sense of safety—that was distinct: she had left it behind her there forever" (*WD* 152). In its place is the liberating, yet terrifying, open question of how to live without any of the old, usual supports, divested of any familial or social relations. Sir Luke's advice opens Milly up to an understanding of her existential aloneness that she recognizes as putting her in touch with humanity at large:

> No one in the world could have sufficiently entered into her state; no tie would have been close enough to enable a companion to walk beside her without some disparity. She literally felt, in this first flush, that her only company must be the human race at large, present all round her, but inspiringly impersonal. (*WD* 152)

Once divested of the "old sense of safety," Milly finds herself reduced "to her ultimate state, which was that of a poor girl—with her rent to pay for example—staring before her in a great city" (*WD* 155). The meeting with Sir Luke had been "directly divesting, denuding, exposing" and this has forced her once again to confront the idea of her death. The difference between this and her apotheosis at Matcham, however, is that this time Sir Luke has supplied her with "some queer defensive weapon" (*WD* 152). What is this weapon? Although Milly (like most critics) understands the doctor as referring to the question of volition, of will, Sir Luke's formula that "she could live if she would" can equally be read as a question about desire, "would" understood in its archaic meaning of to want.[27] In effect, Sir Luke intimates to Milly that, in order to survive her confrontation with death, she must find something or someone to love, thereby transforming her traumatic "apotheosis" into the open question whose Freudian overtones are unmistakable: What, as a woman, does she want?[28]

The mystery surrounding Milly's illness now begins to clear once we realize that it is precisely in order to be able to keep living in the face of the knowledge of death that Milly becomes "ill."[29] Rather than "surrender" to Lord Mark and her apotheosis, Milly vows to fight, and the way she does this is by interposing something between herself and her knowledge of her mortality. This "queer defensive weapon" is quite simply, as Strett well knows, the question of her desire. How does desire ward off death? As Scheherezade of the *Arabian Nights* discovered long ago, desire defers death by substituting dissatisfaction in its place. Desire rearranges a deadlock into a temporal series whose primary characteristic is persistent failure. But this failure is precisely what keeps desire (and the subject) alive: desire's endless dissatisfactions maintain the fantasy that complete satisfaction (which is of course nothing other than death) will eventually be attained, but just not yet. By becoming ill or, as we might as well now say, becoming "hysterical" (a desiring subject), Milly embarks on the tortuous pathways of desire that, for as long as it remains dissatisfied, defends her against her "apotheosis."

The problem remains, however, that Milly no more knows the answer to Sir Luke's question of her desire than did any of Freud's patients. What does she do then? Like any good hysteric, she turns to another woman to learn the truth about her desire. In a stroke of inspiration, Milly decides to copy someone who really does seem to know what she wants, Kate Croy, the "handsome girl" with the enviable "talent for life." In this, Milly is simply taking her own advice to herself at the National Gallery when she muses how she ought to have been a lady-copyist. Kate will show her what and how a woman desires. But first she must find out what it is that Kate wants.

IV

A word of caution here. It is important not to mistake the three-way relation between our main characters for René Girard's triangular structure of desire in his well-known study *Deceit, Desire and the Novel*.[30] Briefly, Girard observes how the modern condition is characterized by a fundamental lack of foundation. But instead of looking "freedom in the face," people are horrified by the loss of guarantee previously provided by God and fall back on "substitute gods" in compensation. They turn to each other and gain self-definition through imitating what they perceive as another's desire. All desire is thus mimetic for Girard, filtered through a mediator who is the only one to desire spontaneously. Therefore, if we were to translate James's novel into Girardian terms, Kate should play the role of mediator for Milly: Milly will copy Kate's desire because she doesn't know what she wants for herself. This mimetic dimension is certainly at play in the novel but it is important to note how this pattern does not tell the whole story. Although, on one level, Milly does identify mimetically with Kate, taking Densher as her object, it is crucial to remember, as the scene in the National Gallery makes clear, that Milly also simultaneously identifies with Densher. The structure is therefore redoubled just at the point where the two women's looks cross one another, overlaying the dual exchange of looks with a third viewing position that is structurally in excess of both of them.

In contrast, Girardian triangular desire simply replicates the pattern of antagonism that we saw operating at the beginning of the novel. In the Girardian triangle, the third position, the object, is nothing more than a simple token that shuttles between rivaling subjects, intersecting the competing desires. As such, it has no power of reconfiguring the relation between the two subjects. Although various permutations of this structure are possible, which Girard traces in terms of the mediator's increasing proximity to the subject, the basic pattern remains the same one of imaginary rivalry that we saw dominating the social world of James's novel before Milly's arrival on the scene. In other words, and counterintuitively, the Girardian triangle remains a duality of reflective antagonisms as the desiring subject competes furiously with its mimetic double for an essentially irrelevant and replaceable object.[31] James on the other hand, introduces something completely different into the equation.

What is this difference? The difference is that, whereas the Girardian subject imitates the other by copying its desire, James's subject, Milly, does not know what the other (Kate) wants. Until her traumatic illumination by Lord Mark, Milly remains—to some extent—ignorant of the truth of Kate's desire. And it is this question, this lack of knowledge as to what Kate wants (which is also the question of what her, Milly's, own value is for Kate, that is, what it is that Kate wants from Milly) that can be said to sustain Milly's life. Once her question has been answered, once she discovers the truth about Kate's relationship with Densher, her entire fantasmatic structure dissolves. What keeps her alive, in other words, is not Densher's love, as the sentimental reading of the novel would have it. It seems clear that on this score Densher's overtures toward Milly were less than convincing, and it would take a character with considerably less of the "wisdom of the serpent" (WD 141) not to see through the impression he makes, which Kate describes as "a clever cousin calling on a cousin afflicted, and bored for his pains" (WD 280). What keeps Milly alive, rather, is the open question of Kate's desire which, so long as it remains unanswered, maintains Milly on the path of desire, that is, on the path toward answering Sir Luke's question of what it is that she, as a woman, wants.

Another way of understanding this is to put it into the linguistic terms with which we began this discussion: what sustains Milly is her constant failure to find a name that would completely describe her. This failure transforms her experience of something that is permanently unrepresentable, namely, her essential identity in death, into the much more manageable, because temporally displaced, idea of the unnameable whose crucial difference lies in the promise this formulation holds out that there might be a word that could adequate to her, if one could only find the right name. It implies, in other words, a subtle shift from the certain, metaphysical impossibility of representing something that lies beyond the limits of our representational capacities, on the one hand, to the deferred possibility implied by reducing the problem to a linguistic question of naming, on the other.

How does this transformation of the unrepresentable into the unnameable occur? The next time Milly sees Kate after her visit to the doctor and the crisis in Regent's Park, she once again discovers that strange otherness that comes from seeing her friend as if through Densher's eyes: "Just so was how she looked to him, and just so was how Milly was held by her—held as by the strange sense of seeing through that distant person's eyes" (WD 157). The meaning of Kate's look suddenly comes to Milly in a flash: "it struck our young woman as absurd to say that a girl's looking so to a man could possibly be without connexions;

and the second [effect] was that by the time Kate had got into the room Milly was in mental possession of the main connexion it must have for herself" (*WD* 158). Identifying with Densher, Milly discovers in a flash who it is that Kate desires. The immediate result of this knowledge is to hold back from Kate the details of her visit to the doctor: "'You mean you've been absurd?' 'Absurd.' It was a simple word to say, but the consequence of it, for our young woman, was that she felt it, as soon as spoken, to have done something for her safety" (*WD* 158).

Two points need to be made at this juncture. The first is that, although at this moment Milly intuits the meaning of Kate's look as signifying her desire for Densher, she spends the rest of the novel trying to test this, shall we say, unconscious, knowledge against what Kate and everyone else tell her. The difference can be described as that between knowledge and belief. Although she "knows" from this point on that Kate and Densher are lovers (a knowledge on which she constructs her own mimetic desire for Densher), Milly believes Kate's denials insofar as they give her the freedom to embark on her own path of unsatisfied desire in her romance with Densher. Second, this flash of insight provides her with an understanding of how desire organizes itself around a prohibition. Comprehending, finally, the meaning of their joint refusal to mention Densher's name to each other, Milly intuits how prohibition has the power to transform impossibility into deferred possibility. Applying this discovery to herself, Milly immediately refuses anyone any knowledge about her own condition, forbidding anyone to as much as mention the possibility of her being ill. In doing so, Milly creates the conditions to uphold the fantasy that there really is a word that would adequately describe her—that language really can say everything—if one could only find the right name. It is, as Kate astutely gleans, the "conspiracy of silence" itself, then, that subsequently sustains Milly's life:

> [Kate] grasped with her keen intelligence the logic of their common duplicity, [. . .] easily saw that for the girl to be explicit was to betray divinations, gratitudes, glimpses of the felt contrast between her fortune and her fear. [. . .] That was it, Kate wonderingly saw: to recognise was to bring down the avalanche—the avalanche Milly lived so in watch for and that might be started by the lightest of breaths. (*WD* 262–63)

So whatever else one might want to charge Kate with, she at least must be credited with showing Milly a way out of the fatal deadlock of her apotheosis, and of presenting an alternative (and, as I will elaborate, a specifically ethical) approach to the question of the limits of representation. For Kate shows Milly how to rearrange a representational impossibility into the productive, because temporal, series that is desire.

Milly's strict prohibition forbidding anyone to refer to her "illness" must be understood, then, as having no other function than to carve out a space in which she can try on the different names she manages to draw out of everyone around her (except of course Sir Luke who responds, proto-analytically, to her demands merely with the "crystal-clean [. . .] empty cup of attention" [WD 142]). But because none of the names will ever be adequate for the hysterical subject whose dissatisfaction is constitutive, because there is always something more that escapes every one of the attempts to name her, Milly avoids becoming trapped by them, at least for as long as something remains outside the representational system that cannot be said. Until that moment, when Lord Mark's avowal effectively closes the circuit of representation and fixes her as an object, what does Milly do in her short life? She does nothing but generate names from everyone around her in response to her constant demand, "Why do you say such things to me?" (WD 171)—Who am I? What do you take me for?

The constant production of new names sustains not only Milly's life, but in the process contributes to increasing the possibilities for language's signification. For the names Milly receives from her friends are not medical diagnoses but metaphors: the dove, the princess, the American girl. But these figures seem strange in comparison to the metaphorical language in which James saturates the rest of the novel's prose. Isn't there something a little contrived about these figures? Don't they seem to jump out and demand another kind of attention than the rest of James's metaphors? Compare, for example, how effortlessly James inserts his metaphor of embroidery into the scene at Matcham where Milly gets a first good look at the way Aunt Maud "works" everyone into her system: "[Lord Mark] seemed slowly to pass and repass and conveniently to linger before them; he was personally the note of the blue—like a suspended skein of silk within reach of the broiderer's hand. Aunt Maud's free-moving shuttle took a length of him at rhythmic intervals; and one of the accessory truths that flickered across to Milly was that he ever so consentingly knew he was being worked in" (WD 133). In contrast, the metaphors surrounding Milly seem almost too forced and contrived. Why does James make Milly's metaphors so anomalous? The answer can only be because these metaphors are not simply metaphors but are them-

selves the forms of Milly's symptoms; these names are the peculiar products of her perpetually failed attempt to put herself wholly into language.
As such, they demand attention and interpretation, much in the way the
hysteric's symptom presents itself for decoding to hear its hidden mes-
sage about desire. For as we know, the hysterical symptom is the attempt
to communicate an idea that has been unable to gain representation
through the usual channels due to repression. The conversion symptom
therefore makes use of what it has to hand, namely, fragments, parts of
the body that can be mobilized to represent the content of the repressed
idea without its being noticed by the censoring agency. Symptoms are,
thus, themselves forms of metaphor, as Gilbert Chaitin notes, insofar as
they join previously unconnected ideas together to form a meaningful
unit.[32] Like Milly's metaphors, they, too, are strange and disruptive, dis-
turbing the regular functioning of the body, sticking out and requiring
further interpretation.

IV

To summarize, the metaphors proliferating around Milly are the products
of her attempt to find names to substitute for the unspeakable, names
which, while they help to plug the gap left by the unrepresentable, nevertheless always fall short of filling it in. But this falling short is the very gap,
it turns out, that sustains Milly, it is what keeps her alive.

Shortly afterward Milly shifts her entourage to Venice and sets up her
"court" in the Palazzo Leporelli. Early twentieth-century readers would
have been alerted to the specifically aesthetic meaning of Milly's choice of
Venice as the place she will stage her hysterical fantasy. Following the mid-
century publication of Ruskin's influential account of the Byzantine and
Gothic architecture in *The Stones of Venice*, Venice had by the late nineteenth century become a privileged signifier for art and for aestheticism
generally. It was *The Stones of Venice* that Walter Pater (one of Susan
Stringham's favorite authors) implicitly revised in his history of *The
Renaissance*; it was to Venice that Whistler retreated after his disastrous
libel case against Ruskin. Venice, by the time of James's novel, had
become symbolic of the central tenets of aestheticism whose association
of excessive beauty with fatal decay found its penultimate expression in
this city, "most beautiful of tombs."[33] By choosing Venice, Milly cannot
fail to have had some of this in mind.

What does Milly do there? In keeping with the pervasive aestheticism of the place, she holds a party that she stages, or at least so Susan imagines, as a living Veronese painting. In fact, two paintings by Paolo Caliare detto Veronese are usually named as the ones James had in mind when Susan whimsically explains the composition to Densher: "'[I]t's a Veronese painting, as near as can be—with me as the inevitable dwarf, the small blackamoor, put into a corner of the foreground for effect'" (*WD* 297), and Densher, "'the grand young man who surpasses the others and holds up his head and the winecup'" (*WD* 298). The first painting identified by Holland still hangs in the Venice Academy where James first saw it during his visit to Venice in 1870.[34] It is called "The Supper in the House of Levi" and it depicts an episode from the Book of Luke where Christ dines with his disciple Matthew, along with a group of publicans and sinners. The contrast in this painting between a serene, pensive Christ in the center of the painting and the riotous publicans around him is frequently taken to reflect back on the image of a saintly Milly surrounded by "sinners."

The second painting is "The Marriage Feast at Cana" hanging in the Louvre in Paris. In this painting, Christ again attends a banquet, this time a wedding feast where the host ran out of wine. This episode from John 11, 1–11 is Christ's first miracle when he changes the water into wine. As Holland notes, this event prefigures the later Christian sacrament where, during the last supper, Christ invites his disciples to eat of his body and drink of his blood. It is this painting, with its sacramental implications, that lends itself particularly well to the Christian allegorical reading of Milly's "sacrifice": forgiving her false friends, Milly, like Christ, willingly sacrifices herself and in the process redeems Densher's moral consciousness, resulting in a wholescale transformation of their social world, founded this time on love rather than exchange. Both paintings thus lend credence to the influential "moral" reading of the novel, identifying Milly with Christ who, radiating resplendently from the center of the paintings, and surrounded by "enemies" masquerading as friends, is cruelly betrayed and sacrificed.[35]

To my mind there is no question that in this novel James was as concerned as ever with exploring moral and ethical questions. The problem with the allegorical Christian/moral reading, however, is that in pitting Kate and Milly against one another in a moral drama of betrayal and redemption, it fails to take account of the insistent triangulation that I have been arguing plays such an important role in this novel. The alle-

gorical reading remains caught in the oppositional paradigm that characterized the early part of the novel, whose dominating trope, as we saw, was
reciprocity. It neglects to account for the new discursive space opened up
by Milly's arrival on the scene. This was the space I identified as opening
up the possibility of desire. And it is only from this perspective, from the
place of desire, I assert, that we can begin to understand the ethical
dimension of *The Wings of the Dove*.

To recall briefly, we saw how for Holland and Brooks the novel's ethical concerns are intimately connected with the question of the limits of
representation. The problem for these critics resides in the question of
how to approach the "abyss of meaning" lying hidden at the center of the
novel, and given form in the shape of Milly and her mysterious illness.
However, we have seen how Milly's illness is in fact nothing but a con-
certed and systematic attempt to defend against the unrepresentable
through the transformation of its terms into the deferred possibility
implied by the unnameable. This deferral describes the structure of unsatisfied desire that subsequently sustains Milly's life, the desire that becomes
both thematized and formalized in the novel in terms of language's continual failure ever to completely represent her. Now, Holland argues that
this aspect of James's literary style—his characteristic syntactical method
of "approach and withdrawal"—represents the formal expression of
"mourning" for what is beyond language, whose fate, like Milly's, is to be
forever inaccessible. For Holland, this beyond of representation can only
be memorialized in the ambiguous tribute of art which, like Kate and
Densher, must always "betray" what it seeks to represent. What Holland
neglects to realize, however, is that this failure or "betrayal" is precisely the
solution to Milly's problem. For it is only by failing to represent everything
that language, like desire, can hold Milly's apotheosis at bay.

As Milly's retreat toward the aesthetic realm implies, the importance
of the role of art identified by Holland is crucial here. But, because of
his insistence on reading the novel as a tragedy, Holland misses a very
important point: the aesthetic works here in the service of Milly's desire;
the aesthetic becomes one of the very last barriers that she erects against
the unrepresentable. By putting herself "into" a Veronese painting,
Milly enlists the aesthetic as the means for staging her commitment to
desire, which is nothing other than her commitment to maintaining the
gap between unconscious knowledge and belief or, to put it slightly differently, to keeping open the question of what it is that Kate (woman)
really wants.[36]

Let us look more closely at this scene. By this point in the novel, Milly's direct consciousness has long been lost to the reader and the scene is related from Densher's point of view, through whose eyes we see the entire Venetian episode. Densher, accordingly, sees Milly through his habitual metaphorical lens as the "American girl," but he notices how Milly seems this night to be "acquitting herself [. . .] as hostess [. . .] under some supreme idea, an inspiration which was half her nerves and half an inevitable harmony" (*WD* 302). Densher recognizes that Milly's performance this night is put on almost entirely for the benefit of Sir Luke Strett who has arrived in Venice for his vacation. It was for Sir Luke that she finally sheds her little black dress and appears "for the first time in white" (*WD* 301):

> Milly came down after dinner, half a dozen friends [. . .] having by that time arrived; and with this call on her attention, the further call of her musicians ushered by Eugenio, but personally and separately welcomed, and the supreme opportunity offered in the arrival of the great doctor, who came last of all, he felt her diffuse in wide warm waves the spell of a general, a beatific mildness. There was a deeper depth of it, doubtless, for some than for others; what he in particular knew of it was that he seemed to stand in it up to his neck. He moved about in it and it made no plash; he floated, he noiselessly swam about in it, and they were all together, for that matter, like fishes in a crystal pool. (*WD* 301)

It is Kate, however, who draws Densher out of his reverie and points his particular attention to the pearl bejeweled Milly. For once, Milly strikes him as outshining Kate. Her sudden, unexpected gloss diminishes the "handsome girl" who Densher finds suddenly "wanting in lustre" (*WD* 303); comparing the two women, Densher sees Milly surprisingly supplanting Kate, who seems to have mysteriously changed places with her, as if "she might fairly have been dressed tonight in the little black frock, superficially invisible, that Milly had laid aside" (*WD* 303). But Milly's valiant effort to "deceive" the doctor as to the state of her health—her sudden radiance—is unmasked by Kate who sees through the performance, telling Densher "she isn't better. She's worse." Milly's effort, in other words, her "supreme idea," derives from her losing battle with her apotheosis. Her improvisation on a theme by Veronese represents her last-ditch effort to hold death at bay.

The question is, in what sense can the aesthetic be enlisted for Milly's cause? James's (or Milly's) choice of Veronese gives us a clue. The first of the Veronese paintings Holland indicates, "The Supper in the House of Levi," is also known as the Last Supper. Both paintings therefore carry an implied reference to Christ's final meal with his disciples, one of whom, Judas, has of course betrayed him for silver, resulting in Christ's sacrifice on the Cross (and the identification of Kate with Judas is now a commonplace in *The Wings of the Dove* criticism[37]). Christ's enjoining of his followers in the Last Supper to partake of his body is the precursor to the later Christian Eucharist, symbolic of Christ's continuing presence on earth following his sacrificial death. In this ritual, the transubstantiation of the bread and wine into Christ's flesh and blood is taken as the guarantee of the miracle through which Christ's death on the cross has the effect of "killing" death, by promising an afterlife together with him and God in heaven. But in *Totem and Taboo*, Freud famously offers another reading of the Christian myth.[38] Freud sees the Christian Eucharist as a version of the ancient totemic sacrificial meal, developed in reaction to what he hypothesizes was the founding act of the earliest civilization, the killing of the primal father. The totemic meal symbolizes a repetition of that earliest crime, but with a difference. By repeating, in the cannibalistic totemic meal, the death of the primal father, the community of brothers celebrate the rule of law that emerged after the father's death. How did the rule of law take over? In the Freudian myth the brothers kill the father in the expectation of having access to the women of the tribe themselves. But instead, after his death, they discover that what had been previously prevented by the father—their enjoyment of the women—was now impossible; each of the brothers represented an equal match for the others so that, failing an utterly destructive struggle of all against all, they were obliged to make all of the women of their tribe off limits, with the result that the first law, the law against incest was instituted.

Freud hypothesizes that the earliest societies were thus founded on the collective guilt following the crime against the father. In the sacrificial meal, this guilt is atoned for by the killing of one of their own, according to the ancient rule of "talion."[39] Freud notes how the totemic meal therefore symbolizes both a repetition of the guilty deed, at the same time as it represents a guarantee among the brothers that such a deed will never be repeated toward any of them. The totemic sacrifice is thus an ambivalent or contradictory event. Why should the crime be repeated in the sacrifice? Freud claims that its supplementary function is to remind the father that he is dead, that is, to guarantee that the rule of the brothers has supplanted him. This is also one of the central meanings that Freud discovers in the

Christian sacrifice. The Christian sacrifice is the staging of the installation of a son in the Father's place. As Freud puts it, a "son-religion displaced the father-religion" (*TT* 191); "The Christian communion [. . .] is essentially a fresh elimination of the father, a repetition of the guilty deed" (*TT* 192).

In Freud's interpretation, then, the Christian sacrifice portrays the symbolic staging of the ascension of the rule of law that puts one of the brothers into the place where the Father used to be. The Christian sacrifice replaces the primal "Father of enjoyment" with his representative, the symbolic Father, the one whose sacrificial death guarantees that the primal Father will remain dead, replaced by the law of prohibition. Christ thus figures as an ambiguous sign: his sacrifice points to the Father's absence, to the founding negation, the original crime, that constituted the community of brothers. But because this negation cannot be represented, because lack is constitutively unrepresentable, it can only take positive form in the shape of a signifier whose presence paradoxically signifies absence. This signifier, Christ, has no other function, then, than that of marking within the community of brothers the place of the absent Father whose death founded that community.

Readers familiar with Lacan will readily recognize the "paternal metaphor" in this description, which denominates the way the Nom du Père (the No/Name of the Father) comes to substitute for the missing signifier for woman's desire (the desire of the mOther).[40] What is striking is the way a structure very similar to this substitution is played out in the James novel. Where the scene in the National Gallery gave us a geometrical space that exceeded the play of identifications between Kate, Milly, and Densher, opening up the static circle of reciprocity into the triangle of desire, the Christian sacrificial narrative depicts the way this excessive or impossible space is filled out, given body, in the shape of a signifier whose sole function, it turns out, is to erect a barrier against that space. If, in the National Gallery scene, a space was opened up which, we might as well now say, heralded the lack of a signifier for Kate's (woman's) desire (insofar as it opens up for Milly the riddling question as to what it is that Kate wants from her, subsequently sending her off on her life-prolonging desiring path in search of its answer), the Christian sacrifice demonstrates how one signifier, Christ, can take on the burden of marking the place where that missing signifier should be. But, as Freud emphasizes, this place-marking is also, simultaneously, the guarantee that the missing signifier will never be filled in; the Christian sacrifice is also the guarantee against the *return* of the primal Father.

Marking his absent place, the Christ signifier also functions to remind the Father that he is dead.

So when Milly stages her party as an imitation of a Veronese painting, and puts herself into Christ's place as the sacrificial object, we can say that, in so doing, she assumes the burden of Christ's substituting principle. Imitating Christ, Milly puts herself into the space where the absent signifier for Kate's desire should be, not in order to fill it (that is, to answer it definitively), but to guarantee that it will never be filled in completely. Assuming the Christ function, Milly commits herself to defending the empty space of the question of woman's (Kate's) desire. The question remains how this is different from Milly's previous generation of metaphoric symptoms. This time, faced with her losing battle against her apotheosis, Milly cuts right to the heart of the structure and installs herself as the very principle of substitution itself. What is this principle? Freud would call it primary repression, *Ur-Verdrängung*, the principle of the founding negation that originally divided the subject. If previously Milly generated metonymies of metaphoric names as a defensive strategy of deferral against the unrepresentable, now she throws herself into the breach of language itself in a final attempt to hold open the question of woman's desire. In her imitation of Christ, Milly assumes the signifier that marks the place of the founding negation—which is nothing other than the bar of metaphor in its other register, that is, not as the principle of identity critiqued in the first chapter, but as the principle of substitution—the originary crime that inaugurated the differential system of deferral that is (metonymic) desire.[41]

So far this only explains the *content* of the primary narrative of aesthetics that Milly enlists to defend against, and, as we now see, to serve in defense of the unrepresentable (through keeping the question of what Kate wants open). But I indicated earlier that the aesthetic *itself* plays a very specific role in this theatrical production. Let us, therefore, look again at the description of Milly's party. What is most striking is the way Milly's sudden radiance cuts through the bath of beatific mildness, causing Densher to see Milly and Kate in exchanged places. Milly's sudden beauty, in other words, has an important part to play in her staging of her commitment to (Kate's unknown) desire.

It is to Kantian aesthetics again we must turn in order to make sense of this. As we recall, for Kant, what gives us pleasure in regarding a beautiful object is not any intrinsic quality of the object itself but rather the subjective feeling that results from a certain interplay of the faculties of imagination and understanding as the latter, freed from the requirement to present a concept under which to subsume the manifold, is given over to "free play." This is what enables Kant to claim the universality of the aesthetic judgment: as we saw in the previous chapter, objects of aesthetic judgments please "universally" because what pleases us is not the object but the free play of the faculties of imagination and understanding acting in harmony together. Since everyone possesses these faculties, this is a pleasure that can be shared by everyone. Kant writes, "[T]he judgment is called aesthetical just because its determining ground is not a concept, but the feeling (of internal sense) of that harmony in the play of the mental powers, so far as it can be felt in sensation."[42] This pleasure is nothing other than the delight felt when the sensible manifold exhibited by the imagination is unexpectedly discovered to be in harmony with the laws of the understanding, even though there was no imposition of those laws, as there was in the cognitive judgment. The result is that the object appears to us in reflective judgment as if it, like us, was related to a final cause, which is the meaning of Kant's assertion of the beautiful object's "purposiveness without purpose"—the object seems to possess a "subjective finality," which in rational beings is our supersensible vocation, morality[43]

Although this operation only gives us a partial presentation of the supersensible in the form of what he calls a "symbolic hypotyposis," since Kant is careful to restrict the presentation to an operation of analogy rather than claim the direct, sensible presentation of Reason found by his followers Fichte and Schelling in the "intellectual intuition," nevertheless, in our judgment of beauty we gain an apprehension of the way the sensible and intelligible worlds possess an unexpected correspondence. Beauty "bridges" the sensible and supersensible realms by disclosing how our limited, phenomenal view of the world is, when under the conditions of aesthetic judgment, already contemporaneous with the realm of the beyond.

In his discussion of Hegel's response to Kant, however, Slavoj Žižek makes an important observation. Žižek argues that, counter to the Idealist tradition through which Hegel is usually read—where the Hegelian Aufhebung is taken as "closing" the Kantian divide—such a reading actually results from a misunderstanding of Hegel. What Hegel does with Kant, Žižek asserts, is the opposite. Rather than "deliver" the Kantian divide in the unity of Substance and Subject under the Idea, Žižek argues that Hegel's signature reversal instead accounts for the way the divide itself is the product of a perspectival illusion seen from the phenomenal point of view. That is to say, for Hegel, according to Žižek, the beyond of the supersensible is nothing but the "inherent limitation of intuited phenomena" (Žižek 39). Rather than reconciling the realms of sensible and supersensible, Hegel's twist on the Kantian dilemma is to show how "the actual synthesis of the Sensible and of the Intellectual is already effectuated in what was for Kant their splitting" (Žižek 39). In other words, Hegel shows how there is nothing beyond the intuited phenomena, there is no existing "thing in itself." Rather, the concept of the beyond is discovered as an *effect* of the limited phenomenal viewpoint itself. Hence there is no need to postulate a second moment, of bridging, or synthesis, after the first that splits the phenomenal and noumenal realms. The Hegelian Aufhebung, Žižek argues, is nothing but the realization of how the apparent opposition is simply the false perspective seen from one of the ostensible sides of the opposition. Thus the Kantian divide already contains the synthesis of the phenomenal and noumenal realms, since the noumenal realm is nothing but the Understanding's failure to see that the phenomenal is all that there is. As Žižek puts it, the thing-in-itself does not "ontologically precede its loss" (Žižek 39)—there is no realm beyond the signifier. It is the limit itself that creates the illusion of the beyond.

If (Žižek's) Hegel is right, how does this change our understanding of the traditional role of beauty as the means for reconciling the two realms? From this perspective, beauty is what maintains the fiction of the realm of the beyond, even while it is responsible for creating the illusion of it. All representation pretends that there is something beyond itself that it aims at but fails to reach. Beauty is simply an unusually privileged case of such pretense because, not only does it imply the existence of such a beyond, but the aesthetic actually claims to short-circuit the endless representational cycle of positing and reflection (in Holland's terms, language's pattern of approach and withdrawal). Asserting that the "supersensible substrate" appears to us in the apparent "purposiveness" of the forms of beautiful objects, beauty appears to bypass the usual constraints imposed by the Understanding on the objects of the world, giving us a more direct experience of the thing-in-itself. But as it turns out, what both representation generally, and beauty specifically, are complicit in hiding is the fact that the beyond, the thing-in-itself, is simply a product of representation's own activity of failure: the beyond is nothing but an effect of the limit of representation.

As I said, beauty gives the illusion that the thing-in-itself exists and can be reached, at least partially, from the viewpoint of the phenomenal. From this perspective, we can say that beauty has a similar function to desire.

Like desire, beauty projects, if you will, the fantasy that everything really can be said, that a bridge can be formed between two irreparably divided worlds. Beauty thus acts to veil the limit that is the indispensable condition of possibility of representation—the bar of metaphor, the split between signifier and signified—and, in spreading itself out beyond that limit, appears to reconcile an opposition that it has itself created. Yet, as we will see, all the while that beauty is making conciliating gestures toward bridging the Kantian divide, it does nothing but reaffirm the limit.

How does beauty accomplish its illusion? The beauty effect seduces the viewer into believing that there is something beyond phenomenal perception, beyond our representational system, if we could only see past the limits of our phenomenal viewpoint. But while beauty thus seems to fill out the void left by the loss of the noumenal world, by claiming to give it momentarily back to us in phenomenal form, beauty has a peculiar effect: it produces pleasure in the subject. This pleasure, which is derived from the apparent "purposiveness" of the object as it seems to be "for-us," brings us back from the (illusory) opening to the noumenal world and returns us to our limited, phenomenal world. The pleasure found universally in beauty paradoxically lowers our desire for what lies beyond, distracting us, blinding us even, and serves to direct us back to the object world once more.[44]

Although, strictly speaking, what prevents us from obtaining a direct presentation of Reason is a structural impossibility—when Reason reaches its limit, as Kant observes in his first *Critique*, it falls into contradiction with itself—beauty nevertheless implies that that limit can be crossed, allowing us a momentary and partial access to the supersensible realm. But beauty's true role, it appears, is surreptitiously to guard the limit of representation. Beauty, it turns out, is nothing but the effect of representation's limit on the objects of the phenomenal world.

How to clarify this seemingly contradictory point? In the Third Moment of the Analytic of the Beautiful, Kant directs our attention to the way the purposiveness of the beautiful object in aesthetic judgments is directed not toward the object's existence in any way (which would be a teleological judgment) but simply to the object's form. In aesthetic judgment, everything that is connected with interest, or content, or even existence is stripped from the object, leaving it in its essence as pure form:

> The *charm* of colors or of the pleasant tones of an instrument may be
> added, but the *delineation* in the first case and the composition in the

second constitute the proper object of the pure judgment of taste. To say that the purity of colors and of tones, or their variety and contrast, seem to add to beauty does not mean that they supply a homogenous addition to our satisfaction in the form because they are pleasant in themselves; but they do so because they make the form more exactly, definitely, and completely intuitable, and besides, by their charm [excite the representation, while they] awaken and fix our attention on the object itself. (*CJ* 61)

Although, in his First *Critique*, Kant already described the way pure form is directly intuitable in the transcendental aesthetic (as the "pure forms" of space and time), here Kant is concerned not so much with transcendental form, but with the way form is *experienced*. Judgments of taste concern the condition of objectivity as objects are experienced in the world; they inquire into the conditions of possibility that allow an object to show itself, to draw a line around itself, to delimit itself from the as yet undifferentiated manifold. Hence aesthetic judgments, as Rodolphe Gasché has pointed out, inasmuch as they are indeed concerned with something transcendental, namely, the condition of possibility of objects in general, are paradoxically more fundamental than cognitive judgments. Cognitive judgments already implicitly presuppose the aesthetic judgment regarding the condition of possibility of an object, insofar as it is an object.[45]

Kant's discussion of the way aesthetic judgments inquire into the object's form states very clearly what I have been arguing above. For what is form but the drawing of a limit around the field of representation? Form is, quite simply, representation's condition of possibility. We can say therefore that beauty, or more precisely, judgments of beauty, inasmuch as they inquire into the conditions of possibility of an object as it appears to us in its purely formal externality, are nothing other than presentations, not of the supersensible substrate, but of representation's limit. Beauty derives from the effect of the limit of representation. As such, it has much in common with what Kant, in his First *Critique*, designates "transcendental illusion."

Briefly, in his First *Critique*, Kant explains how the transcendental Ideal is the necessary but illusory principle on which all concepts of the understanding are founded. The transcendental Ideal is the idea of totality, the "sum-total of all possibility," whose primordial characteristic is that of "transcendental affirmation."[46] Kant writes,

Logical negation, [. . .] does not properly refer to a concept, but only to its relation to another concept in a judgment, and is therefore quite insufficient to determine a concept in respect of its content. [. . .] A transcendental negation, on the other hand, signifies not-being in itself, and is opposed to transcendental affirmation, which is a something the very concept of which in itself expresses a being. Transcendental affirmation is therefore entitled reality, because through it alone, and so far as it reaches, are objects something (things), whereas its opposite, negation, signifies a mere want, and, so far as it alone is thought, represents the abrogation of all thinghood. (*CPR* 489–90)

Transcendental affirmation, or reason's primordial idea of "the All," is the supreme "reality" that conditions the ground of all things. But to give this idea a concept such as a "being that is one, simple, all-sufficient, eternal, etc." (i.e., the concept of God), Kant warns, is an overstepping of the limits of the purpose and validity of the transcendental idea. He writes, "reason, in employing [the transcendental idea] as a basis for the complete determination of things, has used it only as the concept of all reality, without requiring that all this reality be objectively given and be itself a thing. Such a thing is a mere fiction in which we combine and realize the manifold of our idea in an ideal, as an individual being" (*CPR* 493). Although we need this principle of the totality as the basis for grounding our concepts of the understanding, Kant explains, if we give it any objective validity as a concept, we enter into transcendental error, the "transcendental subreption" or "illusion." But as it turns out, although we need not be "deceived" by it, transcendental illusion is nevertheless "indispensably necessary" for cognition. For in order for the Understanding to reach its greatest possible extension, it inevitably hypostasizes the idea of the totality as a real thing that serves as the "source of the possibility of all things" (*CPR* 495). Now, transcendental illusion occurs when we apply the empirical principle of our concepts as a transcendental principle regarding the possibility of things in general. What is the empirical principle of our concepts? It is nothing other than the aesthetic judgment through which objects can be empirically given to us in their pure form: the circumscribing of the limit that distinguishes an object from the unified manifold. Here is Kant again:

The possibility of the objects of the senses is a relation of these objects to our thought, in which something (namely, the empirical form) can be thought a priori, while that which constitutes the matter, reality in the field of appearance (that which corresponds to sensation), must be given, since otherwise it could not even be thought, nor its possibility represented. Now an object of the senses can be completely determined only when it is compared with all the predicates that are possible in the field of appearance, and by means of them is represented either affirmatively or negatively. But since that which constitutes the thing itself, namely, the real in the field of appearance, must be given—otherwise the thing could not be conceived at all—and since that wherein the real of all appearances is given is experience, considered as single and all-embracing, the material for the possibility of all objects of the senses must be presupposed as given in one whole; *and it is upon the limitation of this whole that all possibility of empirical objects, their distinction from each other and their complete determination, can alone be based* [my emphasis]. (*CPR* 494)

Although we are prohibited from applying empirical principles to transcendental ones, nevertheless, in order to have the most fundamental experience of objects of the senses, insofar as they appear to us in their purely formal externality, we necessarily conflate one with the other: as Kant puts it, the "natural illusion" comes about as a result of the fact that we hypostasize the idea of the totality, because "we substitute dialectically for the *distributive* unity of the empirical employment of the understanding, the *collective* unity of experience as a whole" (*CPR* 494). But this transcendental "subreption" is "indispensably necessary" for the cognition of objects in general as Kant explains:

[Transcendental ideas] have an excellent, and indeed indispensably necessary, regulative employment, namely, that of directing the understanding towards a certain goal upon which the routes marked out by all its rules converge, as upon their point of intersection. This point is indeed a mere idea, a *focus imaginarius*, from which, since it lies quite outside the bounds of possible experience, the concepts of the understanding do not in reality proceed; none the less it serves to give to these concepts the greatest possible unity combined with the greatest possible extension. Hence arises the illusion that the lines have their source in a real object lying outside the field of empirically possible knowledge— just as objects reflected in a mirror are seen as behind it. Nevertheless this illusion (which need not, however, be allowed to deceive us) is indispensably necessary if we are to direct the understanding beyond every given experience (as part of the sum of possible experience), and thereby to secure its greatest possible extension, just as, in the case of mirror-vision, the illusion involved is indispensably necessary if, besides those objects which lie before our eyes, we are also to see those which lie at a distance behind our back. (*CPR* 533–34)

Beauty is, then, nothing but a massively privileged incidence of the indispensable illusion without which we could have no cognition of objects. To put it simply, beauty's promise of the beyond is the necessary fiction that enables us to have experience of the phenomenal world to the extent that that experience is "subjectively objective." But, as it turns out, beauty does nothing other than maintain the limit beyond which there is nothing; the "beauty function," if I may so put it, upholds the limit that protects us from the realization that there is *nothing beyond the limit.*

To return to James. This foray into Kantian aesthetics helps to clarify how, *pace* Holland, language's failure to completely represent the whole is hardly a tragedy. As Kant repeatedly warns, could we indeed have a direct presentation of Reason, the entire system of representation, inasmuch as it is a system of differentiation—of "affirmations" and "negations" to use Kant's terms—would collapse. To see from God's point of view, the point of view of the "intellectual intuition," is to void all oppositions, with the result that we would be crushed under the totalizing weight of the absolute, precluding us, as we saw in the previous chapter, from any possibility of freedom and ethics. Moreover, as we now see, that separation is nothing less than the condition of possibility for experience itself, inasmuch as experience is the experience of the object world, of objectivity in general. For both strictly theoretical and practical reasons, then, Kant insists on the necessity for maintaining the gap between sensible and supersensible realms.

It should be clear from this how Milly's apotheosis is but another name for the (illicit) Kantian totality. It is against this "All," the total fusion of subject and object, that Milly, seeking refuge in (hysterical) desire and, ultimately, the aesthetic itself, defends herself. Far from being a tragedy, it transpires, language's failure to completely represent the whole—the failure that Milly cleaves to in her hysterical insistence on keeping the question of Kate's desire open—is our protection against the illusion of complete satisfaction that language nevertheless holds out in promise. This promise, as Kant also shows, is indispensably necessary for the operation of representation. But to the extent that desire continually aims at missing that moment, what desire and beauty (and, indeed, narrative) have in common is that they all keep us from realizing the ultimate satisfaction which is, as Milly knows, nothing but death itself. It is beauty that leads us into the indispensable illusion at the same time that it keeps us from transgressing the bounds of our phenomenal nature by returning us to our bodies in pleasure.

We can now say that Milly's retreat toward the aesthetic in the final months of her life, far from representing a retreat into a delusory, self-absorbed monism, engages the most vital form of resistance to the threat of her apotheosis that she knows. Milly's "aesthetic" solution, we now see, is nothing but her cleaving to representation's enabling principle, the limit that prevents us from ever reaching total satisfaction.[47] Now we can understand why Lord Mark's avowal of Kate and Densher's engagement was so damaging to Milly. Lord Mark didn't tell Milly anything she didn't already "know," but he collapsed the distance between her knowledge and her belief, the crucial distance that enabled her until that moment to uphold the fantasy that satisfaction really could be reached. Lord Mark's avowal cuts through the sustaining barrier that prevented Milly from learning the truth of her value for Kate; his avowal, in effect, halts the generation of new names by confirming her identity as one thing, as an object. It is this, rather than any romantic disappointment with Densher, or a belated discovery of the evil in the world, that results in Milly's decline: Milly's collapse comes about from having the last barrier between her and the truth of Kate's desire removed. This cuts her off from the chain linking her to Kate and, as Paul Verhaeghe would say, to a possible sexual identity.[48] Now instead of generating new and sustaining failures—linguistic symptoms—Milly suddenly finds herself trapped within the very language that had originally given her the power to resist her apotheosis. With the collapse of the barrier between her and the truth of Kate's desire, language clangs shut on her, like the door of a birdcage, trapping and reifying her.

What happens next? Milly famously "turn[s] her face to the wall" and dies. How do we interpret this act? The obvious, sentimental, answer (Densher's) is of course to say that once Milly discovers the truth of Kate and Densher's relationship, she loses her will to live.[49] Still utterly failing to comprehend what has happened, Densher tells Kate "'One can see now that she was living by will'" (*WD* 357). What Densher fails to realize is that it is Milly's *death*, rather, that represents her final act of will. Turning her face to the wall, Milly deliberately enacts the sacrifice whose function, as Freud tells us, is nothing other than to ensure that the limit remains untransgressed. Dying, Milly puts herself into the breach of language, not to complete the field of representation, but to guarantee that representation remains "not-whole." Milly's sacrifice is thus far from being the final collapse of a disappointed woman; by sacrificing herself, Milly acts in accordance with her desire.

It might seem paradoxical to fight death, as Milly does, with death. For didn't I argue that her entire desiring structure was inaugurated against the threat of death represented by her apotheosis? But a willing death, it seems for James, is quite different from the death that lies in wait for Milly in the collapse of all oppositions, the death by totality. By willing death, in this way, Milly in effect dies in order to "keep dreaming," to maintain the fantasy that has sustained her as a desiring subject, and which, in preserving an area of indeterminacy, prevents her from becoming wholly trapped by language. Milly's death thus recalls, albeit inversely, the dream Freud recounts of the father whose child cries out that he is burning. In the Freudian dream, the father wakes up, *in order to continue dreaming*, that is, in order to avoid the "real" of his dream (where the child's burning reproaches him, as Lacan suggests, for the "sins of the father").[50] Milly, in reverse, dies to avoid waking up; she dies in order to maintain the fantasy whose promise of complete satisfaction is, paradoxically, the guarantee against completing the field of representation. Milly's death is thus, in a very precise sense, a desiring death, a death died in accordance with desire.

As it turns out, Milly's death does indeed have the effect that she willed. For in addition to persuading a skeptical Lord Mark during those brief moments before the crisis in Venice that there is nothing between Kate and Densher, Milly's final act ultimately keeps open the question of Kate's desire. By the end of the novel, as we know, Kate and Densher's relationship has so far deteriorated that, as Kate departs from Densher's lodgings, we are left, famously, with the question of what Kate is going to do. From this perspective, Milly's act has been a resounding success: we no longer know what it is that Kate wants.[51]

V

Lest this discussion seem overly weighted toward Milly who is, after all, only one of James's three "lucid reflectors" in the novel, let us now turn back to Kate and Densher to discover the effect of Milly's sacrifice on them. Densher, as we saw, misunderstands Milly's final act; inverting its meaning, he believes she dies from the loss of the will to live. Kate, however, has a different reading of the event. "'The great thing,'" Kate tells Densher,

> "is that she's satisfied. Which [. . .] is what I've worked for."
> "Satisfied to die in the flower of her youth?"

"Well, at peace with you."

"Oh, 'peace!'" he murmured with his eyes on the fire.

"The peace of having loved."

He raised his eyes to her. "Is that peace?"

"Of having been loved," she went on. "That is. Of having," she wound up, "realised her passion. She wanted nothing more. She has had all she wanted. (*WD* 364)

Critics usually see Kate's argument here as an exercise in sophistry through which she exculpates herself of guilt over Milly's death. A closer look at Kate's behavior throughout the last days of Milly's life, however, reveals a Kate who, while unmistakably engaged in soul searching, does not flinch from the consequences of her actions the way Densher subsequently does. Kate, we remember, recalls later how, throughout her visit to Venice, "her sincerity about her friend [. . .] was deep, her compassionate imagination strong." These things, James writes, "gave her a virtue, a good conscience, a credibility for herself, so to speak, that were later to be precious to her" (*WD* 262). Regardless of what one might think of Kate's "credibility for herself," and many critics fault her on just this point, Kate displays an unbending willingness to look the truth in the face, to exercise her "art of seeing things," as she once taught Milly, "as they were" (*WD* 168).[52]

In contrast, the elaborate ethical gymnastics that Densher performs in order not to face the consequences of his actions, speak volumes. Recall the series of self-justifications Densher makes whose absurdity even he, finally, is not able to repress from himself:

If he positively wanted not to be brought up with his nose against Milly's facts, what better proof could he have that his conduct was marked by straightness? It was perhaps pathetic for her, and for himself was perhaps even ridiculous; but he hadn't even the amount of curiosity that he would have had about an ordinary friend. [. . .] In what therefore was the duplicity? He was at least sure about his feelings—it being so established that he had none at all. (*WD* 296)

Rather than face the truth about their mutual deception, Densher's guilty conscience reverses the argument claiming that, since he has been faithful to Kate, he cannot be said to be responsible for Milly's death: "He was accordingly not interested, for had he been interested he would have cared, and had he cared he would have wanted to know. Had he wanted to know he wouldn't have been purely passive, and it was his pure passivity that had to represent his dignity and his honour" (*WD* 296). The irony of Densher's position, of course, is that, in his insistence on his innocence, on his ethical righteousness, Densher finds himself ultimately forced to betray the sole ethical maxim that he has. What is this maxim? When he finds himself surrounded by the "circle of petticoats" (*WD* 299) in Venice, Densher resolves to follow the "immediate workable law. The law was not to be a brute—in return for amiabilities" (*WD* 285). In order to defend himself against the implied accusation, however, Densher must celebrate in himself the very brutality that he wants to avoid. In order to see himself as not guilty, he must brutalize himself, for what could be more brutish than not having about Milly "even the amount of curiosity that he would have had about an ordinary friend"? Densher's "innocence" is ultimately damning.[53]

At the crux of Densher's moral dilemma is his interpretation of what it means to act. Densher convinces himself that by being purely passive, the mere object of Kate's and Milly's wills, he is excused from all responsibility, and more than once he insists on this point to Kate: "'It's not *I* who am responsible for her, my dear. It seems to me it's you'" (*WD* 236). A few moments later, Densher again rejects any suggestion of his own complicity in the scheme, using his innocence as capital in the sexual bargain he strikes with Kate. To Densher's suggestion that they break off where they are, Kate replies,

> "We've gone too far," she none the less pulled herself together to reply. "Do you want to kill her?"
> He had an hesitation that wasn't all candid. "Kill, you mean, Aunt Maud?"
> "You know whom I mean. We've told too many lies."
> Oh at this his head went up. "I, my dear, have told none!" (*WD* 293–94)

The ethical bad faith of his position, however, is hard even for him to ignore, and Densher finds himself early on seeing "with a certain alarm rise before him that everything was acting that was not speaking the particular word" (*WD* 228). In spite of this, Densher nevertheless continues to pursue his program of total passivity, until he finds, to his relief, that the decision (to deceive Milly) has already been made:

> The system of not pulling up, not breaking off, had already brought him headlong, he seemed to feel, to where they actually stood; and just now it was, with a vengeance, that he must do either one thing or the

other. He had been waiting for some moments. [. . .] He couldn't keep
that up forever; and since one thing or the other was what he must do,
it was for the other that he presently became conscious of having
decided. If he had been drifting it settled itself in the manner of a
bump, of considerable violence, against a firm object in the stream. "Oh
yes; I'll go with you with pleasure. It's a charming idea." (*WD* 234)

What is interesting to note here is the way Densher is only conscious of
his decision as a past act, not one that he is actively making at any present
time. He realizes only afterward that his choice has been made. Again, Densher misinterprets this, believing, as his later, convoluted self-justifications
indicate, that his decision had been made for him by others, that, by keeping still (as Isabel would have said), he remains innocent of guilt. This future
anteriority of Densher's choice (he is always either behind making his decision, or conscious of already having decided) has something in common
with Isabel's choice in *The Portrait of a Lady*. The difference between how
these characters respond to the impossibility of consciously choosing, however, is that, as we saw in the first chapter, where Isabel takes ethical responsibility for a choice that can only in retrospect be assumed to have occurred,
Densher rejects any suggestion of his complicity in the plot and thereby, of
course, proves his guilt. What is Densher guilty of? Lacan would say that he
has given up on his desire, which is the only thing one can be guilty of.[54]
   When is the moment that Densher becomes guilty of ceding his
desire? It is during the scene in San Marco square in Venice when he first
tries to strike his bargain with Kate. Densher insists to Kate that he will
only continue to go along with her plan if she will come to him, to spend
the night in his room. Surely, one might say, Densher's demand instead
proves his desire for Kate? But, in fact, the moment that Densher stops
believing in Kate, trusting her, and demands a sign of her good faith in
return, he gives up on his desire. For, with this demand, he transforms
their relationship from one of mutual irreciprocity—where Densher did-
n't know what Kate wanted from him, but was willing to act for her cause
anyway—back into the cycle of reciprocal exchange. Kate herself understands her "betrayal" by Densher, but despite knowing this, as I will elaborate, she persists in her desire, putting her ethically closer to Milly.
   The more Densher protests his innocence about Milly, the more he
reveals the extent to which he has given up on his desire. In desperation
he turns to Sir Luke who miraculously appears to him to "let him off"
from responsibility, by virtue of their jointly being "men of the world":

> The liberation was an experience that held its own, and he continued
> to know why, in spite of his deserts, in spite of his folly, in spite of every-
> thing, he had so fondly hoped for it. [. . .] He was *being* let off; dealt
> with in the only way that didn't aggravate his responsibility. (*WD* 350)

The result of Densher's ethical maneuverings, coming as an effect of Sir
Luke's "mercy" (*WD* 350) is the tragic (if it wasn't so ludicrous) perception of himself, in a final reorganization of the triangular relationship,
taking Milly's place as the "victim" of his own and Kate's plot: "the effect
of it, Densher would have said, was a relation with [Sir Luke] quite
resembling that of doctor and patient. One took the cue from him as one
might have taken a dose—except that the cue was pleasant in the taking"
(*WD* 351).

Whatever she might feel about the consequences of her actions, Kate,
on the other hand, doesn't flinch from facing them. In the famous scene
of Milly's party, when Densher and Kate finally come to "name names,"
James describes Kate's resolution:

> Now that he was in possession moreover she couldn't forbear, strangely
> enough, to pronounce the words she hadn't pronounced: they broke
> through her controlled and colourless voice as if she should be ashamed,
> to the very end, to have flinched. "You'll in the natural course have
> money. We shall in the natural course be free." (*WD* 308)

Apologists for Kate who emphasize the extent to which she, like Milly, is
trapped by circumstance therefore do Kate short shrift. It seems clear that
James has Kate actively making choices, and accepting full responsibility
for her acts. Kate famously tells Densher "'I don't like it, but I'm a person, thank goodness, who can do what I don't like.' It wasn't till after-
wards that, going back to it, he was to read into this speech a kind of
heroic ring, a note of character that belittled his own incapacity for
action" (*WD* 309). Densher is right, I believe to hear in this speech "a
kind of heroic ring." But in what does Kate's heroism consist?

In some ways, as I suggested, Kate is paired with Milly insofar as they
both are seen to act uncompromisingly in accordance with their desire.
But if Milly's desire aims at maintaining the gap that keeps her from being
completely swallowed up by the representational system, what is Kate's
desire? Like Milly's, Kate's desire is bound up with the word, or name,
that bars access, we might as well now say, to jouissance. Her desire, like
Milly's, is therefore also hysterical insofar as hysterical desire involves a

defense against—and, as I suggested above, the defense of—the gap that prevents the totality from becoming whole.[55]

Recall how everything that Kate subsequently does is in order to rescue her father's name, "the precious name she so liked and that [. . .] wasn't yet past praying for" (*WD* 22). It is for the sake of her father's name that she ultimately constructs her plot for Densher and Milly. The name is, if you like, the "support" of her desire, it is what gives her world meaning and consistency, and for which she is willing to risk everything. In a telling speech to Densher who, once more pressuring her to give some sign of her love, accuses her of risking nothing, Kate responds that she is risking her all:

> It made her keep her eyes on him, and he could thus see that, by one of those incalculable motions in her without which she wouldn't have been a quarter so interesting, they half-filled with tears from some source he had too roughly touched. "I'm taking a trouble for you I never dreamed I should take for any human creature." (*WD* 307)

The idea that Kate really does risk everything becomes clear when one tries to follow through the logic of her act. Although most critics see her as cruelly and coldly calculating when she instructs Densher to pretend to love Milly, if we take literally what the novel tells us, there is no guarantee that Milly will die. In fact, unless Kate has better knowledge about Milly's condition even than Sir Luke Strett, by putting Densher into Milly's way, surely she is creating the only conditions under which, as far as she knows, Milly's life will be saved. This is a point that seems to evade many critics who are intent on reading the novel through a tragic moral paradigm. Kate hears quite clearly from everyone concerned that Milly will live if she wants to, if she can find someone to love. There is no guarantee, then, that Kate's plan won't misfire, that she won't lose Densher either to a living Milly, or finally to a dead one. And of course the latter is what finally happens. By the end of the novel, Kate and Densher's relationship collapses under the strain of their different individual responses to what has happened. Milly's death has come between them. But although the collapse of their relationship is usually taken as the sign of Densher's "moral transformation" and Kate's inability to learn from Milly's forgiving gesture, that is, their relationship collapses because of Kate's moral failure, what really divides the couple is their different responses to the unrepresentable, now embodied in the absent figure of Milly. What divides the couple, that is, is the difference between an ethical and an aesthetic response to the question of the limit of representation.

After Densher returns to London he receives a letter from Milly which, he understands, had been deliberately timed to arrive on Christmas Eve. The next morning, Christmas Day, he runs into Maud at Sir Luke's home and learns from her what he has already suspected, that Milly is dead. Densher then takes the letter to Kate, unopened, as a "tribute," he says, of his faithfulness to her. Meeting her at her sister's home where she has returned to look after her stricken father, Densher presents Kate with the letter which, he says, represents his own "sacrifice" in return for the sexual one she made for him according to their bargain in Venice:

> "You played fair with me, Kate; and that's why—since we talk of proofs—I want to give *you* one. I've wanted to let you see—and in preference even to myself—something I feel as sacred."
> She frowned a little. "I don't understand."
> "I've asked myself for a tribute, for a sacrifice by which I can peculiarly recognise—"
> "Peculiarly recognise what?" she demanded as he dropped.
> "The admirable nature of your own sacrifice. You were capable in Venice of a splendid act of generosity." (*WD* 393)

Kate hesitates but on Densher's insistence takes the letter.

> "To hold it," she brought out, "is to know."
> "Oh I *know*!" said Merton Densher.
> "Well then if we both do—!" She had already turned to the fire, nearer to which she had moved, and with a quick gesture had jerked the thing into the flame. He started—but only half—as to undo her action: his arrest was as prompt as the latter had been decisive. He only watched, with her, the paper burn; after which their eyes again met. "You'll have it all," Kate said, "from New York." (*WD* 393–94)

Two months later, a second letter arrives, the one from Milly's lawyers in New York containing the details of her bequest. Densher also gives this letter to Kate unopened, in order, as he tells Kate later, to test her. When Kate appears unexpectedly at Densher's lodgings and indicates to him that she has read the letter, he responds by saying "'I wanted—oh yes, if that's what you wish to ask me—to see what you'd do.' [. . .] 'I wanted—in so good a case—to test you'" (*WD* 400).

Densher's interpretation of Kate's actions toward Milly's last communications has set the standard by which Kate is usually judged but, for the

reasons I will indicate below, I find that Densher's supposed ethical transformation is fundamentally flawed. To use Densher's ethics as the standard against which Kate's must be judged is, therefore, untenable. Densher makes his disappointment in Kate quite clear to her, indicating that
to his mind the proper, ethical response would have been to have returned
the letter to the lawyers, unopened but accompanied by "an absolutely
kind letter" (*WD* 399). As Densher sees it, this gesture would have
"squared" him ethically with Milly, returning her gesture with a compa-
rably generous act of refusal. But Kate immediately recognizes the real
meaning behind his intended gesture; she understands that Densher's
ethics are founded on an essentially aesthetic principle: Kate questions
Densher, "'So that if cognisance *has* been taken [of the amount of the
bequest] [. . .] it spoils the beauty?'" (*WD* 400).

In what way is Densher's ethical transformation flawed? Wanting
Kate to return Milly's bequest unopened, Densher implicitly reasserts the
bargaining principle that, as I showed, Milly's entire trajectory was dedicated to dissolving. Densher wants to exchange generosity with generosity, not understanding the fundamental asymmetry that a generous act
assumes. He is unwilling or unable to put himself into the terrifyingly
passive, disempowered position that the gift requires of the receiver, if it
is indeed an authentic gift and not part of the cycle of exchange. Milly's
intention is quite clear on the authenticity of her gesture; her gift arrives
on Christmas Day, continuing her allegorical association with Christ. For,
as God's "gift" to humanity, Christ, in the Christian narrative, is an
authentic act of God's love and forgiveness for our original sin. In the radically asymmetrical gesture of the gift, Christ assumes the burden of our
guilt and pays, with his body, for our crime.

The aesthetic dimension of Densher's ethical transformation is apparent in his reaction to Kate's destruction of Milly's letter. James describes
how, in the weeks following their meeting at Kate's sister's house, Densher
turns repeatedly to the thought of Milly's letter and how he would never
know what it contained. James writes,

> he took to himself at such hours, in other words, that he should never,
> never know what had been in Milly's letter. The intention announced
> in it he should but too probably know; only that would have been, but
> for the depths of his spirit, the least part of it. The part of it missed for
> ever was the turn she would have given her act. This turn had possibil-
> ities that, somehow, by wondering about them, his imagination had
> extraordinarily filled out and refined. (*WD* 398)

Nursing this idea, Densher takes it out in his private hours: "He kept it back like a favourite pang; left it behind him, so to say, when he went out, but came home again the sooner for the certainty of finding it there. Then he took it out of its sacred corner and its soft wrappings; he undid them one by one, handling them, handling *it*, as a father, baffled and tender, might handle a maimed child" (*WD* 398).

Kenneth Reinhard observes how Densher's obsessive mourning for Milly's memory is not the Freudian process of remembering in order to forget. He argues, "Rather than remembering, Densher 'takes to himself' the trace of Milly's unread letter, melancholically incorporating it as something he can neither remember nor forget, an 'ache in the soul' with which he has identified" (Reinhard 133). As Reinhard notes, Densher's "incorporation" of Milly effectively ensures that the cycle of betrayal and sacrifice that is Milly's legacy will continue. Instead of accepting her gift (and thereby breaking up the cycle), Densher's memorializing in effect repeats Milly's drama in the images he uses to conjure up her memory: "cherished as a 'maimed child,' and sacrificed again and again, 'like the sight of a priceless pearl cast before his eyes [. . .] into the fathomless sea'" (Reinhard 134).

Now, one of the strangest aspects of hysteria is the way it can be catching. As Teresa Brennan has noted, the hysteric's discourse is characterized by an interchangeability of positions, leading her to surmise that in one sense, "an emotion is an entity in its own right. If one party drops it, the other picks it up."[56] In his obsessive repetition of the sacrificial narrative, Densher can be said to have inherited Milly's desire, to have "caught" her hysteria. By failing to mourn Milly, and by incorporating her instead, Densher condemns himself to the endless cycle of betrayal and sacrifice. Hence Densher's ethical attitude remains fundamentally aesthetic in its principle, condemned to repeat forever the repetitive cycle of approach and withdrawal performed by language under the capture of the aesthetic's positing of the beyond. Can we not say, then, that Densher has indeed learned from Milly's ethics of desire and, in so memorializing her—in his endless repeating of the primary aesthetic narrative of betrayal and sacrifice—Densher maintains her desiring legacy by guaranteeing that the field of representation remains incomplete? Doesn't Densher's, then, also exemplify an authentically ethical act? The answer is no. As we saw with Isabel in the previous chapter, the burden of interpreting how the Kantian categorical imperative translates into action remains solely with the individual. There is no content to the ethical imperative, no maxim that tells you what you must do (as for example, "you must keep the field of representation incomplete at all costs," etc.). The difference between Milly's and Densher's acts, the difference that makes Milly's an authentic and Densher's an inauthentic one, is that, where Milly's hysterical solution is an act of her own invention tailored to the singularity of her own unique set of circumstances, Densher, revealing his origins as the son of a "lady-copyist," merely imitates her ethical act. When Densher refuses Milly's gift, he refuses to assume the responsibility that would make the act his own. By merely repeating Milly's drama of betrayal and sacrifice, Densher gets stuck in the stultification of another's desiring pattern or neurosis. Once again purely passive, Densher is unable to act, unable to create for himself the meaning of the circumstances in which he finds himself.

When Kate destroys Milly's letter, on the other hand, she signally refuses to take on the transmission of Milly's hysteria. Kate rejects Densher's aesthetic response, refusing to put herself into Milly's place and to continue her hysterical drama. Kate can be said, therefore, to represent a different way of responding to the unrepresentable. Instead of aestheticizing her, Kate acknowledges the traumatic testimony Milly leaves behind—"'We shall never be again as we were'" (*WD* 403)—but refuses to pass it on in a perpetual, hysterical metonymy. One might say that, in destroying Milly's letter, she "sends" it back to Milly: Kate breaks up Milly's hysterical cycle that never stops asking the Other to tell her what kind of thing she is. Kate's destruction of Milly's letter turns the tables on Milly, leaving the dead woman's legacy finally and radically open to interpretation. Like Milly, then, and unlike Densher, Kate creates for herself the ultimate meaning of Milly's act. In this sense, she must be seen as being much closer, ethically, to her friend than to her former lover.

VI

When, at the end of the novel, Densher forces Kate to make a choice between him without Milly's money, or the money without him, Kate finds herself again in the situation with which the novel began. Remember how this choice is a false one—Kate cannot choose between love or money because, as Reinhard observes, neither choice "can fully retain its value apart from the other; to choose either is at the same time to lose something essential to both" (Reinhard 136), (at least according to the conventions of nineteenth-century romance). Kate's answer to this first false choice was to transform it into the new terms of desire and duty. But we can see now that for Kate this second opposition resolves itself through the discovery of how desire and duty are not really opposed. Kate's desire is on the side of duty. What is Kate's desire? We saw how everything she did was in order to rescue her father's name. Why is the name so important to her? It is because it is the symbolic signifier for her mother's unrepresentable desire. It is for the sake of her mother's desire, it turns out, that Kate subsequently sacrifices her all: "'That's all my virtue,'" she tells Densher early on in their relationship,

> "a narrow little family feeling. I've a small stupid piety—I don't know what to call it." Kate bravely stuck to that; she made it out. "Sometimes, alone, I've to smother my shrieks when I think of my poor mother. She went through things—they pulled her down; I know what they were now—I didn't then, for I was a pig; and my position, compared with hers, is an insolence of success." [. . .] Densher watched, decidedly, as he had never done before. "And the fact you speak of holds you!"
>
> "Of course it holds me. It's a perpetual sound in my ears. It makes me ask myself if I've any right to personal happiness, any right to anything but to be as rich and overflowing, as smart and shining, as I can be made." (*WD* 59)

Kate's desire is precisely for the thing that will give body to her mother's desire, the name that substitutes for it in the symbolic order. Kate's duty is thus identical to her desire: to rescue the name that substitutes for, and that (partially) fills, the gap in the field of representation. Kate's desire is, therefore, like Milly's, a hysterical desire.

Yet by the end of the novel Kate finds she has lost everything; she has given up both love and money, she has lost Densher as well as Aunt Maud. But even this, it seems, is not enough. Kate finds herself at the end of the novel having also given up the very thing for which all the other sacrifices were made. For the sake of her father's name, Kate has had to sacrifice even the name itself. Once she has given in to Densher's sexual blackmail, Kate no longer has her name intact, an act whose ramifications must be seen in the light of the conventions of nineteenth-century morality where a woman's honor and reputation were the sole value that she had to bring to marriage. As a "fallen woman," Kate now has not only no future, but not even a name. She has erased herself from the linguistic community more thoroughly than even her father did, for when a man creates a scandal, he still remains within the signifying system, albeit as an outcast. But a woman's scandal, according to nineteenth-century mores, relegates her strictly to nonexistence. According to the society in which she lives, Kate now belongs to that strange world of the living dead or, as Lacan would say, the space "between two deaths." Having sacrificed her good name, she has lost her identity in the symbolic order. The only options left to a woman of Kate's position would then have been suicide, prostitution, or to join the other women without signifiers of their own, as a nun in the convent. For the convent's primary function, Alenka Zupančič has argued, is to "make real death coincide with symbolic death."[57] The convent removes such women from circulation in the symbolic, immuring them until real death coincides with their symbolic death. Renouncing her name for the sake of the name itself, Kate has effectively committed symbolic suicide, an act that puts her in the company of other famous women whose uncompromising pursuit of their desire has been discussed by Lacan, namely, Antigone and Sygne du Coûfontaine.[58]

But Kate's uncompromising pursuit of her desire, which leads her finally to give up even that for the sake of which all of her other sacrifices were made, identifies her ethical orientation as being that of the drive, rather than, like Milly's, of desire. For Zupančič has shown how desire and drive have a strange relation to one another: drive appears at the far end of desire. Zupančič writes, "even if there is no common measure between desire and drive, at the heart of desire a possible passage opens up toward the drive; one might therefore come to the drive if one follows the 'logic' of desire to its limit" (Zupančič 243). Much like the structural paradox of the Möbius strip, when desire reaches its pure state, it changes into the drive. When Kate finds that, in order to be faithful to the Name, she must give it up as merely one more of the empirical series of things she can sacrifice, she has changed gear: she has shifted from desire to drive. As such, she anticipates the topic of my next chapter, which traces this paradoxical logic of the drive in a classic work of James's short fiction.

3

Lighting a Candle to Infinity

"The Altar of the Dead"

In this chapter I want to turn back to some of the issues I began with, back, that is, to what might be considered the "burning" question of ethical thought, the question of universality.[1] It was the concept of universality, after all, that Hegel addressed when he came to consider the dialectic of human and divine laws in his discussion of the Ethical Community in his *Phenomenology*,[2] and it continues to smolder despite the twentieth-century's attempts to "overcome" the great dialectician. The concept of universality has been the target of some of the most sophisticated critiques of contemporary thought and would seem, by now, to have been securely relegated to the ashes of history as embodying the most egregious excesses of nineteenth-century imperialist and totalizing impulses. The universal, it is now assured, is dead: discredited as a concept, and routed from its historic pride of place on the shrine of ethical discourse. Replacing it of course, in a swing typical of such discourse's dialectical progression, is the concept of particularity or, as it is more commonly called, "difference." Difference has long come to dominate contemporary ethical discussions, embodying now the touchstone for ethical action and judgment. Since the great Hegelian "overcoming" represented, culturally, by the new historicism and, philosophically, by deconstruction, ethics has become the ethics of the particular, specifically of the rights of particulars to differ from the all-encompassing, hegemonic Same.

The problem, however, as has been recognized recently by some of the same theorists who originally proclaimed the death of the universal, is that without some workable concept of universality ethics dissolves into mere cultural relativism and the "free play" of endless, metonymic slippage.[3] Without some unifying or, better, *limiting* principle, in other words, judgment (the basis for ethical action) becomes impossible. The question now becomes how to resurrect the concept of universality, but without repeating the excesses and violent impositions that this concept historically has invoked. Can we have a universal that is not inherently totalizing? Does the concept of universality always necessarily ultimately imply the (surreptitious and illicit) dominance of one particular at the exclusion of another?

Henry James's, "The Altar of the Dead,"[4] seems an appropriate place to continue sounding out these questions since, like Hegel's chapter on the Ethical World where the question of the "being" of universality and individuality is first raised, the tale similarly deals with the problem of burial, more specifically, of marking a place for the dead. Although unlike Antigone, who is the central feature in Hegel's discussion, the woman in James's story is neither burying her brother, nor breaking state laws to do so, she nevertheless shares with the Sophoclean heroine a conviction regarding what she considers the appropriate memorial rites to be. Indeed, for both women, it is not so much a question of what is appropriate, but rather of what *must* be done. Each woman, in other words, holds the question of what to do with the dead as possessing a uniquely ethical urgency, an urgency that for us at a first glance might seem excessive. Why should the question of the rites/rights of the dead carry such import to the extent that, at least since Hegel's Antigone, they have come to epitomize for us what is essential to ethics? James's tale gives us some answers.

The story is told through the eyes of the male character, George Stransom, for whom the rights of the dead also matter very intensely. They matter so much in fact for Stransom that he dedicates his life to remembering or memorializing his Dead, at first through intrinsic and later extrinsic means. It is Stransom, as Andrzej Warminski helps us to see in his superb analysis of the tale,[5] who shows us what is at stake in the funereal rites of death. For it is as a consummate dialectician, Warminski argues, that Stransom sets up his altar of the dead, with the aim not of repressing death but of turning it over to the service of life, that is, to dialectize it in a manner reminiscent of Hegel's own "tarrying with the negative." "Death," as Hegel famously puts it in his preface (but worth citing once more), if that is what we want to call this non-actuality, is of all things the most dreadful, and to hold fast to what is dead requires the greatest strength. [. . .] But the life of Spirit is not the life that shrinks from death and keeps itself untouched by devastation, but rather the life that endures it and maintains itself in it. It wins its truth only when, in utter dismemberment, it finds itself. (Hegel 19)

It is for nothing less than to "win truth" from death, we realize, that Stransom sets up his altar, in yet another version of our interminable attempt to wrest necessity from contingency or, as Hegel puts it in the Ethical World, to infuse with consciousness the blind work of Nature.[6] Clearly these are not small stakes. For isn't this ultimately the aim of all literature, art, representation: to negate death, to create a whole out of what is fragmentary, to transform a series of radically contingent events into a coherent, completed narrative necessity?

Like many of James's tales, the plot is fairly simple. George Stransom, a somewhat retiring man, lost his fiancée shortly before their wedding day. All his life he has kept faithful remembrance of her, in particular on the anniversary of her death. To her he constructs an imaginary altar in his mind that in due course also comes to be populated with his other friends who have died. Most notable among these is Kate, the wife of his friend Paul Creston, who died recently in childbirth. Two events occur in close succession that herald a change in the way Stransom pays homage to his Dead. The first is a chance encounter with Paul who, it transpires, has remarried in what Stransom feels to be undue haste and without proper regard for Kate's mourning: "That new woman, that hired performer, Mrs Creston?" Stransom "felt himself grimacing, he heard himself exaggerating the usual, but he was conscious that he had turned slightly faint" (AD 268).

Later that evening, as he mulls indignantly over "the frivolity, the indecency of it" he comes across a newspaper obituary reporting the death of one Acton Hague K. C. B., Stransom's dearest yet irrevocably estranged friend: "the only man with whom he had ever been intimate; the friend, almost adored, of his University years, the subject, later, of his passionate loyalty" (AD 271). Hague has in the past, we learn, done Stransom a terrible wrong which, while never named, has nevertheless destroyed the friendship. With the news of his death, Stransom freezes: "To-day it all seemed to have occurred merely to the end that George Stransom should think of him as 'Hague' and measure exactly how much he himself could feel like a stone. He went cold, suddenly and horribly cold, to bed" (AD 271).

The next day, which happens to be the anniversary of the death of his fiancée, Mary Antrim, Stransom comes across a church in which he rests after his long pilgrimmage to the cemetery where she is buried. There he basks in the radiant light of an altar covered in candles in memory of some recently departed soul, and there he comes to the idea of creating a permanent, physical altar for those of his friends whom he calls his Dead:

> The thing became, as he sat there, his appropriate altar, and each starry candle an appropriate vow. He numbered them, he named them, he grouped them—it was the silent roll-call of his Dead. They made together a brightness vast and intense, a brightness in which the mere chapel of his thoughts grew so dim that as it faded away he asked himself if he shouldn't find his real comfort in some material act, some outward worship. (*AD* 272)

Thus the "Altar of the Dead" is born, a permanent shrine in the church dedicated and paid for by Stransom who ensures that for each of his Dead a candle shall always burn. For each of his Dead, that is, except one, for Stransom vows that he will never light a candle in honor of Acton Hague.

Years go by and he gradually becomes friends with a nameless woman, the same one who was present at the church the day he first conceived of his altar. Like him, she goes regularly to the church to mourn at his altar and, like him, she seems to derive great comfort from the mountain of burning flames. For years they worship together yet with little more knowledge of the shrine's individual significance for each other than they had at the beginning. They nevertheless agree that, after Stransom's death, she will continue to maintain the shrine and light a candle for him, "a candle [. . .] before which all the others will pale" (*AD* 281). This candle, for Stransom, will finally complete the set. The plan gives Stransom much pleasure as he contemplates his death: "He often said to her that since he had so little time to live he rejoiced in her having so much; so glad was he to think she would guard the temple when he should have ceased" (*AD* 282).

One day Stransom arrives at the church to discover a change has occurred. The woman's aunt has died and for the first time Stransom is invited back to the woman's apartment, an invitation that constitutes to Stransom's mind, "an event, somehow; and in all their long acquaintance there had never been such a thing" (*AD* 283). Once there, Stransom makes the momentous discovery that the woman and Acton Hague had been lovers, and that all this time that she had been worshiping at the shrine, it had been for Hague.

Then Stransom understood, while the room heaved like the cabin of a ship, that its whole contents cried out with him, that it was a museum in his honor, that all her later years had been passionately addressed to him and that the shrine he himself had reared had been passionately converted to this use. It was all for Acton Hague that she had kneeled every day at his altar. What need had there been for a consecrated candle when he was present in the whole array? The revelation seemed to smite our friend in the face, and he dropped into a seat and sat silent. (*AD* 285)

The difference this makes between them is profound. When Stransom reveals that he has never lit a candle on the shrine in honor of Hague, the woman declares she can never go back there again: "How can I, then, with this new knowledge of my own, ask you to continue to live with it?" she asks Stransom. How can she go on with the old style of worship, now that they know their irreconcilably different intentions?

"I told you, long ago, that my Dead were not many. Yours were, but all you had done for them was none too much for *my* worship! You had placed a great light for Each—I gathered them together for One!" (*AD* 288)

Stransom protests. He pleads. But the woman is firm and Stransom is dismissed. They see each other again, but not at the church, and Stransom is struck once more by the woman's firmness: "He argued with her again, told her she could now have the altar to herself; but she only shook her head with pleading sadness, begging him not to waste his breath on the impossible, the extinct. Couldn't he see that in relation to her private need the rites he had established were practically an elaborate exclusion?" (*AD* 292).

The worst part of the "difference" that has come between them is the disruption it represents to Stransom's plans for after his death. For now, after what they know, the woman cannot accept the charge of being the eventual "guardian" of his shrine: "[S]he listened to him now with a sort of shining coldness and all her habitual forbearance to insist on her terms" (*AD* 295). Her unspoken terms, of course, are that he must light one more candle, the missing candle for Acton Hague. This Stransom feels he cannot do.

The woman and Stransom are estranged. Stransom feels guilty for depriving the woman of the solace the altar used to give her. He invents excuses; he argues with himself, he tells himself (without sincerity, James notes) that there is no room on the shrine for one more candle. Finally, after much mental shuffling, he arrives at the thought that symmetry requires one more candle. "Symmetry was harmony, and the idea of harmony began to haunt him" (*AD* 298). "'Just one more—to round it off; just one, just one,' continued to hum itself in his head" (*AD* 298). After a bout of illness Stransom returns, weakly, once more to the altar. He loses himself in the vast radiance, but is conscious of a single candle burning more brightly than any of the others. It is the candle for Mary Antrim, "the central voice of the choir, the glowing heart of the brightness" (*AD* 299). Stransom

> bowed his head in submission, and at the same moment another wave rolled over him. Was it the quickening of joy to pain? In the midst of his joy at any rate he felt his buried face grow hot as with some communicated knowledge that had the force of a reproach. It suddenly made him contrast that very rapture with the bliss he had refused to another. This breath of the passion immortal was all that other had asked; the descent of Mary Antrim opened his spirit with a great compunctious throb for the descent of Acton Hague. (*AD* 299–300)

Suddenly Stransom recognizes the prostrated woman before him. It is the old "partner of his long worship." She has come back. Something has changed in her heart, she tells him. "It was as if I suddenly saw something— as if it all became possible" (*AD* 300). Stransom sinks toward her, staring up at the shrine. The Dead, he tells her, are saying to him, "'there's a gap in the array—they say it's not full, complete. Just one more,' he went on, softly,— 'isn't that what you wanted? Yes, one more, one more.' "'Ah, no more,'" the woman wails, as Stransom dies in her arms, "'no more!' [. . .] as if with a quick, new horror of it, under her breath" (*AD* 301).

I

I want to begin by looking at Warminski's argument that Stransom's altar comprises nothing less than the promise of any representational system. This is the promise of a system that claims to give us access to a meaning beyond and above the mere material signifiers that constitute it, the simple but well-established and powerful idea that a phenomenal sign can stand in for a transcendent meaning. The fact that Stransom's is a system designed to mark the continuing existence (in the form of remembrance, or memory) of dead friends simply makes all the more visible the implied promise of all such representational systems, namely, the possibility of transcending our physical state and entering a realm beyond the reach of time and contingency. Systems such as Stransom's, in other words, are designed to allow us to go beyond death, beyond our physical and material limits as phenomenal beings. They constitute nothing less than the conditions of possibility for our acts of intention, and as such enable us, as Warminski puts it, "to recover from the negativity of experience," which can then be retold as a history, that is, as the story of a self's past (Warminski 268). But, as I suggested above, what makes Stransom's such an efficient system is that it is not so much a matter of repressing death as making *death itself* go to work for us. Warminski argues that this is what makes Stransom a dialectician of such "considerable refinement": the realization that even death can be placed in our service as the very means by which contingency, or death, can be overcome.

As Warminski points out, Stransom's altar in fact constitutes the most minimally representational system there is, based on a simple, one-to-one correspondence of signifier and signified. The altar comprises a binary system of inclusion and exclusion: one candle for each dead, except for one, the missing candle for Acton Hague. As such, it is little more than a simple counting system, one that counts presence and absence not unlike the binary computational system of a computer (Warminski 272). But despite, or rather because of, its simplicity, this is a system with infinite variability. Stransom is quite explicit on this point: "To other imaginations they might stand for other things—that they should stand for something to be hushed before was all he desired" (*AD* 275). This is why, once the break between him and the woman has occurred, he imagines that they can nevertheless go on as they had been previously. Stransom, in other words, believes he has already incorporated into his system all the differences that other intentional meanings might proffer. For his is a system with infinite combinatory possibilities, a system "in which endless meanings could glow," enabling him to count and recount his Dead: "He took, in fancy, his composition to pieces, redistributing it into other lines, making other juxtapositions and contrasts. He shifted this and that candle, he made the spaces different" (*AD* 298). The only thing that cannot be changed, the only invariable if you like, is its founding principle, the exclusion of one candle for Acton Hague. This exclusion is what gives Stransom's system its consistency: the candles might exchange places, they may represent different individual intentions—"Stransom divined that for her too they had been vividly individual, had stood for particular hours or particular attributes—particular links in her chain" (*AD* 294)—in other words, each candle can move about in relation to another, but Hague's exclusion is the guarantee that each will find a place after the shuffle, much like in a game of musical chairs. But as we know, something happens to disturb this self-supporting, or "closed tropological system" as Warminski puts it. Something occurs that Stransom can only call, rather vaguely, "an event" but which Warminski, more specifically if no less obliquely, names "reading." He argues, "the happening of 'The Altar of the Dead,' its one event, is reading" (Warminski 262). What does he mean by this?

For Warminski, the critical event occurs, not because it is revealed that Stransom and the woman have different meanings for the shrine, that is, because they have different subjective intentions. This possibility, as we saw, was already encoded within the precise functionings of Stransom's representational system. In fact, Warminski claims, what happens is the exact opposite. The "event" occurs precisely because something falls outside the intended, subjective meanings of both Stransom and the woman, and this occurs because of an act of "reading." For Warminski, the event occurs when the woman "reads" Stransom's "text" (i.e., his representational system) and as a reader "intends a linguistic intention that is utterly outside the grasp of a self or a subject" (Warminski 275). What Warminski is alluding to of course is the inevitable gap that results from all signifying activity, the gap produced when the signifier and signified fail to fully coincide with one another. This gap is the inevitable result of any attempt to make objects of the material world representatives or stand-ins for an external meaning. For on every occasion that some material object becomes "marked" as a sign, something—namely, the object's materiality—falls outside the intending subject's grasp.

So far this is fairly straightforward. Everyone knows by now that linguistic, or really any representational signs, have an uncanny ability to say both more and less than what we mean, and therefore divide us from simple presence. We need only to begin with Hegel's first chapter of the *Phenomenology*, "Sense Certainty," to discover the truth of this, when Hegel disingenuously suggests that writing down the words "Here" and "Now" cannot in itself change the "truth" of their meaning, only to find that this particular "here" and this particular "now" have already changed, disappeared, become, as Hegel puts it, "stale" (Hegel 60). The point for Warminski, and this is the significant "political" purchase of his position, is what we do with this "knowledge." For Warminski, the point is that this discovery, once made, fundamentally changes the conditions for the previous system of signs. That is, it makes it impossible, he says, quoting James, to "return to the old symbols," to recover from the "negativity" of the disruption that such "reading" engenders. Into Stransom's closed circuit of transferential meaning (the system Warminski names "metaphor"), the woman's "reading" erupts as a radically asymmetrical event, undoing the elaborate system of correspondences based on a one-to-one relation. As Warminski puts it, "Rather than his and her altars, his and her metaphors (for the self, for example) that would be united, mediated—if by nothing else, then at least by negation—what we have is his and her metaphors (un-)yoked by a radical (i.e., blind) metonymy in something like a zeugma" (Warminski 276). And as such, with the recognition of this fundamental property of material signs to escape or, to use the terms of the previous chapter, to "betray" the meaning of the intending subject, any attempt to "return" to the old ways of signifying, the old "ways of worship" is in vain. The fact of language's materiality radically destabilizes the system and cuts us off from any return—if, that is, we are to remain faithful to the event that such "reading" engenders, and refuse to repress that knowledge or otherwise engage in an (for Warminski) illicit "aestheticization" and attempt to close that gap.

What is at stake in all of this, as James's text makes so unusually and refreshingly clear, is quite simply the question of a limit, of the exception that creates the rule. We saw how Hague's absence from Stransom's system is the system's founding principle, the law that enables all the other candles to correspond to their signifieds. With Hague's absence as the limit point around which Stransom's representational system converges, the candles must eventually halt their metonymic slide. Marks, letters, signs may indeed "relate only to other marks, other letters, other signs," as Warminski points out, but in order to have the most minimally significatory event, there must be something posited beyond them, a founding principle or Law of laws to which they ultimately refer.[7] But remove that limit—as the woman insists—and there is nothing that guarantees the candles will eventually find a stopping point (since you can always add "just one more" even to infinity, for example, infinity + 1, infinity + 2, etc.). This is scarcely a trivial problem, as Stransom recognizes, since it inflects the entire enterprise of creating meaning, narratives, histories. Indeed it inflects nothing less than the very possibility of a self as a being "having" a past that can be retold, remembered as a history (without which possibility, as Hume discovered, we relegate ourselves to mere, immediate bundles of impressions, existing in isolated moments in time with no means of collecting them together). The limit, in other words, as I have been arguing throughout these pages, is what makes it possible for us to transcend our merely phenomenal state, and enter, with Isabel Archer, a realm of transcendental freedom, to escape, with Milly Theale, the birdcage of language that otherwise threatens to fully entrap us. The limit, I have claimed, is nothing less than the condition of possibility of reason itself, enabling us to be freely acting, conscious beings. Why, then, should the woman demand we give it up? And what are we left with in its place?

For Warminski, of course, the concept of such a limit is merely the embodiment of the mystified, ideologically suspect aesthetic fantasy whose contours are defined by Stransom's metaphorical "economy," which he describes as "the organic, sacrificial, redemptive, aesthetic economy of death and restoration" (Warminski 272). What the woman represents in contrast, he argues, is an other economy, the "mechanical, nonredemptive, non-aesthetic economy of death," whose uncanny, dispiriting presence disrupts and undoes the elaborate fictions of the first (272). Warminski makes much of James's image of "the dreadful clockface of the friend we meet [that] announces the hour we have tried to forget" (*AD* 283) in his characterization of how this other economy disrupts or "disarticulates" (Warminski 284) the celebratory fantasies of the first. Honing in on James's image of a clock mechanically (i.e., nonintentionally) ticking as a figure for the running down of human life—an image that stands in starkest possible contrast to the first economy's incarnational figures that seek to transcend time through a mystified valorization of human "nature," the *face* of the friend we will remember—Warminski emphasizes the purely mechanical, hence, "inhuman" features of this second economy. He writes,

> According to the story's own words, the story's own figures, "human grief," "human time," and "human memory" are not so "human" after all but rather as mechanical and tit-for-tat as the winding-up and working out of dispirited clockwork: the human face becomes a "dreadful clockface" that punctually and inexorably announces the hour of our death. Human memory is, if anything, most inhuman, most mechanical, and most dead, and the most human thing to do about it is, in the story's own words, to try to forget it—forget the inhumanity, indeed monstrosity [. . .] of "human," that is, mechanical and *in*human, time, the bad job of being unto death. (Warminski 267)

What we are left with, in other words, once the economy founded on an exception is destroyed by the nonintentional disarticulations of a "material" reading is, for Warminski, the sheer, senseless, mechanical repetition of language voided of its (illusory) transcendent powers: the ridiculous, inane stuttering of a Stransom at the end of the story, "just one more, just one more." Warminski writes, "What's left is a story of mechanical, dead repetition: the candles continue mechanically to burn; Stransom is reduced to repeating his 'inanity.' Whether he dies or not at the 'end' makes no difference. He has become a counting, re-counting memory-machine—whose memory is not 'human remembrance' but mechanical memory by rote, mere memorization—a computer 'reading over endless histories'" (Warminski 283).

The question is whether this mechanical, dispirited, repetitious "reading" strategy (and despite the often dizzying qualities displayed by *tour-de-force* material readings such as Warminski's own, there is nevertheless a mechanically repetitious quality to "High" deconstruction), whether the workings of this "memory-machine," can ever found a politics or act as a basis for ethical action? If, as Warminski so effectively demonstrates, the very concept of the self gets "undone" by deconstructive reading events, what possibilities are left for subjective agency without which ethics are inconceivable? This is scarcely a new question, having been addressed to deconstruction right from its earliest days but which, to my mind, still has not been satisfactorily resolved. Two possibilities have been posited: the first is to betray the knowledge we have just learned, to "forget" it, as Warminski suggests, and go on as before, at worst in a kind of aestheticizing bad faith, at best in a form of disavowal that holds this knowledge in suspension (as, for example, in Kant's Transcendental Illusion that says, "I know very well that there is nothing beyond the limit but it is a necessary fiction in order for me to have even the most basic cognitive functions"). The other possibility is to accept this tragic knowledge and embrace the repetitious automaton of a symbolic system that can refer only to itself—to its own failure to signify—and try to find some form of political purchase within the excesses of that system, as found in those readings that celebrate the "pleasures of the text," or in the subversive potential of the system's "performative" dimensions.[8] In the language of psychoanalysis, the first response describes the politics of perversion, based on disavowal, while the second describes a politics of psychosis—if such a term is even comprehensible—founded on foreclosure.

It seems clear that if the first response provides at least a foundation for a rigorous, Kantian ethics, even if it continually threatens to double as an ethics of Sade, as Lacan famously showed in "Kant with Sade"[9]—that is, as an ethics of the superego under whom no renunciations can ever be enough—the second seems to offer little more than a voluntarism. This is the idea that changes in deep structures can be made simply by an act of will. Henry's brother William James probably would not have had major problems with such an attitude, famously writing in his journal "my first act of free will is to believe in free will," but it seems to me that Henry had something characteristically more subtle and rigorous in mind. To the question of what is left once the economy of the exception has been undone by "reading," perhaps we should once more read "The Altar of the Dead."

II

Let us go back then to the central image of the story, of Stramson and the woman worshiping "side by side" (*AD* 276). The figure Warminski suggests for this image is the rhetorical trope of zeugma, the yoking together of two opposing semantic features under one grammatical coordination. The example Warminski cites from the text as illustrating this trope is James's description of Stransom's reaction to Hague's death: "[H]e went cold, suddenly and horribly cold, to bed" (*AD* 271). As Warminski points out, what is important in a zeugma is the asymmetry between the grammatical coordination and its semantic opposition, a difference, that is, that is not reducible to either grammar or syntax but lies somewhere in between. It is this asymmetry, this irreducibility of zeugma to come down on one side or the other of grammatical or syntactical laws, that makes this trope emblematic of the "material" reading Warminski proffers. On the one hand, Stransom "reads" metaphorically, returning all his candles to the one exception. On the other, the woman "reads" metonymically: all her candles are for Hague in a relation that is based not on a vertical principle of substitution, but by "contiguity," by a horizontal relation. Warminski cites James's description of the woman's apartment as representative of the way such a metonymic "reading" approaches meaning:

> The place had the flush of life—it was expressive; its dark red walls were articulate with memories and relics. These were simple things—pho-

tographs and water-colours, scraps of writing framed and ghosts of
flowers embalmed; but only a moment was needed to show him they
had a common meaning. (*AD* 284)

Warminski glosses this passage thus: "[H]er 'scraps of writing framed and
ghosts of flowers embalmed' signify their 'common meaning' by contiguity, they are the dead, material remainders of an accidentally contiguous,
material association with Hague, indeed with certain places and
times. [. . .] This is not matter informed, in*formed*, by spirit, but matter
arbitrarily converted to a signifying function by a pure act of the mind"
(Warminski 280).

The difference Warminski wants to make out here is between Stransom's reading as a mystified act of "aestheticization" whereby the gap
between sensible and intelligible realms is plugged by way of an illicit reconciliation attained through the vertical trope of metaphorical substitution, and the woman's "material" act of reading. Her act, according to
Warminski, recognizes the purely formal, that is, contiguous, association
of "marks, letters, signs" with their intended meanings. Because of this
recognition, her reading disrupts Stransom's economy by showing how
the relation between signifier and signified can only ever be horizontal,
that is, signs "mean" only inasmuch as we have "memorized" the arbitrary
relation of signifier and signified. In other words, her reading disrupts the
fallacy of believing we can derive a vertical relation among contiguous elements in a binary system. Any impression of verticality that is produced
is the result of an illicit, aesthetic, mystified, violent act of imposition.
Hence where Stransom imagines representation enables him to transcend
contingency and enter a realm beyond death, the woman's reading reveals
how illusory this promise remains. All meaning, as she suggests, is a
zeugma, the mechanical yoking together or "memorization" of grammatic
and semantic elements. To imagine anything different is to fall into the
error that mistakes an external, contiguous, contingent relation for an
internal, vertical necessity given, most famously, in the Romantic trope of
Erinnerung. As Warminski incisively puts it, "Whereas Stransom is a man
of 'remembrance' [. . .] she is a woman of 'reminders'" (Warminski 280).

The problem begins, however, once we start to track the way the figure of the zeugma operates in Warminski's text. For on the one hand,
zeugma seems intended by Warminski to function as a figure for the
undecidability of the woman's style of reading, which highlights the way
all signs are doubled between their "material" and meaning-producing

functions; in Warminski's terms, between their "grammar" and "seman-
tics." Here zeugma acts as a figure for the woman's "metonymic" or
"grammatical" strategy of reading that "(un-)yokes" signs from their mystified relationships with their signifieds, revealing how meaning is "an act
of memorization," that is, an unnatural relationship. On the other hand,
however, it seems that zeugma is also supposed to act as a figure for the
asymmetrical *conjunction* of both "metonymic" and traditional
"metaphorical" readings together, that is, zeugma is what "happens" when
you place metaphor and metonym side by side. Zeugma is, in other
words, forced to do double-duty as genus and one of its own species or,
to use the text's own terms, as both the "event" *and its own cause.* Zeugma
is both the (metonymical) rhetorical reading strategy of deconstruction,
and the name of the irreducible (metonymical) "event" that occurs when
deconstructive or "metonymical" readings and "metaphorical" readings
occur side by side.

Here we have in a nutshell the "tragedy" of deconstructive readings
(and the preponderance of "tragic" figures in deconstruction, particularly
in the readings of Paul De Man, has often been noted[10]): on the one hand,
in order to perform their act of radical undoing such readings are dependent on the very "master signifier" (the "metaphorical" or "exceptional"
reading strategy such as Stransom's) they set themselves to undo. On the
other hand, because they end up repositing a new (quasi-)transcendental
figure, for example, the zeugma, which in turn must be undone in yet
another act of "reading," each act of reading must endlessly repeat itself in
a reading to the next "power," a situation De Man names in shorthand as
"allegory." Each new reading subsequently "allegorizes" its previous failure
to read in the precise sense that Warminski and De Man give this term,
that is, its failure to fully comprehend and account for the radical implications of language's self-undoing, with the result that its knowledge is "forgotten." To use an image inspired by Stransom's "counting machine," allegory thus functions for De Man and Warminski much the way infinite sets
are constructed in set theory, whereby each sequence to infinity is completed (with what is known as a "limit ordinal," such as omega) only to
begin again (as, for example, infinity + 1, infinity + 2, etc.). "Allegorical
readings," which are nothing but "material" readings to the next degree ad
infinitum, thus comprise the structure of an infinite regress as each new
reading becomes "completed" by a new quasi-transcendental figure which,
in turn, becomes subject to a further "reading." But as the analogy with
omega illustrates, the infinity that deconstructive reading represents is

really *finite*: the infinite ordinal, omega, is the figure of the *completed* infinity. Hence the much touted "infinite divisibility" of deconstruction is in truth the infinite repetition of the finite task that allows one to take one more step and complete an infinity, and then begin again.

It is thus that readings such as Warminski's, for all of their disruption of the symmetrical logic identified with Stransom's metaphorical system, nevertheless remain within a binary system of choice (such as that between metaphor or metonymy). They must proceed on the basis of an either/or: either we have one economy (the illusory, mystified metaphorical economy) or we have the "other" economy (demystified, material, mechanical), but this "other" economy cannot exist in a universe of its own. It is structurally dependent on the first, as Warminski's second use of the figure of zeugma makes apparent: the zeugma marks the *intersection* of metaphorical and metonymical readings. So even if, as Warminski argues, "[I]t is not the decision between metaphor or metonymy [. . .] that counts, but rather their tangle, their mutual intrication, or better, their mutual un-doing" (Warminski 268), allegorical readings ultimately remain caught in the old dialectic of positing and reflection that they set out to undo. And it is for this reason, moreover, that the solution represented by "material" readings in response to the knowledge that all symbolic systems, in order to fulfill their promise, must make (illicit) use of an exception, of the extrasystemic element, inevitably fails from a psychoanalytic perspective. Attempting to theorize the moment when an "event" profoundly disrupts the smooth functioning of a "metaphorically" driven signifying system, material readings can only offer the "dispiriting" solution of the mechanical, arbitrary, repetitive capture of the automaton of language, the very trap that we saw Milly in the previous chapter attempting at all costs to avoid.[11] Again, it appears James can be instructive. It seems that with the woman's insistence that Stransom light the last candle for Hague, James is offering in "The Altar of the Dead" a way of theorizing the "event" that Warminski is correct to identify. Where he goes wrong, however, is in his conceptualization of that event. For what Warminski claims to "happen" is something that occurs at the level of the Symbolic system itself, namely, that the exception, or what Lacan would call the "quilting point," which holds the system in place is routed, disposed of, shown that its "exceptional" nature is illusory, and that it, too, is merely a member of the set it was supposed to describe. But from a psychoanalytic perspective, it is not hard to identify that the "happening" of James's story takes place not at the level of the Symbolic but at the *intersection* of the Symbolic and the Real. To paraphrase and correct Warminski: The happening of "The Altar of the Dead," its one event, is the encounter with the Real (the *tuchè*).

Against Warminski, then, it is James (with Lacan) who shows us another way of conceptualizing the "event" of the tale, such that, instead of condemning us to the endless, senseless repetition of language conceived as a strictly mechanical system of tropes, a different possibility is opened up, enabling us to conceptualize how such a system may after all transcend its limits, but without "forgetting" the hard-won knowledge produced by deconstruction and reverting back to some externally imposed, mystified "transcendental signfied."[12] If deconstruction, in other words, winds up only being able to construct elaborate but strictly isolated chains of readings stretching away to infinity, perhaps James with Lacan can show us a way to link them, to find a way to "yoke" them together? It is to Warminski's figure of zeugma, therefore, that I propose to return, but this time to see if it can be employed to theorize a different conceptual relationship than that of his "(un-)yoking" of metaphor and metonymy. For as I will show, the zeugma in fact offers a rather nifty figure for illustrating not one but the *two* modes by which language fails to live up to its promise of reconciliation. The zeugma, in my reading, provides a figure for the two distinct modes of impossibility represented by psychoanalysis and (De Manian) deconstruction.[13]

III

The difference between the two systems has already been stated: "'I told you, long ago,'" says the woman to Stransom, "'that my Dead were not many. Yours were, but all you had done for them was none too much for *my* worship! You had placed a great light for Each—I gathered them together for One!'" (*AD* 288). If Stransom's was a system designed around a central absence, the woman's is characterized, inversely, by nothing so much as an all-encompassing presence. Hence if Stransom's system is guaranteed by the single candle that escapes his rule (one candle for each Dead), we might say that the woman's is characterized by the fact that there is not one candle on the altar that is not dedicated to Hague. Thus their systems both represent incomplete totalities, but each in different ways. Stransom's will be completed when the last candle is lit. But, as Stransom is all too aware, this projected completion of the system will also entail the collapse of the system (which is why he puts so much store by the thought that the woman will act as a "guardian" to the shrine, that is, to continue his existence after his death). Indeed Warminski already makes the convincing point that the missing candle for Hague actually, coterminously, represents the missing candle for Stransom, so that Hague is somehow Stransom's "alter/altar ego":

> Once when she had discovered, as they called it, a new star, she used the expression that the chapel at last was full.
> "Oh no," Stransom replied, "there is a great thing wanting for that! The chapel will never be full till a candle is set up before which all the others will pale. It will be the tallest candle of all."
> Her mild wonder rested on him. "What candle do you mean?"
> "I mean, dear lady, my own." (*AD* 281–82)

The woman's system, meanwhile, although there is nothing missing, is nevertheless not whole. That is to say, for the woman, even though there is not a single candle that is not for Hague, all the candles together still do not constitute a totality. No matter how many more candles are to be lit, in other words, it would still not be enough as James, in a strange blurring of aural and visual metaphors makes clear: "The light she had demanded for his [Hague's] altar would have broken his [Stransom's] silence with a blare; whereas all the lights in the church were for her too great a hush" (*AD* 291).

The best way to conceive of the difference between the two systems is found in Kant's discussion of logical antinomies toward the end of his *Critique of Pure Reason.* Here Kant enunciates what appear to be logically contradictory statements but which, as Joan Copjec points out, in fact turn out to be "contrary" statements. The distinction is that between a statement whose opposite is its negation (contradiction), and a statement whose opposite doesn't so much negate the first statement but rather asserts a different positive (contrary). Unlike with contradictory statements, with contrary oppositions, as Copjec notes, a possibility is left open that both statements may turn out to be true or false.[14]

The antinomic statements concerning us here are those that Kant gives, appropriately enough for my discussion, regarding magnitude, namely, the attempt to think the world as a totality. Two antinomies are posited: the statement that the world has a beginning in time and a limit in space, and its opposite, that the world has no beginning in time and no limit in space. Taken as contradictory statements, we have to choose between either one of the statements as true. Taken, however, as contrary statements, Copjec argues, a solution is found in showing how both statements make an illicit assumption of existence about the world.

In order to make a determinant judgment about a possible object of experience, Kant demonstrated in the First *Critique* how it is necessary for that object to be given in the transcendental intuitions of time and space. However, as Kant argues (and subsequently demonstrates in his Analytic of the Sublime in the *Critique of Judgment*), the absolute totality of phenomena cannot be given in phenomenal form, that is, in the successive or regressive apprehension of space and time, but only simultaneously, either as a concept of the Understanding or, in special cases, as an Idea of reason: "[W]e have the cosmic whole only in concept, never, as a whole, in intuition."[15] Therefore, the attempt to make a determinant judgment about the universe as a totality is illegitimate; *both* statements are false, the first because it attempts to legislate on a noumenal object (the "cosmic" totality) with phenomenal laws (a beginning in time and limit in space), the latter because it claims that phenomena may be approached from a noumenal perspective (no beginning in time and no limit in space, i.e., a "God's-eye" view of the world). Kant explains, "All beginning is in time and all limits of the extended are in space. But space and time belong only to the world of sense. Accordingly, while appearances *in the world* are conditionally limited, *the world itself* is neither conditionally nor unconditionally limited" (*CPR* 458). The implications of this are spelt out by Copjec: "[T]he world is an object that destroys the means of finding it; it is for this reason illegitimate to call it an object at all. A universe of phenomena is a true contradiction in terms; *the world cannot and does not exist*" (*Read My Desire* 220, her emphasis).

Hence we must, with Kant, reject both antinomies. The first statement, that the world has a beginning in space and a limit in time, is false. For this would imply that we could have a perception of the boundaries of space and time, an empirical perception, that is, of what Kant calls "empty time and empty space" at the edges of our phenomenal space and time. "But such an experience, as completely empty of content, is impossible," Kant asserts, and "[c]onsequently, an absolute limit of the world is impossible empirically, and therefore also absolutely" (*CPR* 457). This means, as Copjec glosses Kant, that "there can be no limit to phenomena in the phenomenal realm, for this would mean the existence of a phenomenon of an exceptional sort, one that was not itself conditioned and would thus allow us to halt our regress, or one that took no phenomenal form, that is, that was empty: a void space or a void time" (*Read My Desire* 220).

But it does not mean that we must conclude from this that the world is infinite. Rather, the statement of antithesis, that there is no beginning in space and no limit in time, does not mean that we can make a cosmological jump and conclude that phenomena can after all be apprehended as a whole, or noumenally (as Kant's followers, Fichte and Schelling, came to suggest with their concept of the "intellectual intuition"). As Copjec again explains, "[O]ur acknowledgement of the absence of a limit to the set of phenomena [. . .] obliges us to recognize the basic *finitude* of all phenomena, the fact that they are inescapably subject to conditions of time and space and must therefore be encountered one by one, indefinitely, without the possibility of reaching an end, a point where all phenomena would be known" (*Read My Desire* 221). Hence, as Kant writes, "[T]he regress in the series of appearances, as a determination of the magnitude of the world, proceeds *in indefinitum*" (*CPR* 457).

With this "mathematical" antinomy of Kant's some of the positions of the previous discussion are repeated. For doesn't Kant's negative answer to the first antinomy describe very precisely the position Warminski is arguing? According to Kant, there is no signifier external to the system, no outside to language that will guarantee it and hold its signifiers in place. But, as I said, this does not mean, with Warminski, that all we are left with is the senselessness of a system shorn of its transcendent powers and reduced to the inane, mechanical stuttering of an automaton. As the second, "affirmative," answer to the Kantian antinomy demonstrates, it is precisely *because* there is no limit to the phenomenal, because there is no point from which we can phenomenally apprehend the totality, that we can nevertheless create a structure that *both* fulfills the promise of meaning (i.e., a system that keeps the signifiers from their endless metonymic slide), *and* ensures that it will never form a totality, a whole (from which one could see it from the perspective of the outside). What strange kind of a system is this?

It is to the concept of infinity that we must in fact turn if we are to successfully theorize how such a system might be possible.[16] As we saw, one method for generating the infinite hierarchies of allegorical readings was through the use of something I called a "quasi-transcendental" (e.g., Warminski's zeugma), which I identified as possessing a function structurally similar to the element in set theory called a "limit ordinal." A limit ordinal is simply the element which represents the completion of an infinite series of steps—the smallest of these is known in set theory as omega, the limit of our ordinary discrete counting process, the completed set of all natural numbers. From omega, however, it is always possible to begin a new series of steps (omega + 1, omega + 2 . . .) all the way up to omega + omega, which is the next limit ordinal, and then go beyond that (omega + omega + 1, etc.). Omega*omega is thus the omega-*th* limit ordinal and so on. As we saw with regard to deconstructive readings, with a procedure like this we are always either *completing* a series of infinity or *beginning* another.

A distinction is made in mathematics, however, between "ordinal" and "cardinal" numbers: the ordinal number represents the counting action implied by that number. It describes the way any number is the result of an addition that begins with 0 and adds as many unit steps as are given. So effectively, each ordinal is really the "set" of all previous ordinals coming before it, beginning with the first ordinal, the empty, or null set. The cardinality of a number, on the other hand, is the *naming* of that unit amount once the computation is completed. The cardinal number, in other words, represents the size or "number of elements" of the set it describes, in abstraction from the order in which they have come to be in the set. Now, set theory tells us that as long as we are dealing with finite sets, the ordinality and cardinality of numbers is identical. 1 + 1 + 1 + 1 = (both ordinal and cardinal) 4, that is, it took exactly *four* steps to get to the size of 4. Once we launch into the realm of infinity, and specifically of infinite sets, however, the two do not usually coincide. There are infinite ordinals and infinite cardinals. Omega, the first infinite ordinal, is also the first infinite cardinal, since it marks the transition point between the finite and the infinite. As a cardinal it is known as Aleph-zero, $\aleph_0$.

What is the difference between omega and Aleph-zero? The difference has to do with something called "equipollence," which is the relation between two sets that obtains when they have the same "size" regardless of any ordering of their elements. Two sets are equipollent when their contents can be placed in a one-to-one correspondence—thus, for example, the set of squares of integers is equipollent to the set of integers: each integer can be matched, one-to-one, with its own square. Stransom's altar of candles, for example, was a set in a relation of equipollence with the Dead it was to commemorate. Infinite sets can be conveniently defined as just those sets which are equipollent to the proper subsets of themselves.

Now, omega + 1 is equipollent to omega and also to Aleph-zero. But although omega + 1 is larger than omega, its cardinality remains the same:

Aleph-zero. How is this possible? How can you add 1 to infinity and, on the side of ordinality get something bigger (i.e., be able to count it), but still remain with the same cardinality? And if this is nevertheless the case, how do you then go beyond the cardinality of Aleph-zero? Is there anything larger? The answer to the first question is that the cardinality of omega + 1 remains the same as that of omega (i.e., Aleph-zero) because omega + 1 is, precisely, "countable." That is, you can always rearrange the entire contents of the last set by gathering it together into a new set and then add one more to it. As David Odell puts it,

> you can rearrange its contents placing the one infinite term "omega" that it contains at the beginning, matched with the "zero" of omega, and then match up the remainder of the two sets in a natural way since they both now consist of a single "run-out" to infinity. Similarly an infinite set like omega + omega which contains two "run-outs" to infinity can be matched to omega with its single "run-out," by interleaving the elements, and even omega*omega with its infinitely many "run-outs" can be cleverly folded and laid point for point alongside omega. (Odell)

In fact every new infinite ordinal created from omega in this way is "countable" in this sense. Think of it as analogous to the Kantian successive apprehension of phenomena—we can indefinitely keep adding one more to the set of infinity, *but its cardinality will remain the cardinal infinite, Aleph-zero.* To get beyond Aleph-zero (which, to continue the Kantian analogy, is something like the "Idea" of infinity supplied by Reason in the sublime[17]) we must make use of a certain general property of sets, which is as follows: a set is never equipollent to its power set (the set of *all* its subsets).

First, here is the definition of a cardinal number: a cardinal number is an ordinal that is not equipollent to any *smaller* ordinal. Now, one of the beauties of "Cantor's paradise" is the way that it permits us to go beyond Aleph-zero in an utterly different way from how the infinite ordinal omega was produced (that is, not by the limit of calculable accretions): if an infinite set is not equipollent to its power set, this means that the power set must possess a *larger* cardinality. This is known as Cantor's theorem: the power set of *x* is bigger than *x*. Odell explains how,

> by using the Power Set Axiom we can create sets which can in no way be counted by Aleph-zero, for example the power set of omega, and under a generally assumed principle called the Axiom of Choice, this

means that there is an endless series of ever larger infinite ordinals none of which are equipollent to any ordinal smaller than themselves. These are known as the Alephs, the sequence of infinite cardinals.[18]

These Alephs can be written: $\aleph_0$, $\aleph_1$, $\aleph_2$, [. . .] $\aleph_\omega$, $\aleph_{\omega+1}$, [. . .], and so on, where the subscripts run through the entire range of ordinals. Of course, because of the way these infinite cardinals are created, they advance in orders of magnitude that are vastly greater than that of the infinite ordinals. Odell explains: "$\aleph_1$ is the limit of all the infinite ordinals that can be counted by omega, such as omega + omega, omega*omega, and every other ordinal created in this way and many more besides. $\aleph_2$ is the limit of all ordinals countable by $\aleph_1$ and so on."[19]

Now, bear with me for just a minute longer before I return to Kant and James. Just as omega was designated a "limit ordinal," at the boundary of finite and infinite, it ought to be possible to create what's known as a "regular limit cardinal." No finite limit process ever suffices to reach omega so, as Odell explains, a regular limit cardinal would be "a cardinal that can only be reached by taking an infinite sequence of steps through ever larger cardinals, but such that the ordinal of *any* such sequence of steps must be the same as the cardinal itself." Omega, he says, has this property. Omega, in its cardinal form as Aleph-zero, is such a regular limit cardinal: "Omega is the only thing that can count omega, no matter how giant the steps we take we never get there any sooner." But are there any others? These are known as Inaccessible Cardinals, and if they existed they would be not merely "super"-Alephs, that is, Alephs that equal their subscript, but "super-super [. . .]"-Alephs to any degree.

Keith Devlin has shown how any attempt to find an Inaccessible Cardinal will necessarily fail, since the existence of an Inaccessible Cardinal is equivalent to the consistency of set theory, which is known to be unprovable from Gödel's Theorem.[20] Nevertheless, as Devlin also argues, and here we begin to come back to James, although their existence can never be proved using the tools and axioms of set theory, such cardinals nevertheless are implied by the system's own rules.[21] What does it mean for there to be an Inaccessible Cardinal? As Odell explains, this would be an uncountable object *produced within a system and which justifies that system and which therefore can never be found, but which "holds open" all the (conceivable or accessible) infinities below it.* It would be like a strange invisible asymptote interrupting the seemingly endless generation of infinite sets, a (false-) ceiling in the infinite but one that is not imposed from a place outside the set universe but generated internally within it. This would be a limit strictly *internal* to the counting system and, as such, as Odell points out, would possess a very peculiar property: it is only when seen from within the system that it looks impossibly huge and Inaccessible. "As something attained," he says, "it immediately suggests an outside to the system, a larger system, and looked at from there, from the perspective of God, or the Kantian totality, it might well seem as if it were never really inaccessible at all, just an anonymous limit ordinal, possibly even a countable ordinal, or a minor Aleph. The larger system, the imagined God's eye view, would of course in turn have its own inaccessible internal limit."

We arrive once more back in Kantian territory, for isn't this exactly what the "affirmative" answer to the mathematical antinomies describes? What we have is a system whose ability to "count" everything that "counts" depends on a certain stumbling block generated within the system itself, a blind spot that can never be proven but on which the entire iterative process depends. But this does not entail an illegal superimposition of a noumenal or God's eye perspective. It is, rather, produced by the phenomenal, counting system *itself.* Thus we have a nominally consistent system that, while strictly infinite (i.e., not a totality) is nevertheless internally bounded by some strange unphenomenalizable fact. We cannot "count" it using our regular, phenomenal successive and regressive counting system, but nor can we say it is an illegitimate external imposition since it is structurally implied by the very system itself. But hence, to recall Copjec again, what the absence of an (external) limit to the set of phemomena implies is *not* that we are sent floating off into some transcendental ether of infinity but rather that

> the absence of a limit to the set of phenomena [. . .] obliges us to recognize the basic *finitude* of phenomena, the fact that they are inescapably subject to conditions of time and space and must therefore be encountered one by one, indefinitely, without the possibility of reaching an end, a point where all phenomena would be known. (*Read My Desire* 221)

We can neither create a total set where everything would be eventually counted, but nor can we make a cosmological leap into a God's-eye view. We might say that we are "bounded" by our very infinitude, and for this reason must take phenomena "one by one."

Now it should be clear how with such a concept of an unprovable but structurally implied internal limit, the problem of deconstruction's "finite" infinitude disappears. This internal limit is what "quilts," as Lacan would say, the field of representation, enabling substitutive (vertical), not just contiguous (horizontal) relationships to form between signifiers.

IV

Now that I have mentioned Lacan, there is no need to try to disguise the fact that what I have been describing in this foray into Kantian philosophy and introductory set theory is of course nothing other than the structure of what he calls the "formulas of sexuation."[22] And in fact we might as well begin to use his terms, finally, since it is, after all, nothing other than the impossibility of the "sexual relationship" that James's tale describes.[23] Returning to Warminski's figure of zeugma, what is revealed by the preceding discussion are the two, fundamentally asymmetrical modes by which Stransom and the woman respond to the "failure" of language, to the fact that, as Lacan famously puts it, "there is no sexual relationship" (i.e., that language cannot "say it all," that there is no direct, legitimate bridge between phenomenal and noumenal realms). Stransom, as we saw, constructs an external limit in his attempt to ward off this knowledge, but this is an attempt that can last only so long as that limit is not breached. This was also Milly's response in *The Wings of the Dove*, as it was Isabel's in *The Portrait of a Lady*. What these two Jamesian heroines had in mind was to transform the structural impossibility of the sexual relationship into a positive form, that is, into a prohibition, thereby sustaining the fantasy that everything really could be said, that there really would be a "sexual relationship," if one could only get past the barrier obstructing it. Thus, I argued, Isabel's act is to be read as a defense of the limit that marks the gap between phenomenal and noumenal realms, since it is that limit that also guarantees our freedom. Similarly, in *The Wings of the Dove*, we saw how Milly also dedicates herself to preventing a certain limit from being crossed when, at the cost of her own life, she throws herself into the breach of language in a last-ditch attempt to prevent the representational system from closing in around her. With "The Altar of the Dead," however, the terms have significantly changed in what can best be described in psychoanalytic terms as the shift from an "ethics of desire" to an "ethics of drive." Now, instead of defending the limit, James's heroine finds that the only ethically tenable position is to demand that it, too, be finally removed, along with everything else that one was prepared to give up in its name. If the first two novels I discussed described the ethical acts through which James's heroines maintained fidelity to the protective limit that keeps us from the horrific Real of *jouis-sance* (that limit being the phallus), "The Altar of the Dead" thus requires an even greater fidelity: it demands that we give up the very limit itself for which we made every other sacrifice. Thus we saw Kate at the end of *The Wings of the Dove* anticipating this position. Having given up not only her (prospective) fortune, her fiancée, all her hopes and dreams for future happiness, even her own sense of ethical fitness toward her friend, for the sake of her father's name, she finds herself at the end of the novel having had to give up even the name itself and, as a now "fallen" woman, has utterly erased herself from the symbolic realm to dwell for the rest of her days in a kind of life-in-death or death-in-life, the state Lacan calls being "between two deaths."

But to return to "The Altar of the Dead." Surely one might say that Stransom, too, ends up in a position similar to that of Kate, in a state of what we might call, after Lacan, the "subjective destitution" that accompanies an ethical act? Doesn't he undergo exactly the same sort of ethical transformation, with its concomitant dissolution of the self when, after weeks and weeks of internal conflict, he finally gives in to the woman's demand? James is quite explicit about the process of Stransom's self-unraveling as he finally reaches the point where he recognizes that "Symmetry was harmony, and the idea of harmony began to haunt him" (*AD* 298). "'Just one more—to round it off; just one, just one,' continued to hum itself in his head" (*AD* 298). The problem with Stransom's position is made with characteristic clarity by James:[24] it is on the basis that "symmetry was harmony" that Stransom is finally led to give up the limit. It is thus on the basis of *aesthetic* grounds, in other words, rather than ethical ones, that he is induced, finally, to agree to "just one more." For "'isn't that what you wanted?'" he asks the woman, imagining he is dying to fulfill her wish, "'Yes, one more, one more.'" But as James's text makes clear, this is not at all what the woman had in mind: "'Ah! no more, no more!'" she wails under her breath.

What, then, did the woman have in mind? It is hard to give a positive answer for a woman who has so far been presented only in negative terms. Describing her, James tells us "She had no colour, no sound, no fault, and another of the things about which [Stransom] had made up his mind was that she had no fortune" (*AD* 276). We don't even know her name, although we do know she has two of them, her own and the pen name under which she publishes. Her sole act in this story is, in a sense, negative. All she really does, when you come right down to it, is say "no"—no to Stransom's refusal to light Hague's candle, no to his dying capitulation to what he thinks is her wish. She is, in other words, an embodiment of a resistance. What is she resisting? Clearly she is resisting the aesthetic workings of a system founded on an exclusion. But she is also resisting Stransom's last attempt to reconcile "his and her altars" as Warminski put it so memorably. In response to his (aesthetic) reconciling "one more," she wails "no more."

I find that what she conveys here in this desperate, despairing wail is a gesture of resistance to the idea that ethics can ever be formalized as a discourse (as when, for example, Stransom believes all he has to do is concede to her demand, and add—aesthetically or ethically, it doesn't matter which—the last remaining "one"). That is to say, by this final "no" the woman expresses a resistance to the idea that ethics can ever be reduced to a Law or set of laws according to which we must then act—even if that Law, as my examples of Isabel and Milly demonstrate, bears very little in common with the more conventional understanding of ethical laws (as linked to the idea of a "Good"). No, the woman's resistance embodies the ethical demand that insists on the removal of even that last limit; her resistance conveys the way ethics must always *escape* our attempts to pin it down, to consolidate it, such that, as we know from Kant, we will never cognize the totality of the meaning of our actions, that is, whether or not our act has been ethical. Nevertheless, as Isabel discovered, we must act anyway, we must make choices but, as James expresses so beautifully with this story, true fidelity means maintaining a resistance against ever thinking we can reach the "ethical" as such, i.e., as a limit that must be defended at all costs. Something, James seems to be saying, always escapes our infinitude—namely, precisely our finitude. It is our *finitude* that demands we take every moment, every singular situation on a one-by-one basis for action.

Aren't we then left in a double bind, as deconstructivists like to say? Aren't we poised forever like Buridan's ass (as Odell would say) over our first choice, whose impossibility of making causes us to ethically starve to death? Must we assume, pragmatically, something equivalent to an "Axiom of Choice," that says that every possible choice for a first member of a set has already, infinitely been made? No, no (as the woman would say), and still no. We are not in a double bind *because our infinitude is internally bounded.* We must make choices. But we must not be pragmatic and betray an "event" *just because it forces us to confront a logical and epistemological impossibility.* It is this, I think, that is expressed by the idea of the "not all" of the Kantian antinomy, and by Lacan's feminine side of the formula of sexuation:

> *There is not one x that is not submitted to the phallic function.*
> *Not all (not every) x is submitted to the phallic function.*[25]

Like the woman in James's tale we each have two "names," Real and Symbolic.[26] We are creatures of two irreconcilable realms. Possessing both "ordinality" and "cardinality," we bisect infinity with our finitude. Hence something always escapes our symbolic determinations—the Lacanian "no, that's not it" that emerges every time we try to pinpoint our fundamental essence (or, under the condition of objectivity, whenever an object of demand falls short, which it always will, of the ever-elusive object (a), the object cause of desire that can have no phenomenal form). But this does not mean, as deconstruction has it (or at least would seem to have it[27]), that we are sentenced to inhabiting the world of mechanical determination. The Real may be unreachable, uncountable, like an Inaccessible Cardinal, but it nevertheless exerts effects on us and our signifying system. Although we can never "count" it, can never have phenomenal apprehension of it, its structurally implied presence enables us to transcend our finite, ordinal series.

V

We can now begin to extrapolate some of the practical implications, in the Kantian sense, of the idea of the mathematical not-whole exemplified by James's heroine in "The Altar of the Dead." For what this mathematical structure seems to suggest is a way of theorizing a concept of universality from within the realm of singularity. As with the internally bounded infinite set, it might now be possible to conceive of a universal that doesn't externally impose a set of attributes onto particulars as, for example, most egregiously in the nineteenth-century figures of the scientific, disinterested observer, the universal subject as a "subject without properties" whose trajectory is toward ever-increasing abstractions and, hence, atrocities in the twentieth century. Notably, the first place we came across this idea of a "humanity at large" was nowhere other than in Kant's own descriptions of the aesthetic judgment that enables the individual to join momentarily with all other subjects: aesthetic judgment is the power to judge "which in its reflection, takes account *(a priori)* of the mode of representation of all other men in thought, in order, as it were, to compare its judgment with the collective reason of humanity" (*CJ* 136). (And, as everyone knows, it was nothing other than Kant's *Critique of Pure Reason* that was famously lying on Göbbels's bedside table the day the Americans arrested him after finally taking Berlin).[28]

The contemporary ethical theorist who has most effectively suggested such a way of conceiving of this "other" universal is Alain Badiou. Badiou's work represents a sustained investigation of the mathematical "truths" of set theory extrapolated into the empirical world of living, acting bodies. Because of his specialized terminology, his use of the word *truth*, for example, his work at first sight seems strangely out of touch with contemporary ethical and political developments: after "deconstruction," which I put in quotes to signal that I mean the developments coming after the moment of what I call "High" deconstruction, that is, the infiltration of some of "High" deconstruction's insights into cultural studies and identity politics (which actually represents a kind of "aestheticization" of deconstruction in the precise sense of its being the "Schillerization" of deconstruction),[29] I say, after "deconstruction," we all "know" that truth is a bad word, that there is no truth, but only relative truths specific to historical and cultural contingencies.

But it is precisely against this complacent "knowledge," supposedly given us by "deconstruction," that Badiou orients his discourse of ethics. For Badiou, ethics is not about guaranteeing the right to difference, but about the creation of a Same. Badiou's translator, Peter Hallward, puts Badiou's political and ethical aims succinctly:

> Whereas the deconstructive project is determined to fold every emergence of the new back into a structure of iterability and repetition, [. . .] if there is a task *specific* to politics, it must be to find clear and universal principles of justice that *break* with the infinite complexities and complicities of history, the interminable "negotiations" of culture and psychology. And thereby to allow something *else* to take place.[30]

Thus Badiou takes exception to what he considers the obscenities of what carries itself off for ethical discourse today, in the form of the discourse of human rights, whose founding assumption is that of the right of cultures to differ, but that something nevertheless, a "universal" human right, holds us in common. This is based on a false Kantianism, the idea that "there exist formally representable imperative demands that are to be subjected neither to empirical considerations nor to the examination of situations; that these imperatives apply to cases of offense, of crime, of Evil; that these imperatives must be punished by national and international law" (Badiou 8). The problem lies of course in its false Kantianism: the idea that an ethical imperative can be formalized, and then applied to contingent situations to serve as an absolute principle (this was Kant's own "mistake" as Zupančič has observed, when, in response to the Benjamin Constant controversy, he seemed to argue that, no matter under what conditions, one must always tell the truth).[31] From this position, however, human rights discourse derives a concept of universality that, as Badiou points out, is nothing other than the spectatorial but no longer "disinterested" subject of aesthetic judgment: "the sympathetic and indignant judgement of the spectator of the circumstances" (Badiou 9). What is more, its "ethics" are an ethics of defense, whose concomitant implication is that the subject is fundamentally acted on, a victim, rather than an actor herself. Badiou writes, it "equates man with his animal substructure, it reduces him to the level of a living organism pure and simple" (Badiou 11). Ethics, on the other hand, for Badiou, have to do with what in us goes beyond the merely animal, with what is "immortal" or "infinite" in us: "if 'rights of man' exist, they are surely not rights of life against death, or rights of survival against misery. They are the rights of the Immortal, affirmed in their own right, or the rights of the Infinite, exercised over the contingency of suffering and death" (Badiou 12).

The ethics of human rights, it turns out for Badiou, are merely the latest version of the nineteenth-century imperialist "civilizing" drive, the political imposition of cultural and economic hegemony disguised as a discourse of ethics. For as he points out, actions taken in the name of human rights invariably offer the same, potent images of the West as a force for "good" against the barbaric practices of at least some version of the East. We are still in Thomas De Quincey's old dialectic of the self-consolidating other (the exotic Near East) and the non-self-consolidating other (the Far East). As Badiou argues, "this celebrated 'other' is acceptable [to human rights discourse] only if he is a *good* other—which is to say what, exactly, if not *the same as us*" (Badiou 24). The right to difference, in other words, is upheld by human rights discourse only for as long as the other remains within the limits of acceptability for our own (culturally specific) sets of prejudices, as the example of female circumcision and other such "barbaric" practices demonstrates. As soon as the other becomes "really other," we must mobilize against it. Human rights discourse is thus a kind of cultural relativism but a relativism that is really an imperialist universalism in disguise.

But even if cultural relativism remains faithful to its own premises and refuses to surreptitiously insert a hidden universal, it comes up against the same problem we already saw with regard to deconstruction: under the terms of cultural relativism, ethics as a category must disappear, since relativism tells us we cannot make judgments about actions. At its purest, cultural relativism is nothing but nihilism. But Badiou holds that ethics is a category that we need now more than ever. He says, "It is only through a genuine perversion, for which we will pay a terrible historical price, that we have sought to elaborate an 'ethics' on the basis of cultural relativism. For this is to pretend that a merely contingent state of things can found a Law" (Badiou 28).

The task of ethics, for Badiou, involves fidelity to something he calls, in terminology that ought to be quite familiar to us by now from James, an "event." An event is "a breakdown of the count." It is what demonstrates the previous system's "law" by articulating its central "void" or impossibility. Each "event" thus possesses its own "truth," which is the particular way in which the "event" is attested to, the way one remains faithful to it. We might say that the "truth" is the way an "event" is imbued with historical content. Badiou gives Haydn's reinvention of classical music at the end of the Baroque period as an example of an event:

> at the heart of the baroque style at its virtuoso saturation lay the absence *[vide]* (as decisive as it was unnoticed) of a genuine conception of musical architectonics. The Haydn-event occurs as a kind of musical "naming" of this absence *[vide]*. For what constitutes the event is nothing less than a wholly new architectonic and thematic principle, a new way of developing musical writing from the basis of a few transformable units—which was precisly what, from within the baroque style, could not be perceived (there could be no knowledge of it). (Badiou 68–69, translator's square brackets)

But although "truths" are articulated in specific historical circumstances, this does not mean truths are thus merely relative. Inasmuch as they express the central void or impossibility of a previous system of knowledge, the invisible "law of the count" that couldn't be articulated from within the previous historical system of knowledge, truths do indeed take place in contingent space and time. But insofar as every "truth" is the historical articulation of a transhistorical necessity, that is, an "event," it cannot be said to be relativist. It may, and indeed must, have specific historical and cultural content, but what each "truth" in its specific and historical fashion articulates is the Same: a "truth" tells us an "event" has occurred, that is, the count has broken down. Truths then, in Badiou's specific use of the term, signify the contingent, phenomenal eruptions in space and time of a transhistorical, or "infinite" event—they are the manifestations, if you like, of an impossibility, the bizarre eruption of an Inaccessible Cardinal into a system that cannot count it. Truths of course occur within the counting system (there is nothing "beyond" it). They testify, however, to an encounter with something that is strictly impossible but *generated by the system itself.*

Badiou's concept of the relationship between the event and its truths thus helps us to get "over" one of the interminable feminist stumbling blocks with Freud, his "truth" of the phallus. The psychoanalytic concept of the phallus is a "truth" in this specialized sense: it is the expression in uniquely contingent sets of circumstances (nineteenth-century Vienna, a struggling former neurologist trying to form a medical practice for middle-class women who were coming to him with bizarre symptoms to be cured), of an encounter with a transfinite event. The hard "rock" of the phallus, the master signifier, is simply not replaceable by any of the alternative, shall we say, "mistress signifiers" proposed by psychoanalytic feminists, for the reason that none of these other, contingent, replaceable signifiers (e.g., the breast, etc.) carry the burden of conveying the "breakdown of the count," that is, that an "event" has occurred. Why not? It is because within psychoanalysis the phallus is the sole signifier whose very meaning is its failure to signify—it is what *ruins*, as Copjec puts it, "the possibility of any simple affirmation or negation" (*Read My Desire* 215). The phallus, we might as well now say, is the element of impossibility within the psychoanalytic system and as such cannot simply be replaced by any other signifier—this would be like saying just any old cardinal can become an Inaccessible Cardinal *without changing everything else in the system.* Mathematically, this doesn't make any sense.

It is for this reason, too, that anthropological attempts to prove that psychoanalysis is merely culturally specific and has no application to members of other cultures are misguided. (In response to one such contemporary attempt, to Malinowski's claim that the Trobriand Islanders were "uncastrated," Freud memorably responded "Was, haben diese Leute keinen Anus?"). But the point is that what enables psychoanalysis to claim to have "universal" truth is that its "truth" is the truth of a fidelity to the event. When psychoanalysis states its truth, "every speaking being is castrated," it is a particular, contingent way of saying, "the count has broken down," something structurally impossible has happened, we have run up against an Inaccessible Cardinal. Ethics is to be found in the act(s) of remaining faithful to a "truth." But, Badiou cautions, we must not make the mistake of believing, as we try to remain faithful to the truth, that our truth is absolutizable. Any attempt to give positive attributes to a truth, even to say absolutely that our truth is a truth, is to fall into what Badiou considers "evil." Evil is to imagine that anything can be done in the name of our truth for its own sake. (The example of course he gives is Nazism which for Badiou represented not a "truth" but the simulacrum of a truth. Badiou claims Heidegger made his egregious mistake because he imagined he was witnessing a truth, whereas what he saw was a simulacrum: "When a radical break in a situation, under names borrowed from real truth-processes, convokes not the void but the 'full' particularity or presumed substance of that situation, we are dealing with a *simulacrum of truth*") (Badiou 73).

There are many historical, that is, contingent articulations of "truths" that emerge when the count breaks down, when an "event" occurs. Badiou gives examples of "events" occurring across four "conditions" of philosophy, or "generic processes": love, art, science, and politics:

> The French Revolution of 1792, the meeting of Héloise and Abélard, Galileo's creation of physics, Haydn's invention of the classical music style. . . . But also: the Cultural Revolution in China (1965–67), a personal amorous passion, the creation of Topos theory by the mathematician Grothendieck, the invention of the twelve-tone scale by Schoenberg . . . (Badiou 41)

What is the "truth" we are living today? I assert that it is nothing other than deconstruction itself (i.e., what I am calling "High" deconstruction in order to differentiate it from the bastardized version found in cultural studies and identity politics). *(High-) Deconstruction articulates the central void of psychoanalysis.* Now, before the Lacanians get all hot and bothered, and before the deconstructivists begin clapping themselves on the back, crowing "We knew all along that the master signifier was a phallogocentric concept, the last vestiges of a theology that must be overcome," let me be very precise about this. Deconstruction is nothing other than the act of remaining faithful to the "event" of psychoanalysis. It is a strict "fidelity," that is, an act of love toward psychoanalysis, as Derrida himself has suggested.[32]

Again, let me explain very carefully what I mean by this. What deconstruction "articulates" in the only way possible for it is the central void of psychoanalysis that Lacan calls the Real. I can imagine my deconstructive readers now throwing up their hands in horror, for isn't the Real exactly the kind of "theological" concept that deconstruction categorically demands we must give up, that must be allowed to "undo" itself and be overcome? Wasn't the Real, in its Symbolic guise as the master signifier,[33] simply the "blind spot" of psychoanalysis that it was unable to see but that we, from the higher-deconstructive rung of the Hegelian ladder, can identify in all of its illusory, mystified, aesthetico-theotropic glory?

Here is my assertion. What deconstruction does—and this is why it is strictly an *act of fidelity to psychoanalysis*—is attempt to articulate the encounter with the Real, that is, with a strictly impossible but structurally neccessary element that it has no means of "counting." From its "finite" perspective, deconstruction can never form a concept of the Real, the structurally internal limit that prevents endless metonymic slide. But, nevertheless, deconstruction remains infinitely faithful to this Thing that it has absolutely no means of comprehending, of "counting," of forming any kind of phenomenal presentation for. How does deconstruction remain faithful to the Real? Through the only means available to it in its finite, counting system: through its continual *failure* to form a concept of it. Every time deconstruction aims for this event, every time it tries to "count" it, deconstructive readings inevitably fall back on the old symbolic divisions of metaphor and metonymy. Deconstruction does not, and *cannot* by its own system's rules, allow for a concept of the Real. But in its endless, repetitive readings, deconstruction signifies nothing other than that it has bumped up against the Real: an "event" has occurred, something structurally greater than the system itself has impossibly fallen out of the system.

Thus it is that I assert that deconstruction is the "truth" of psychoanalysis in Badiou's sense. It is the contingent, historical articulation of the psychoanalytic "event." But because this "event" is strictly unphenomenalizable, deconstruction remains faithful to it in the only means it has available: through the "negative presentations" *of its failure to count it.* Deconstructive readings thus will always stumble on this structural impossibility of the Real but not be able to see it for what it "is," that is, see it from outside the finite system. Deconstruction's very "fidelity" in fact consists in its categorical refusal to make what it considers an illegitimate "leap" to the Real. But it nevertheless doesn't stop articulating the truth of psychoanalysis negatively, through its perpetual *failure* to count the Real. Deconstruction therefore has something in common with the imagination in the Kantian sublime. The experience of the sublime marks the encounter with something that is strictly impossible for the phenomenal system, with something that is structurally in excess of the system, but which nevertheless exerts uncanny pressure on that system. Since we cannot, from our phenomenal perspective, account for it in any way, all we can do is testify to its presence negatively, through the articulation of an experience of failure.

Hence, from its finite perspective, deconstruction will always fail to "see" the Real, which functions much like an Inaccessible Cardinal for its system and whose inside/outside paradox was already described. For if deconstruction could see from a psychoanalytic perspective, it would recognize that what it thinks is "impossible" is actually its own system's condition of possibility. Deconstruction will always stumble against what we might as well now call "castration"—the fact that all speaking beings are split, that language always divides us from full presence—but instead of seeing this fact from psychoanalysis's perspective of the Real (i.e., that it is precisely castration that enables us to perform creative, nonmechanical acts), it remains stuck in the stuttering of the Symbolic. Deconstruction cannot conceive of any other register than the binary Symbolic system of language, thus it takes this "fact" as evidence that we are finite, mechanically determined creatures who imagine in a kind of aesthetic fantasy that we are free. But Lacanian psychoanalysis, which does possess a concept of the internal limit of the Real, recognizes that the "fact" of castration is nothing other than our condition of possibility for freedom—it is what enables us to transcend the limits of our finite system *by means of an element that is internal to the system itself.*

Hence again, as I said, deconstruction will never be able to assimilate the psychoanalytic concept of the Real because, from its "finite" perspective inside the system, the concept of the Real looks like a theology. Deconstruction imagines that the Real requires us to have "faith" that it exists. It imagines psychoanalysis requires a kind of illicit "leap" by which we can transcend the limits of our finite system. As I hope my discussion of the two forms of infinity clearly shows, it is only from within this finite counting system (of deconstruction, of an "ordinal" counting system) that this appears so. But because, of course, we can never go "outside" this system (there is nothing beyond language), we cannot see the way this Real would look from outside. Nevertheless, as Odell suggested with regard to the Inaccessible Cardinals, could we have such a viewpoint, *the Real would look just like any other countably infinite cardinal.* This is to say, although it is strictly impossible for us finite, deconstructive beings to be able to "count" the Real, it is nevertheless *not* a "theological" concept but, rather, a necessary if necessarily impossible member of the count.

But here is the crux of the issue. Precisely because deconstruction is unable to form a concept of the Real—precisely because it will always stumble upon this peculiar property of infinite systems to inscribe within themselves an internal limit, yet without being able to account for it—deconstruction behaves very much like a trauma victim, endlessly going back over the same traumatic event, forever trying to incorporate an irreducible element into its own set, to account for something that it cannot count.[34] Deconstruction can never be "done" with the Real, although it can never know why. For this reason, I assert, it is a strictly *ethical* discourse in the precise sense I have been elaborating here. But let me say at once that deconstruction is ethical not because it "overcomes" the violence of the Hegelian *Aufhebung,* not because I believe it is right that infinite divisibility is all there is, not because of the profound implications such quasiconcepts as "différance" or "materiality" have for the future inventions of political and ethical communities, and so on. I especially do not believe it is ethical because it asserts primacy to the "rights" of difference over monolithic Identity. It is ethical, that is, not for any of the reasons that deconstruction itself ("High" or "low") believes itself to be "ethical." Deconstruction is ethical because it is the contemporary discourse today that repeatedly performs the encounter with an event whose terms are strictly impossible for it to comprehend. Deconstruction is the discourse that remains undyingly faithful to the "event" that is structurally implied by its own system, yet of which it can never have any phenomenal presentation. As I said, the Real is this concept for deconstruction. It is like deconstruction's Inaccessible Cardinal, the one blind spot, the cyst in the iterative process around which its entire discursive structure is built. But although it can never adequately account for this Real, deconstruction nevertheless is the discourse that maintains strict fidelity to it, as the endless, repetitive productions of deconstructive readings have demonstrated. Deconstruction, to paraphrase Lacan, *doesn't stop not reading the Real.*[35]

Badiou tells us if we absolutize a truth we slip into evil. Deconstruction shows us how we can remain faithful to an event inasmuch as it escapes us, inasmuch as its "truth" always remains in excess of the system that has created it. This, too, I think is the significance of the woman's return to the altar (a certain plot detail that Warminski strangely avoids mentioning in his reading). For her, too, an "event" has occurred: "It was as if I suddenly saw something—as if it all became possible," she tells Stransom (*AD* 300). What the woman suddenly "sees" is that true fidelity to the event requires that we keep something "unnameable" to ourselves, as Badiou would say, that we enable something always to be able to escape.[36] For imagining that we have possessed the whole truth, we slip into evil. If the woman categorically demanded that Stransom give up the limit—if this was her limit, if you like—her return to the altar at the end of the story suggests that this limit, too, has had to be given up, along with all of the other things that that limit required we give up. In order to approach ethics, in other words, the ethical limit must join all of the other, contingent objects in the series of things that ethics demands we give up in its name.[37]

Lacan claims ethics occurs at the intersection of the Symbolic and the Real.[38] Let me now try to paraphrase him: ethics "happens" when we come up against the internal limits of our signifying system but nevertheless remain faithful to what is, strictly speaking, "impossible" for us.

VI

Thus, we might ask, deconstruction or Lacan? Of course, to imagine that we have to make a choice between deconstruction and psychoanalysis is a fallacy. That is, it is only from within one of the positions that it looks like an either/or choice. From the other it does not look that way at all. Each opposing assertion, "There is only infinite divisibility" and "Not only is there not only infinite divisibility but this not infinite divisibility is the precondition of our ability to perform creative, i.e., 'uncountable' acts" is, in a sense, "true." That is, the seemingly conflicting statements of deconstruction and psychoanalysis are, like Kantian antinomies, not contradictions but *contraries*. They each express the "truth" of their own mode by which the "sexual relationship" (language) fails. This is why, I think, the experience of reading each of them is so convincing (and also so confusing since, without this realization of the two modes of failure, we imagine we have to make something like a "choice" between them, and be "faithful" to one or the other).[39] For all of its endless critique of the "ideological" (i.e., aesthetic) character of the master signifier (troped most usually as metaphor), De Manian deconstruction remains indissoluably wedded to this limit that it says we categorically must not transgress, the limit of our finite counting system. Hence it represents an ethics founded on the "masculine" side of Lacan's formulas of sexuation (as indeed do Isabel's and Milly's ethical solutions, see the graph below[40]). Psychoanalysis, while also being wedded to the limit, shows how we may choose between the exception and something else. Like the feminine side of Lacan's graph, psychoanalysis gives us a structure of both/and.[41] For, like women, psychoanalysis presents a doubled relationship to the phallic function (the fact of castration, the gap between signifier and signified, between phenomenal and noumenal realms). It suggests we are both entirely submitted to it (there is not one that is not), at the same time as something always, impossibly (from the finite, phenomenal point of view), escapes: not all women are submitted to the phallic function.[42]

TABLE 1
Lacan's Formulas of Sexuation

Masculine Side		Feminine Side	
$\exists x$	$\overline{\Phi x}$	$\overline{\exists x}$	Φx
$\forall x$	Φx	$\overline{\forall x}$	Φx
There is at least one x that is not submitted to the phallic function. All x's are (every x is) submitted to the phallic function.		There is not one x that is not submitted to the phallic function. Not all (not every) x is submitted to the phallic function.	

Can we say, then, that in its critique of what we might now call the Imaginary lure of aesthetic reconciliation, deconstructive ethics are those specific to an "ethics of desire" in Lacan's sense, that is, an ethics of the Symbolic Law whose sole ethical demand is to ensure against a certain limit from being transgressed? Responding both negatively and positively to the antinomy of the split in our being, on the other hand, Lacanian psychoanalysis represents an ethics founded on the *intersection* of the registers of the Symbolic and the Real. As such, the ethics of psychoanalysis carries a double structure, representing an ethics of both desire and of drive. Rather than opposites, then, psychoanalysis and deconstruction must be viewed as discourses in a relation to one another not unlike that between desire and the drive. To use one of Lacan's frequent metaphors, the relation between psychoanalysis and deconstruction emerges according to the logic of the Möbius strip. Taking deconstruction—like desire—literally, one ends up at the psychoanalytic concept of the Real: at the far end of desire, you have reached the drive.

To clarify this, let us return to the concerns raised in "The Altar of the Dead." If Warminski was right to underline the illusory nature of Stransom's aesthetic attempt to defeat death, does this then mean that death remains our limit? As I have shown, psychoanalysis indicates that there is indeed something "beyond" death if I may be forgiven for expressing it in such a way. What psychoanalysis suggests is that death can no longer be considered our limit but *not* because we make a leap of faith into the unknown, into the absolute of a God's-eye perspective once we die. Psychoanalysis is not a theology. The lack of a limit demands that we recognize a certain immortality but this is an immortality of the finite, counting system itself. That is to say, as Copjec has formulated it, the immortality psychoanalysis recognizes is not that of the soul, but of the *body*, the immortality of the phenomenal world. This seems like a bizarre prospect. Isn't the phenomenal world precisely what is subject to the endless round of death and birth? And isn't it thus precisely for this reason that we perform our endless attempts at wresting something immortal from the inescapable fact of our death—to infuse contingency with necessity? Isn't this the reason, in other words, why art and literature and the creation of all new knowledge continues to possess such a uniquely privileged place in our culture, despite all of the debunkings of the recuperative aesthetic fantasy that have taken place over the past century?[43]

Psychoanalysis asserts that the body is immortal. But this assertion must not be confused with a teleological concept of immortality, such as the immortality of a species beyond and above the being of each individual member. Psychoanalysis, like deconstruction, is resolutely opposed to such a universalizing teleology that would imply a point of view like that of God or of the (misunderstood) notion of Hegel's Absolute Spirit, that is, as implying the illegitimate assumption of an external position from which we can view the phenomenal totality. As we have seen, psychoanalysis, like deconstruction, is resolutely opposed to the illegitimate leap that such a viewpoint would demand. But where, then, resides this bodily immortality? The answer, seemingly paradoxical as it sounds, is that it is found in the death drive.

The death drive is perhaps one of the most misunderstood of the Freudian concepts which, it must be stated clearly, *does not mean the drive toward death*. Rather, the death drive, as Freud elaborates it in *Beyond the Pleasure Principle*, is the drive toward an earlier state of things. It is a backward drive, aiming for a prior moment, rather than a forward headlong sprint into death. What is this prior moment the death drive is aiming for? It is what Freud (a little imprecisely) calls "inertia," the hypothesized moment of unity before the splitting of signifier and signified; the moment before, that is, the interposition of the radical cut that severs us from an original state of ideal unity, named by psychoanalysis as the mother-child dyad (but also readily recognizable in the various forms it assumes throughout the Romantic tradition and beyond, as the tragically lost, prelapsarian state existing prior to the cut of self-consciousness that irreparably splits us from our original unity with nature, for example, Blake's "innocence," Schiller's "naive," Wordsworth's "child," De Quincey's brother/sister unity, etc.).

But psychoanalysis recognizes how, even within this hypothetical unity, something is already out of joint; the ideal mother-child unity is primordially disturbed by what Copjec calls a "structural flaw." This flaw is the enigma of the mother's desire, which the child has no way of understanding. Copjec writes, "The child cannot comprehend the mother's comings and goings; where or why she goes; what she wants from her child to make her want to stay."[44] Because of this unknown quantity, as Copjec argues, the mother/child unity "severs the dyad from the start" (*Giving Ground* 253). One would think, then, that this primordial loss within the hypothetical unity would be "catastrophic," as Copjec puts it, "bankrupting life of all pleasure and thus making death preferable to life's desolation" (253). One would think, therefore, that the death drive really does mean the drive toward total annihilation. But, as she points out, the very thing that causes the separation leaves something behind, which is nothing other than the signifier itself: the "mute, inert signifier, which refuses to yield up its meaning." And it is this strange, "riddling remainder," as she puts it, "that derails the drive from its path of total destruction" (*Giving Ground* 253). This uninterpretable signifier is of course what Lacan calls the object (a), the "little piece of the Real" that is left over from the signifying cut, forever haunting the Symbolic system with its uncanny, irreducible presence. This little leftover, taking various objective forms as the Lacanian objects (a) (the gaze, the breast, the mouth, etc.), interrupts the drive's aim, and enables it to find satisfaction in the detours it makes around these small doses of *jouissance.*

Thus the very thing, as Copjec has said, that severs us from our state of absolute *jouissance* (which of course never existed anyway), becomes the means by which another kind of satisfaction is attained. If this is beginning to sound a little like the Freudian concept of sublimation, it is not surprising, since as Copjec has also pointed out, all drives are sublimations. Sublimation, in Freud, involves the process by which a drive may be deflected from its immediate target in an object, but nevertheless obtains its aim. Freudian sublimation is "the satisfaction of a drive without repression."[45] In its circular tours around the objects (a), the drive realizes a form of pleasure that both "breaks up" and "brakes" as Copjec puts it, the drive's push backward to an "earlier state of things," enabling it to content itself with the "small doses" of *jouissance* that saturate these "objects." Note, of course, these are not phenomenal objects but Real ones. But as Real objects they can take on a sort of phenomenal form in the objects of demand, seeming to appear within these phenomenal objects as a kind of ghostly shimmer that disappears as soon as you get too close. Or, to use a less aesthetically driven expression, the Real "appears" in those objects of the phenomenal world that for some unknown reason generate a feeling of excessive pleasure/horror when encountered; when, for no apparent reason, some ordinary phenomenal object produces an affect that is completely in excess of the sum of its qualities. This, too, is a definition of sublimation: Lacan, fine-tuning Freud, describes sublimation as the act of "rais[ing] an object [. . .] to the dignity of a Thing" (*Sem.* VII, 112). When, in the pursuit of desire, the desiring subject comes too close to such an object, the appearance immediately vanishes, leaving the subject only to his or her interminable frustration, to the realization that "that's not It," before heading on to the next object of demand that seems to encapsulate the sought-after Real object. But inasmuch as this endless, metonymic pursuit of desire futilely circles around its endless objects of demand, the drive is nevertheless obtaining satisfaction *from the search itself.*

We can now explain in what sense the body is "immortal" for psychoanalysis. The immortal has to do with what is "in us more than ourselves," to use a Lacanian phrase; with what manages to escape all of our Symbolic determinations, the "little piece of the Real" that remains left over after the signifying cut of castration. In its objective form, this piece of the Real is called the object (a). In its subjective form, it is the "void" that constitutes the Lacanian subject as it mysteriously appears and fades within the signifying chain. Immortality for psychoanalysis thus has to do with the strange ways the death drive inscribes itself on our bodies, a testament to something that is prior to "ourselves" (ourselves, in the sense of a Symbolic identity, which is of course the only possible identity). The drives mark the traces of impossibility onto our bodies, they are the physical inscriptions (the "truth" if you like) of an encounter with something that is prior to the presence and absence of phenomenal life and death and, hence, "immortal." Thus Stransom was, in a sense, right when he intuitively set up his altar with the idea that symbolic representation would somehow help him to defeat death. But where he went wrong was in imagining it was by way of imposing an external limit to its field that his aim could be accomplished. Psychoanalysis asserts that representation is both the cause and the cure of our condition as castrated beings. In the strange, enigmatic, unanswerable materiality of the signifier that derails the death drive and sends it into its circular tours around the object (a), psychoanalysis discovers a form of immortality.[46]

But doesn't deconstruction also, famously, possess a concept of materiality, developed more extensively the later writings of De Man who in his essay, "Phenomenality and Materiality in Kant," outlines a concept of Kantian aesthetic vision that bears certain striking resemblances to the Lacanian Real?[47] When, in this essay, De Man describes Kantian "materialism" as a purely ocular vision, devoid of all conceptual input and what he calls "teleological interference," he begins to trace out a concept of materiality that is far from being simply the reciprocal obverse of consciousness or "phenomenality." The materialism alluded to in this essay is described in terms of a nontropological, nonfigurable, purely formal vision that merely takes in what the eye sees. Such nonphenomenal vision, De Man reads Kant as saying, occurs outside of any cognitive understanding, economic exchange or the anthropomorphism that enables us to comprehend the phenomenal world as a mirror image of our own consciousness. In direct opposition to everything we thought we knew about Kantian aesthetics, De Man asserts that it is with this uncanny "material" vision that Kant's critique of the aesthetic culminates: "in a formal materialism that runs counter to all values and characteristics associated with aesthetic experience" (De Man 83).

Here De Man outlines an aesthetic experience at the heart of the Kantian critique that bears little or no resemblance to the traditional concept of aesthetic reconciliation that has so long been the target of his deconstructive critique, but seems to have much in common with the senseless materiality of the signifier as it is taken up and pursued by the drives in Lacan. Perhaps it should come as no surprise, then, that for De Man too, this materiality is closely bound up with the body, yet not the organically unified, that is, Imaginary, body but a strangely dismembered, objectified body. De Man cites Kant as saying:

> The like is to be said of the sublime and the beautiful in the human body. We must not regard as the determining grounds of our judgment the concept of the purposes which all our limbs serve [. . .] and we must not allow this unity of purpose to influence our aesthetic judgment (for then it would no longer be pure). (De Man 88)

Here he glosses Kant with the following comment that under the conditions of aesthetic judgment we must, effectively, "consider our limbs, toes, breasts, or what Montaigne so cheerfully referred to as 'Monsieur ma partie,' in themselves, severed from the organic unity of the body, the way poets look at the oceans severed from their geographical place on earth" (88). In De Man's reading of Kant, aesthetic vision amounts to a bizarre "disarticulating" vision which, far from reconciling phenomenal and noumenal realms, seems to entail an encounter with an object world that is neither phenomenal nor noumenal but somehow, impossibly, *experienced* in what Lacan would call the "Real" of their extra-Symbolic state; an encounter with the nonphenomenalized, disarticulated, obtrusive, strictly speaking unthinkable *parts* of the body as they are given as sheer, senseless "materiality."

Of course the difference between De Man's concept of materiality and the psychoanalytic concept of the Real of the drives lies in the absence of enjoyment from De Man's scheme. The aesthetic vision De Man outlines is aesthetic precisely because of its character of disinterestedness: when we see aesthetically, we perceive without any interest in the being or existence of the object, whereas the drives have nothing other than to do with enjoyment and its satisfaction. However, with this concept of materiality De Man seems to admit the conceptual necessity of a limit point that lies not so much "outside" the grasp of language and phenomenal consciousness but rather within it, in the imposing, ineluctable, ungraspable, indeed *traumatic* presence of the world's body in its unphenomenalizable thinghood.[48] With this notion of materiality, De Man seems to come closest to recognizing the theoretical necessity for a concept of something like set theory's internal limit, a positive concept of impossibility around which the entire cognitive, phenomenal—Lacan would say Symbolic—system revolves.

De Man's revision of the Kantian aesthetic in fact provides another, alternate articulation of what I would want to call the ethicized aesthetic as it emerges in the three James texts we have been discussing. What De Man seems to be proposing is a form of vision that somehow, impossibly, "sees" the world in a state prior to the symbolic processes or categories enabling cognition. But this is clearly no leap into the noumenal totality. De Manian aesthetic vision, like Isabel's kaleidoscopic perception, entails a receptivity to particularity that refuses to gather it together under a conceptual whole or totality. Rather, in seeing aesthetically, De Man appears to be saying, we experience the perceptual field *as if it were* in an original state, prior to the primary signifying cut that first separated the phenomenal objects from the infinite manifold. Aesthetic perception is thus neither Real nor Symbolic, in Lacanian terms, but somehow located right at their intersection, a sort of paradoxical phenomenalization of the impossibility Lacan calls the Real.

In itself, such a mode of vision remains purely "aesthetic" (in the sense of having no pathological, political or ethical "interest"). What gives it its ethical character is the way such a form of vision demands *action* from us. As the title of Kant's Third *Critique* makes clear, the continuing significance of the aesthetic lies in the surprisingly traditional-seeming demand it makes on us for judgment. What I hope my discussion of the three acts in James enables us to see is the way aesthetic experience obliges us to confront what are essentially two fundamental ethical choices: one choice, the choice taken by Isabel Archer, Milly Theale, and implicitly by De Manian deconstruction, responds to the aesthetic experience of impossibility through the exigency of the phallus, that is, it comprises an ethical choice that is expressed through a fidelity to the Symbolic law whose proper function is to protect us from the horrific Real of our jouissance. In such cases, the choice—which in Lacanian terms is the choice of a "masculine sexuation"—subsequently devolves to one of its three possible symbolic phenomenalizations named by psychoanalysis as the anxiety neuroses: the foreclosure of the phallus (psychosis), its disavowal (perversion), or its repression (hysterical/obsessional desire). De Manian deconstruction, like Isabel and Milly, is a choice in favor of repression—as Warminski puts it, we must "forget" the encounter with the Real that material/aesthetic vision puts us in touch with in order to continue defensively producing our infinitely creative signifying processes inside the field of the Symbolic.[49] The ethics of deconstruction, in other words, represent an ethics of hysteria, an ethics of fidelity to the phallic signifier whose function is to mark the place of Real impossibility within the Symbolic field.

The other choice is notoriously less easy to give an account for. This is the choice that enables one to escape the phallic function but, as my discussion should make clear, it is obvious that this is as far from a psychotic foreclosure or a perverse disavowal of the phallic signifier as could be. In his *Encore* Seminar, Lacan explains this choice, the psychic choice of a "feminine sexuation," in terms of a relation not to the phallus but to the signifier for the lack in the big Other $S(\cancel{A})$. This entails a relation to Otherness that has nothing whatsoever to do with the phallus, comprising a form of satisfaction that Bruce Fink glosses as a "jouissance of love" (Fink 120). How one arrives at this nonphallic jouissance of love is famously left unclear by Lacan, which in itself perhaps serves to indicate its fundamentally non-Symbolic, that is, inarticulable, character. In place of further explication, Lacan leaves us instead with exemplars, figures from the mystical and literary traditions such as Saint John of the Cross, Saint Teresa, Hadewijch d'Anvers, a short list to which I should like to add James's unnamed woman from "The Altar of the Dead." With these figures, however, Lacan gives an indication that it might somehow be possible to dwell ethically in the Real, which is to say in an unmediated, that is, unphallicized relation to the lack in the big Other.

One of Slavoj Žižek's favorite closing tactics in his books is to ask the question, "Desire or drive"? My discussion is intended to illustrate the acutely *aesthetic*, in the sense that I have outlined it here, nature of this question. For this is quite simply the question posed to us by aesthetic experience, a question that demands actionable judgment from us: are we masculine or feminine, do we choose desire (founded on phallic jouissance), or the drive (the Other jouissance)? As I have shown, aesthetic experience is nothing but an encounter with the limit of the Symbolic realm, the *tuchè*, an encounter with the Real which, as such, imposes an ethical demand on us. The ethics of our response lies in our infinitely creative, singular ways of maintaining fidelity to this impossibility at the heart of experience.

De Man's essay on the Kantian sublime seems an appropriate place to end this discussion of aesthetics and ethics, given the way Kantian philosophy has served as a kind of court of last appeal throughout this book.

For in the sublime's play of the faculties a sort of allegory of the relation I have been describing between De Manian deconstruction and psychoanalysis can be discerned. When, under the conditions of the sublime, the imagination strives to present the unrepresentable, it experiences its famous "blockage" in its failure to phenomenalize what is intrinsically unphenomenalizable. Although the imagination fails, it all the same expands its presentational powers in its abortive effort. Yet we also know that the sublime is characterized not by one but by two moments, the second of which occurs when, through a kind of perspectival shift, a presentation of the totality is ultimately achieved, albeit in a negative form. The failed presentations of the imagination, in other words, together generate a form of presentation in the *negative space* of their collective failures to present the whole. This is, I think, the accurate way to conceive of Kant's Idea of the totality in the second moment of the sublime. Far from being the illicit superimposition of an external limit-concept outside the phenomenal system, the Idea of the totality is generated *internally*, from the collective failed presentations of the imagination.

Isn't it precisely this kind of relation that inheres between our two discourses which, as we saw above, correspondingly describes the relation between desire and the drive? When, in its endless, futile, circular metonymic paths, the desiring subject continually fails to achieve its goal in an object, some form of satisfaction is nevertheless attained by the drive from the very failures of the search itself. Similarly, in its circular, repetitive, as I have argued, *ethical*, failures to arrive at a definitive internal limit-concept such as the Real, deconstruction all the same negatively traces out the psychoanalytic internal impossibility without which ethics, as the philosophy not only of freedom but of right, that is, nonrelative, judgment, is otherwise meaningless.

After presenting his revised version of the Kantian *Augenschein*, De Man notes how another, competing narrative immediately begins to take over the philosophical text that the critic describes in terms of allegory. De Man observes how, at a certain point, Kant's analytical argument suddenly dissolves into "a story, a dramatized scene of the mind in action" in which the "faculties of reason and imagination are personified and anthropomorphized [. . .] and the relationship between them is stated in delusively interpersonal terms" (De Man 86–87). What De Man draws attention to is the way allegory seems to generate itself spontaneously in and around the moment of impossibility as it appears in Kant's text. Erupting almost simultaneously with Kant's disarticulating concept of aesthetic vision, allegory emerges here as Kant's formal vehicle for managing the ramifications of the material vision. The implications of this, I think, are clear: to the extent that most of us are neither saints nor madwomen, Real or material vision in itself can possess no intrinsic ethical or political value. It is only through our allegorical—symbolic, *beautiful*—articulations of it that the Real can play a viable, that is, productive role in ethics, namely, as the infinitely creative, symptomatic forms through which we as subjects give it negative expression. In much the same way, allegory must generate itself here in my text in order to manage the impossible confrontation between De Man and Lacan, and between aesthetics and ethics. Clothing impossibility in symptomatic form, allegory bears ethical-aesthetic testimony to an impossible encounter with the Real.

In closing, it occurs to me that some readers might be surprised by my contention that Henry James provides a literary framework from which to launch a critique of contemporary ethical and aesthetic discourses. When most people think of James, after all, it is hardly as a figure for intense ethical and political engagement—James is no Byron romantically launching off to fight for the cause of Greek independence, he is no Pablo Neruda, or Malraux carrying on resistance activities against fascist obscenities. Indeed, if anyone still thinks much of James at all it is most likely as a rather effete, slightly porcine, perhaps somewhat stuffy bachelor pacing back and forth in his upstairs room in Lamb House, Rye, occasionally roundly pronouncing an impossibly well-turned phrase, complete with punctuation, to his "stenographer," Theodora Bosanquet, before setting out for an afternoon of cycling in the Kentish countryside on one of those absurd early bicycles. But this is the same James who, when it was not evident that America would actually, finally join the First World War, feeling such profound indignation at what he considered his country's failure not of political but *ethical* responsibility toward Europe, performed a creative, autonomous act. Changing nationalities, James declared himself anew and self-authored himself as a British citizen. This, too, is the same James who, supremely revulsed by the unspeakable horrors of the Great War, decided like some of his younger contemporaries, the budding generation of modernists, that literature in its present form was no longer capable of performing adequate acts of representation. He stopped writing. But rather than retreat into a realm of silence, James's last years were spent visiting wounded soldiers in British hospitals whom he proceeded to "entertain," as he put it, by regaling them with his extraordinary powers of speech.[50] A preposterous image isn't it? There is delicate, fastidious, discriminating James proceeding to spin his exorbitant sentences, his elaborate metaphors, while all around him men are dying from the most horrific and grotesquely inflicted wounds. Preposterous, I said, but as James and Lacan have shown us throughout this discussion, all ethical acts have something preposterous about them. What this image of James's last days shows us very precisely is the way ethics intersects, cuts across, *(un)-yokes*, as Warminski would say, the registers of the Symbolic and the Real. What this image of James also suggests, however, is a figure for the only ethics that psychoanalysis recognizes: the ethics of speaking well.

Notes

PREFACE

1. Jacques Lacan, *The Four Fundamental Concepts of Psychoanalysis*, ed. Jacques-Alain Miller, trans. Alan Sheridan (New York: Norton, 1978), 272. I am indebted to Ed Pluth for certain clarifications of the distinction between the *passage à l'acte* and the act *tout court*.

2. Certain of Slavoj Žižek's formulations seem to imply this kind of ethical trajectory. See, for example, the final chapter, "The Breakout," in *The Fragile Absolute or, Why Is the Christian Legacy Worth Fighting For?* (London: Verso, 2000), 143–60.

3. See, for example, the issue of *Umbr(a): Science and Truth* (2000).

4. Søren Kierkegaard, *Kierkegaard's Writings, IV: Either/Or Part II*, vol. 2, ed., trans., intro. and notes Howard V. Hong and Edna H. Hong (Princeton: Princeton UP, 1987), 219.

5. Sigmund Freud, *Totem and Taboo*, trans. and ed. James Strachey, intro. Peter Gay (New York: Norton, 1989), 92. Jacques Lacan, *The Seminar of Jacques Lacan, Book VII. The Ethics of Psychoanalysis 1959–1960*, ed. Jacques-Alain Miller, trans. and notes Dennis Porter (New York: Norton, 1992), 216–17.

CHAPTER 1

1. Henry James, *The Portrait of a Lady*, ed. Robert D. Bamberg, Norton Critical Edition, 2nd ed. (New York: Norton, 1995), 360. Further references in the text as *PL*. See Dorothea Krook, *The Ordeal of Consciousness in Henry James* (Cambridge: CUP, 1962).

2. Lawrence Buell, "Introduction: In Pursuit of Ethics," *PMLA* 114.1 (1999): 7–19, p. 7.

3. My debts to these latter two should be evident throughout.

4. Jonathan Freedman, "James, Pater, and the Dreaming of Aestheticism," *Isabel Archer*, ed. Harold Bloom (New York: Chelsea, 1992), 152–63.

5. The phrase is from Bersani. See Leo Bersani, *The Culture of Redemption* (Cambridge, Mass.: Harvard UP, 1990).

6. Emmanuel Levinas is an important philosophical resource for this contemporary "revival" of ethics, but so-called political readers of Derrida such as Christopher Norris must also be considered part of this attempt to shift the terms of deconstruction toward political and ethical questions, a concern that has already occupied J. Hillis Miller for many years. More recent theorists of ethics in literary studies include Adam Zachary Newton, *Narrative Ethics* (Cambridge: Harvard UP, 1995); Tobin Siebers, *The Subject and Other Subjects: On Ethical, Aesthetic, and Political Identity* (Ann Arbor: U of Michigan P, 1998) and Alan Singer, *The Subject as Action: Transformation and Totality in Narrative Aesthetics* (Ann Arbor: U of Michigan P, 1993).

7. Laurel Brake notes the general enthusiasm for German theology, philosophy and letters in mid-nineteenth-century Britain. See Laurel Brake, *Walter Pater* (Plymouth: Northcote House, 1994), 17–18.

8. For a discussion of Isabel's perceptual blindness, see Mary Cross, *Henry James: The Contingencies of Style* (New York: St. Martin's P, 1993), 63. Moody, on the other hand, accuses Isabel of a deliberate moral blindness. See A. D. Moody, "James's Portrait of an Ideal," *The Magic Circle of Henry James: Essays in Honour of Darshan Singh Maini,* ed. Amritjit Singh and K. Ayyappa Paniker (New York: Envoy P, 1989), 21–40, p. 25.

9. Elizabeth Sabiston, "Isabel Archer: The Architecture of Consciousness and the International Theme," *The Henry James Review* 7 (1986): 29–47.

10. John H. Smith, *The Spirit and Its Letter: Traces of Rhetoric in Hegel's Philosophy of Bildung* (Ithaca: Cornell UP, 1988), 30–31.

11. Immanuel Kant, *Critique of Practical Reason,* trans. T. K. Abbott (New York: Prometheus Books, 1996), 116. Henceforth cited in the text as *CPrR*.

12. For a more detailed discussion of this ironic solution, see Singer, 141–43.

13. Hayden White, *Metahistory: The Historical Imagination in Nineteenth-Century Europe* (Baltimore: Johns Hopkins UP, 1973), 34.

14. Paul De Man, "The Rhetoric of Temporality," *Blindness and Insight* (Minneapolis: U of Minnesota P, 1983), 218.

15. Dorothy Berkson, "Why Does She Marry Osmond? The Education of Isabel Archer," *American Transcendental Quarterly* 60 (1986): 53–71.

16. Donatella Izzo, "*The Portrait of a Lady* and Modern Narrative," *New Essays on The Portrait of a Lady,* ed. Joel Porte (Cambridge: CUP, 1990), 33–48, p. 37.

17. Carol Vopat, "Becoming a Lady: The Origins and Development of Isabel Archer's Ideal Self," *Literature and Psychology* 38 (1992): 38–56, p. 43.

18. Berkson, 59.

19. Paul B. Armstrong, "Freedom and Necessity: The Servile Will and *The Portrait of a Lady,*" in *The Phenomenology of Henry James* (Chapel Hill: U of North Carolina P, 1983), 99–135.

20. Philippe Lacoue-Labarthe and Jean-Luc Nancy, *The Literary Absolute: The Theory of Literature in German Romanticism,* trans. Philip Barnard and Cheryl Lester (Albany: SUNY P, 1988).

21. Paul De Man, *Aesthetic Ideology*, ed. and intro. Andrzej Warminski, Theory and History of Literature 65 (Minneapolis: U of Minnesota P, 1996). See De Man's discussion of the symbolic and schematic modes of metaphorical representation in "The Epistemology of Metaphor," Sheldon Sacks ed., *On Metaphor* (Chicago: U of Chicago P, 1978), 11–28.

22. Martin Swales, *The German* Bildungsroman *from Wieland to Hesse* (Princeton: Princeton UP, 1978), 28–29.

23. This is not to belittle the often powerful and sensitive readings of the novel represented by this tradition, most displaying an acute awareness of James's deliberate intent to leave his heroine *"en l'air."* My point, rather, is to show how such an approach is structurally unable to account for what I consider to be the specifically ethical dimensions of Isabel's final act.

24. For more on this basic structure, see Georg Lukács, *The Theory of the Novel*, trans. Anna Bostock (Cambridge: MIT, 1971).

25. On the "Edwardianism" of *The Portrait of a Lady*, see Scott F. Stoddart, "'The 'Muddle' of Step-Parenting: Reconstructing Domestic Harmony in James and Forster," *Family Matters in the British and American Novel*, ed. Andrea O'Reilly Herrera, Elizabeth Mahn Nollen, Sheila Reitzel Foor (Ohio: Bowling Green, 1997), 115–48, p. 116.

26. Tracing the history of the idea of the beautiful soul, Norton remarks how the *Bildungsroman* itself emerges from the earlier, eighteenth-century tradition of presenting literary portraits for general edification. Robert E. Norton, *The Beautiful Soul: Aesthetic Morality in the Eighteenth Century* (Ithaca: Cornell UP, 1995), 153.

27. In a memorable passage in his autobiography, Thomas De Quincey writes, "Let a man meditate but a little on [causation] or other aspects of this transcendental philosophy, and he will find the steadfast earth itself rocking as it were beneath his feet; a world about him which is in some sense a world of deception; and a world before him which seems to promise a world of confusion, or a *'world not realised'*" (De Quincey's emphasis). Thomas De Quincey, *The Collected Writings of Thomas De Quincey*, vol. 2, ed. David Masson (London: Blackwell, 1897), 101.

28. The parallels between Isabel's repetition and the Kierkegaardian concept of repetition are striking. In each case, repetition marks the shift from an aesthetic into an ethical mode through an encounter with something beyond the realm of experience proper. See Søren Kierkegaard, *Kierkegaard's Writings, VI: Fear and Trembling/Repetition*, ed. and trans. Edna H. Hong and Howard V. Hong (Princeton: Princeton UP, 1983).

29. Michael Gilmore, "The Commodity World of *The Portrait of a Lady*," *New England Quarterly* 59 (1986): 51–74, p. 73.

30. Maria Irene Ramalho de Sousa Santos, "Isabel's Freedom: Henry James's *The Portrait of a Lady*," in *Henry James's* The Portrait of a Lady, ed. and intro. Harold Bloom (New York: Chelsea, 1987), 117–20, p. 125.

31. See the Judge's discussion of choice in the "Balance between Esthetic and Ethical," in Søren Kierkegaard, *Kierkegaard's Writings, IV: Either/Or. Part II*, ed. and trans. Howard V. Hong and Edna H. Hong (Princeton: Princeton UP, 1987), especially 213–23.

32. See Slavoj Žižek, *The Indivisible Remainder: An Essay on Schelling and Related Matters* (London: Verso, 1996), 169. Alan Singer arrives at a similar point in *The Subject as Action* where he makes an analogy between his formulation of an ethical subjectivity founded on transformability and the Kantian reflective judgment. See Singer, 225–26.

33. Gasché argues similarly when he cautions against a tendency among some identity theorists to conflate the philosophical concept of identity with empirical psychological and sociological identities. See Rodolphe Gasché, *Inventions of Difference: On Jacques Derrida* (Cambridge, Mass.: Harvard UP, 1994), 206–7.

34. Theodore Adorno, *Negative Dialectics*, trans. E. B. Ashton (New York: Continuum, 1973).

35. See, for example, David Lloyd, "Race Under Representation," *Oxford Literary Review* 13 (1991): 62–94.

36. Naomi Schor, "French Feminism Is a Universalism," *differences* 7.1 (1995): 15–47, p. 22.

37. Ernesto Laclau, *Emancipation(s)* (London: Verso, 1996).

38. Linda G. Zerilli, "This Universalism Which Is Not One," *Diacritics* 28.2 (1998): 3–20, p. 11.

39. Paul De Man, *Allegories of Reading: Figural Language in Rousseau, Nietzsche, Rilke, and Proust* (New Haven: Yale, 1979), 63 n. 8.

40. *The Complete Notebooks of Henry James*, ed. intro. and notes Leon Edel and Lyall Powers (New York: OUP, 1987), 15.

Chapter 2

1. Henry James, *The Wings of the Dove*, ed. J. Donald Crowley and Richard A. Hocks (New York: Norton, 1978). Further references in the text as *WD*.

2. Peter Brooks, *The Melodramatic Imagination: Balzac, Henry James, Melodrama, and the Mode of Excess* (New Haven: Yale UP, 1976).

3. Laurence Bedwell Holland, *The Expense of Vision: Essays on the Craft of Henry James* (Princeton: Princeton UP, 1964), 320.

4. Tzvetan Todorov, "The Structural Analysis of Literature: The Tales of Henry James," *Structuralism: An Introduction*, ed. David Robey (Oxford: Clarendon, 1973), 73–103, p. 75.

5. William James to Henry James, letter dated May 4, 1907, in *The Letters of William James*, ed. Henry James (Boston: Atlantic Monthly P, 1920), cited in the Textual Appendix, Crowley and Hocks, ed. 413. On the contemporary reception of the novel, see Kumkum Sangari, "*The Wings of the Dove*: 'Not Knowing, But Only Guessing,'" *The Henry James Review* 13 (1992): 292–305.

6. Josef Breuer and Sigmund Freud, *Studies on Hysteria*, trans. James and Alix Strachey, ed. Angela Richards (London: Penguin, 1974), 57.

7. See F. O. Matthiessen, *Henry James: The Major Phase* (Oxford: OUP, 1946), 67.

8. For a fascinating discussion of how the trope of metaphor itself is implicated in a similar congealing of the text's contingencies, see Gert Buelens, "Metaphor, Metonymy, and the Constitution of Identity in *The Wings of the Dove*," *Canadian Review of American Studies* 31 (2001): 409–28.

9. The idea that Alice's mysterious illness was hysterical in origin was already raised as early as 1868 after her first collapse. See the letter from Mary Walsh James to Garth Wilkinson James April 5, 1868. "It is a case of genuine hysteria for which no cause as yet can be discovered." *The Death and Letters of Alice James: Selected Correspondence*, ed. and essay Ruth Bernard Yeazell (Berkeley: U of California P, 1981), 11. Alice's final diagnosis and death from cancer in no way rules out the possibility that she was suffering from hysteria throughout the major part of her short life.

10. Sharon Cameron is one of the few other critics who argues in favor of a psychological reading of Milly's illness. See Sharon Cameron, *Thinking in Henry James* (Chicago: U of Chicago P, 1989).

11. Their acts are further linked together in the painterly imagery surrounding them, as Lionel asks for the "final, fatal sponge" to be applied, while Milly, turning her face to the wall, unmistakably recalls the fate of Mrs. Brash, the "Beldonald Holbein" in James's tale of the same name. In this story, the Lady Beldonald has become jealous of her friend Mrs. Brash who has been discovered as a rare beauty by a painter, and, as the "Holbein," has supplanted and outshined her patron. In a similar gesture of generosity toward her friend, Mrs. Brash makes the ultimate sacrifice and, like a painting, "turns her face to the wall." Interestingly, Pater used the same phrase to describe Antony Watteau's death in "A Prince of Court Painters," *Imaginary Portraits* (London: Macmillan, 1910), 43.

12. *The Notebooks of Henry James*, ed. F. O. Matthiessen and Kenneth Murdoch (New York: Oxford UP, 1947), 169. Cited in Crowley and Hocks, 446.

13. Among the less obvious pairs of characters are Densher and Maud who figure as a kind of comedic parody of the young lovers. James observes how the young man said to Mrs. Lowder, "very much as one of a pair of lovers says in a rupture by mutual consent 'I hope immensely of course that you'll always regard me as a friend,'" 66. Densher conveys as much to Kate when he admits, "'I quite suspect her of believing that, if the truth were known, she likes me literally better than—deep down—you yourself do,'" 69. Among the lesser characters we find reflective doubles in the depressing two Misses Condrips, sisters of Marion's late husband and cautionary warnings to our pair of sisters, Kate and Marion. Even Susan's and Kate's antitheticality sheds itself momentarily in their each sharing the burden of being the younger of a pair of sisters. Further unexpected pairs are suggested by the animal imagery of the novel. Although as a hovering eagle, "with a gilded beak as well, and with wings for great flights," 60, Maud's is clearly more of a predatory image than Milly's dove, the combined bird imagery suggests an unexpected correlation between the two (wealthy) women, one which is further strengthened in the scene when Maud, trying to discover Densher's whereabouts through Milly, acquires Milly's own signature characteristics: "It was in the tone of the fondest indulgence—almost, really, that of dove cooing to dove—that Mrs. Lowder expressed to Milly the hope that it had all gone beautifully," 172.

14. On the "new relationship" between language and power ushered in by the French revolution, see François Furet, *Penser la Révolution Française* (Paris: Gallimard, 1978).

15. Although Kate claims not to know her value to Aunt Maud (a statement which is dubious in itself) she at least understands the principle of the exchange, if not the specified value she holds.

16. See Julie Rivkin, *False Positions: The Representational Logics of Henry James's Fiction* (Stanford: Stanford UP, 1996).

17. See W. Graham, *The One Pound Note in the History of Banking in Great Britain* (Edinburgh: James Thin, 1911), 5, quoted in Rotman, 48.

18. See Fernand Braudel, *Capitalism and Material Life, 1400–1800*, trans. Miriam Kochan (London: Weidenfeld & Nicolson, 1967), 359.

19. Recall Milly's account of her "used-up relatives, parents, clever eager fair slim brothers—these the most loved—all engaged [. . .] in a high extravagance of speculation," 113.

20. Slavoj Žižek, *Tarrying with the Negative: Kant, Hegel, and the Critique of Ideology* (Durham: Duke UP, 1993), 28–29. Further references cited in the text.

21. Brian Rotman, *Signifying Nothing: The Semiotics of Zero* (Hampshire: Macmillan, 1987), 49. Such a "variable subject" is one of the forms taken by what Rotman identifies as a "meta-sign" whose analogues can be found in the invention and adoption of the number zero, the vanishing point of Renaissance painting, and the inscription of the musical notation for silence, the rest. He writes, "Each meta-sign [. . .] disrupts the code in question by becoming the origin of a new, radically different mode of sign production; one whose novelty is reflected in the emergence of a semiotic subject able to *signify* absence." Such signs usher in a "new semiotic space, one which relies essentially on a reference to the absence of signs that were previously [. . .] conceived in terms of a positive, always present, content." See especially, 55–56.

22. The obvious example of this place changing is when Milly comes to substitute for Kate in Densher's affections. Toward the end of the novel, this substitution is completed when Densher, at Milly's party, famously sees Milly supplanting Kate in beauty. But the novel is pervaded with this strange propensity. Densher's first meeting with Milly, for example, has him initially approaching her with "pity" only to find Milly turning the tables on him, and pitying him in her place: "That was the way the case had turned round: he had made his visit to be sorry for her, but he would repeat it—if he did repeat it—in order that she might be sorry for him," 227. The idea that Densher subsequently comes to insert himself in Milly's place, as I go on to argue, is foreshadowed in the doubling of the Regent's Park scene where Densher, a day later, follows Milly's footsteps to end up, perhaps, on the same bench. Densher's identification with Milly is complete when he inherits her signature characteristics of the dove: "For him too in this position, be it added—and he might positively have occupied the same bench—various troubled fancies folded their wings," 192. The difference between these substitutions and the previous pattern of reciprocal inversion is the difference that Milly's entire desiring trajectory, as I argue below, is dedicated to maintaining: substitution is organized around a foundational cut, or primordial negation.

23. For Mitchell, the difference between these two moments, however, consists in that "Kate was creating the appearance she wanted to see, whereas Milly accepts an identification others merely happen to recognize." Lee Clark Mitchell, "The Sustaining Duplicities of *The Wings of the Dove*," *Texas Studies in Literature and Language* 29.2 (1987): 187–214, p. 200.

24. Nicola Bradbury, "'Nothing that Is Not There and the Nothing that Is': The Celebration of Absence in *The Wings of the Dove*," *Henry James: Fiction as History*, ed. Ian F. A. Bell (London: Vision, 1984), 82–97. Marcia Ian, "The Elaboration of Privacy in *The Wings of the Dove*," *ELH* 51.1 (1984): 107–36, p. 119.

25. Kenneth Reinhard, "The Jamesian Thing: *The Wings of the Dove* and the Ethics of Mourning," *American Quarterly* 53 (1997): 113–46, p. 127.

26. James makes this point even more explicitly in *The Ambassadors* when, using the same metaphor, he has Strether comment how "after a real apotheosis [. . .] there's nothing *but* heaven." Henry James, *The Ambassadors*, ed. S. P. Rosenbaum (New York: Norton, 1964), 265.

27. Sir Luke Strett's advice that she could live if she would is therefore analogous to the Lacanian analyst's question to the hysteric "Che vuoi?," (What do you want?). As one of the "highest scientific minds" in his profession, Strett ought to have been at least familiar with the rising profession of psychoanalysis and Freud and Breuer's "talking cure" treatment of hysteria as the attempt to articulate unconscious desire.

28. Freud makes the same connection in his paper "On Narcissism" where he argues, "a strong egoism is a protection against falling ill, but in the last resort we must begin to love in order not to fall ill." *The Freud Reader*, ed. Peter Gay (New York: Norton, 1989), 552–53.

29. The sequential, almost causal link between the experience in front of the Bronzino and Milly's visit to the doctor has been noted by Cameron, but while Cameron argues that it is the "thought of death" that kills Milly, she fails to make the next step to recognize how Milly's illness is nothing but a defense against that thought. See Sharon Cameron, 127–30.

30. René Girard, *Desire, Deceit and the Novel: Self and Other in Literary Structure*, trans. Yvonne Freccero (Baltimore: Johns Hopkins UP, 1965).

31. The competition occurs regardless of whether the double engages in the struggle or not. Girard notes how the double's refusal to engage in mimetic rivalry simply unleashes the most obsessive form of mimetic desire such as found in Dostoevsky and Proust. See 68–69.

32. Gilbert Chaitin, *Rhetoric and Culture in Lacan* (Cambridge: CUP, 1996), 209.

33. Henry James, "The Grand Canal" (1892), *Italian Hours* (New York: Grove P, n.d.), 32. The importance of Venice for English aestheticism and the Decadent movement has been discussed by Sergio Perosa. See his essay "Literary Deaths in Venice," *Venetian Views, Venetian Blinds: English Fantasies of Venice*, ed. Manfred Pfister and Barbara Schaff (Amsterdam: Rodopi, 1999), 115–28. See also Jonathan Freedman, *Professions of Taste: Henry James, British Aestheticism, and Commodity Culture* (Stanford: Stanford UP, 1990).

34. Leon Edel, *Henry James: The Untried Years, 1843–1870* (London: Hart-Davis, 1953), 306.

35. See F. O. Matthiessen, *Henry James: The Major Phase* (London: OUP, 1944).

36. For a discussion linking the hysteric's desire to the lack of a signifier for "The Woman," see Paul Verhaeghe, *Does The Woman Exist? From Freud's Hysteric to Lacan's Feminine*, trans. Mark du Ry (London: Rebus, 1997, rev. ed., 1999).

37. For example Brooks (1976), 184.

38. Sigmund Freud, *Totem and Taboo*, trans. and ed. James Strachey, intro. Peter Gay (New York: Norton 1989). Henceforth cited in the text as *TT*.

39. On the paradox of the "founding law," see Robert Paul, *Moses and Civilization: The Meaning Behind Freud's Myth* (New Haven: Yale UP, 1996). Paul writes, "The founding deed itself demands just retribution by virtue of the law it brings into effect. The cosmogonic deed of the culture hero, insofar as it is a disruption of the previous order, not only brings the law into existence but also thereby condemns itself with the same law," 75.

40. See Lacan's explication of the "paternal metaphor" in *Écrits*, the substitutive procedure where the Name of the Father stands in for the unrepresentable "desire of the mOther." Jacques Lacan, *Écrits: A Selection*, trans. Bruce Fink in collaboration with Héloise Fink and Russell Grigg (New York: Norton, 2002), 190.

41. It is in this sense that the hysteric "wants to be the phallus," as Soler asserts. But we must be careful not to make the mistake of thinking this means that the hysteric wants to assume the "fullness" of the phallus in the face of the lack of guarantees presented by the man's failure. The phallus, in Lacan, is the signifier that signifies *lack*. Thus the hysteric's aim is not to fill in the gap posed by the missing phallus, but to ensure that the gap remains open. By "becoming" the phallus, the hysteric guarantees that the field of representation remains incomplete, that is, that the question of woman's desire will never be satisfactorily answered. For further discussion of the triangular structure characteristic of hysteria, see Colette Soler, "Hysteria and Obsession," *Reading Seminars I and II: Lacan's Return to Freud*, ed. Richard Feldstein, Bruce Fink, and Maire Janus (Albany: SUNY P, 1996), 248–82. See also her essays "The Symbolic Order (I)" and "The Symbolic Order (II)" in the same volume.

42. Immanuel Kant, *Critique of Judgment*, trans. and intro. J. H. Bernard (New York: Hafner P, 1951), 65. Henceforth cited in the text as *CJ*.

43. But unlike teleological judgments that are directed toward the purposiveness of the object's existence, aesthetic judgments are directed toward the way the object appears to us in its form. See below for further discussion of the aesthetic judgment and form. I am indebted to Rodolphe Gasché for clarifying these and other points in my discussion of Kant.

44. Lacan discusses beauty's blinding effect in his reading of Antigone in *The Seminar of Jacques Lacan, Book VII, The Ethics of Psychoanalysis, 1959–1960*, ed. Jacques-Alain Miller, trans. with notes Dennis Porter (New York: Norton, 1992), 281.

45. Unpublished seminar notes, SUNY Buffalo, 1996. Gasché explains how, in the aesthetic judgment, this appearing of the object in its object-hood remains a "subjective"

process, that is, there is no question of the object's existence, which would concern the objectivity of the object. See also his book, *The Idea of Form: Rethinking Kant's Aesthetics* (Stanford: Stanford UP, 2003).

46. Immanuel Kant, *Critique of Pure Reason*, trans. Norman Kemp Smith (New York: St. Martin's P, 1965), 489. Henceforth cited in the text as *CPR*.

47. Note that Milly's "aesthetic" solution is, therefore, not a sublimation. Although fantasy and sublimation have very similar structures, the crucial difference is that while fantasy occurs in the modality of desire, sublimation has to do with the satisfaction of the drives.

48. See Verhaeghe's discussion of Dora's case for this point, 64–65. A note of clarification is necessary. Although Verhaeghe argues that Dora aims to avoid the "lack in the Other," it should be clear from my discussion how the hysteric's desire effectively safeguards that lack even while her entire desiring structure is an attempt to fill it in. This is only possible with a signifier that signifies its own absence, that is, the phallus.

49. Critics who read the novel through what Sangari has called the implied reading position therefore agree with Densher that once Milly discovers the evil in the world, she stops willing life and dies. Although her gesture has been interpreted both positively and negatively (i.e., as the final gesture of forgiveness found in the religico-aesthetic interpretations of Matthiessen or Goode, or as the final defeat of goodness by a corrupt world that Heyns, Stowe, and Janssen, to name just a few, see in the novel), both interpretations rely on Densher's misreading of her death as the failure of will. As I argue below, Milly's death is precisely an act of will.

50. See Lacan's discussion of this dream in *The Four Fundamental Concepts of Psychoanalysis*, ed. Jacques-Alain Miller, trans. Alan Sheridan (New York: Norton, 1981), 34.

51. The question of Kate's future remains one of the text's quandaries for critics. Those who side with Kate tend to emphasize her resilience (see, for example, Hutchinson). Those who castigate her argue that she fails to learn the moral lesson that Densher earned so painfully, and therefore represents a triumph of the sordid world of exchange (Heyns, Krook, Stowe). Still others celebrate the "uncertainty" that surrounds Kate's future (such as, for example, Mitchell, Rowe, Bradbury). No critic, as far as I can tell, has analyzed the ethical dimension of this uncertainty, however, namely that it represents the success of Milly's ethical determination to keep the question of woman's desire open.

52. Kate's "credibility for herself" is taken by many as a sign of the triumph of the tawdry pragmatism of her reality. This position is only tenable if one holds to a strict moral opposition between Milly and Kate. I am, of course, arguing differently.

53. The pairing of Densher and Lord Mark I mentioned earlier becomes more pronounced after this scene, and it is striking how Densher persistently describes Mark as a "brute" as when, back in London, he asks Kate of Lord Mark, "what has the brute to do with us anyway?" 387.

54. Lacan, Sem. VII, *Ethics*. Lacan writes, "The only thing one can be guilty of is giving ground relative to one's desire," 321.

55. Lacan has shown how the Name/No-of-the Father *(le nom du père)* is one of the means for ensuring against such a totalization. Bruce Fink is especially illuminating on this

156 NOTES TO CHAPTER 3

point. Fink indicates that the Name-of-the-Father, as the primordial signifier that stands in for the mother's desire, gains full dialectical articulation only within the signifying system through what he calls "a further separation" that allows a number of ways for the paternal function to operate. Hence the paternal function may take form variously "as the Father's Name *(le nom du père)*, the father's no-saying *(le non du père)*, or prohibition, the phallus (as signifier of desire), and the *signifier* of the Other's desire, S(A)." Bruce Fink, *The Lacanian Subject: Between Language and Jouissance* (Princeton: Princeton UP, 1995), 57.

56. Teresa Brennan, *The Interpretation of the Flesh: Freud and Femininity* (London: Routledge, 1992), ix.

57. Alenka Zupančič, *Ethics of the Real: Kant, Lacan* (London: Verso, 2000), 133.

58. For a discussion of Lacan's reading of Antigone, see Žižek, *The Ticklish Subject: The Absent Center of Political Ontology* (London: Verso, 1999), 263–64. For a detailed analysis of the Claudel play, see Zupančič, 170–246. Zupančič quotes Lacan as saying "suicide is the only successful act," a statement that Žižek glosses as meaning precisely such an act of symbolic suicide (as opposed to real suicide that remains part of the system of demand). See Zupančič, 20, n. 7.

CHAPTER 3

1. This chapter is dedicated to the memory of my father, David Stowe Asche.

2. G. W. F. Hegel, *Phenomenology of Spirit*, trans. A. V. Miller, foreword J. N. Findlay (Oxford: OUP, 1977).

3. Jacques Derrida's famous political "turn" in his later work coincides with a renewed interrogation of limit concepts such as the Law of laws. See, for example, "The Laws of Reflection: Nelson Mandela in Admiration," in *For Nelson Mandela*, ed. J. Derrida and M. Tlili (New York: Seaver Books, 1987). Judith Butler, too, seems to have conceded something in her recent work to her Lacanian critics, Copjec and Žižek. See Slavoj Žižek's chapter on Judith Butler in *The Ticklish Subject: The Absent Centre of Political Ontology* (London: Verso, 1999). See also Joan Copjec's critique of Butler in the final chapter of *Read My Desire: Lacan Against the Historicists* (London: Verso, 1994), 201–36. For Butler's response, see Judith Butler, Ernesto Laclau, and Slavoj Žižek, *Contingency, Hegemony, Universality* (London: Verso, 2000).

4. Henry James, *Collected Stories*, vol. 2 (1892–1910), sel. and intro. John Bayley (New York: Knopf, 1999), 265–301. Further references in the text as *AD*.

5. Andrzej Warminski, "Reading Over Endless Histories: Henry James's 'Altar of the Dead,'" *Yale French Studies* 74 (1988): 261–84.

6. See Hegel's discussion of Antigone's act of burying Polyneices: "Blood-relationship supplements [. . .] the abstract natural process by adding to it the movement of consciousness, interrupting the work of Nature and rescuing the blood-relation from destruction," 271.

7. St. Augustine was one of the first to theorize how this view of language is essentially theological. Words point to things, but things are themselves pointing to God, the ultimate signified. As John Freccero explains, "The metaphor of God's book halts the infinite series by ordering all signs to itself. In germ, this is the foundation of Christian allegory and of salvational history." John Freccero, "The Fig Tree and the Laurel: Petrarch's Poetics," *Literary Theory/ Renaissance Texts*, ed. P. Parker and David Quint (Baltimore: Johns Hopkins UP, 1986), 20–32, p. 24. This is, of course, the heart of the deconstructive critique of Lacan, that his system is "theological" in this precise sense.

8. I am referring to the celebratory politics that accompanied deconstruction's appearance in Anglo-American English departments throughout the 1980s. Feminist deconstructive critics were particularly prone to this kind of celebratory (misreading) of deconstruction's political potential. For an example of this kind of work in James studies, see Mary Cross, *The Contingencies of Style* (New York: St. Martin's P, 1993). For the "performative" politics of deconstruction see Judith Butler, *Gender Trouble: Feminism and the Subversion of Identity* (New York: Routledge, 1990).

9. Jacques Lacan, "Kant with Sade," trans. James B. Swenson, Jr. *October* 51 (1989): 55–77.

10. See Neil Hertz, "Lurid Figures," in *Reading De Man Reading*, Lindsay Waters and Wlad Godzich, eds. (Minneapolis: U of Minnesota P, 1989), 82–104.

11. Here is another of the necessary "paradoxes" of deconstruction: for a discourse that tells us all we can do is mechanically stutter "I cannot read my own text, I cannot read my own text," deconstructive readings express this "truth" in quite extravagantly beautiful ways. The thrill that comes from reading essays by De Man and his followers from the '80s, the period of "High" deconstruction, is incomparable.

12. One need only to look back at the "Theory wars" of the 1980s to be struck again by the rhetorical virulence of both the attacking and defending positions regarding deconstruction (of which Warminski's essay is a classic example when he uses James to defend "material" reading against the "new historicism"). An analogy might be made between the resistance of English departments to deconstruction's "truth" and that which Cantor faced at the end of the nineteenth century when he first "completed" infinity, a strength of resistance that may indeed have resulted in his insanity.

13. Let me clarify how, by "deconstruction," I am referring exclusively to the rhetorical or "material" reading practice pioneered by De Man, not to Derrida whose work can be said to include a concept of ethical decisionism not too dissimilar to what I outline here. A deeper exploration of the overlap between Lacanian and Derridean and post-Derridean ethical thought would be a different project altogether. A good starting point, however, might be Sarah Harasym's edited collection *Levinas and Lacan: The Missed Encounter* (Albany: SUNY P, 1998).

14. Joan Copjec, "Sex and the Euthanasia of Reason," *Read My Desire: Lacan Against the Historicists* (Cambridge: MIT, 1994) 201–36, pp. 218–19. Henceforth cited in the text as *Read My Desire*.

15. Immanuel Kant, *Critique of Pure Reason*, trans. Norman Kemp Smith (New York: St. Martin's, 1965), 456. All further citations in the text as *CPR*.

16. In the discussion of introductory concepts of set theory that follows, I must make due acknowledgment of the tremendous help provided to me by David Odell, from whose personal communications with me and an unpublished paper, "The Way to Independence: A Journey in Set Theory," much of the following is derived. This section should therefore be read as a strictly collaborative effort.

17. The Kantian analogy breaks down here because while the Idea of Reason in Kant is strictly unphenomenalizable, the infinite cardinal, although uncountable, is nevertheless a property internal to the counting system, not external to it, as the Kantian divide might imply (depending on how we conceptualize the Kantian noumenal realm).

18. Odell observes how "Cantor's Theorem is trivially true for finite sets, since $2 ^ n > n$, for all natural numbers n. More generally, the subsets of a set are formed by abstraction, collecting all the elements which have some common property, so the extent of the power set of an infinite set directly reflects our capacity for abstraction or for making distinctions according to whatever criteria we can come up with amongst its elements. In this sense the power set of an infinite set may vary in size depending on this capacity. Cantor's Theorem really asserts that our capacity for matching up the contents of pairs of (infinite) sets is precisely co-ordinated with our capacity for classifying their contents, so that no matter how finely developed our ability to 'see into' and co-ordinate the contents of infinite sets we can never perfectly match such a set with its power set."

19. Odell continues, "Naturally, one would expect an Aleph to be always much greater than its subscript, as $\aleph_0$ is greater than 0, and $\aleph_\omega$ is greater than omega (= $\aleph_0$). This however is not the case. There are Alephs which equal their subscript, but none that are less. Such "super"-Alephs are easily created by limit processes, and a limit process is always indexed to some limit ordinal which counts off the steps, even and especially when these are infinite."

20. Keith J. Devlin, *Fundamentals of Contemporary Set Theory* (New York: Springer-Verlag, 1979), 117.

21. Odell explains, "The implicit assumption that Set Theory is not inconsistent, and therefore not nonsense, is equivalent to the assumption that the aggregate of all the ordinals (forbidden to be a set, by Russell's paradox) is to all intents and no purposes an Inaccessible Cardinal, quite apart from any other Inaccessibles (unprovably) present within the system."

22. See chapter VII, "A Love Letter," in *The Seminar of Jacques Lacan, Book XX. On Feminine Sexuality: The Limits of Love and Knowledge, 1972–1973*, ed. Jacques-Alain Miller, trans. with notes Bruce Fink (New York: Norton, 1998), 78–82. Further references will be to Sem XX, *Encore*.

23. Shall I venture that all of James's work is in some sense dedicated to exploring the fundamental impossibility of the sexual relationship? There is certainly no shortage of sexual renunciation in his novels, but what I am discussing of course goes a lot deeper than his anti-Victorian thematics of endlessly renunciated love.

24. I may be the only reader of James so far to compliment him on his "clarity." The usual complaint is about the obscurity of his prose. However, I find he is extraordinarily precise when it comes to pinpointing the moment of cross-over between an ethical and an

aesthetic discourse as, for example, when Kate in *The Wings of the Dove,* zeroing in on Densher's real motives for returning Milly's bequest unopened, remarks: "So [. . .] it spoils the beauty?" (*WD* 400).

25. Sem XX, *Encore* 78. For further explication of the formulas of sexuation, see later.

26. Of course this is an oxymoron—you cannot have a "Real" name, since a name is a Symbolic designation. But this analogy with the woman's two names indicates the doubleness I'm trying to highlight.

27. How we understand deconstruction all depends on the status of what Gasché has called "infrastructures"—the quasiconcepts that are produced in the course of a deconstructive reading. See Rodolphe Gasché, *Inventions of Difference: On Jacques Derrida* (Cambridge: Harvard UP, 1994). If they operate as windows to the impossible, then deconstruction seems to offer a similar possibility for freedom as psychoanalysis. If, as Warminski suggests, they must be "forgotten," then the ethical potential of deconstruction would seem to be reduced. Clearly "deconstruction" is not a monolithic entity, or even a particular type of reading strategy but, as I will go on to argue, an *ethical choice.*

28. As I say, "everyone knows," since even if this story isn't true but merely apocryphal, it nevertheless clearly demonstrates some sort of "truth" about Kantian philosophy, or at least a truth popular in the public imagination. This is the fallacy that imagines that Kant, along with Schiller, Nieztsche, and other luminaries of German philosophy somehow "made" fascism happen, a fallacy founded on the idea that Nazism was somehow uniquely specific to Germany and to German people. As Badiou directs us to see, this false ethical discourse, which is ultimately an aestheticization of *political* situations by human rights discourse, enables us to ignore the ways in which fascism can and does occur anywhere and any time, in any cultural and historical specificity.

29. If, as I argued in the first chapter, aesthetic ideology represented a "Schillerization" of Hegel, identity politics performs the exact same "betrayal" of deconstruction's truth. Anthropologizing deconstruction, identity politics mistakes deconstruction's negation for the trope of irony, politically and ethically resulting in the generation of an infinite series of ever smaller and smaller identities, each vying for their own particular "rights." In contrast, as I argued, "High" deconstruction, as represented by a critic like Warminski, demands recognition of how the infinite divisibility of signifiers must finally undergo a process of "reconnecting severed connections" (as Quine would put it). This comes about from the double-duty that a figure like zeugma is obliged to perform in his reading. As we saw, the revised figure of zeugma "reconnects" the severed relationship of metonymy and metaphor once it comes to function no longer as species but as genus, that is, as the figure for the "(un-)yoking" of conventional and deconstructive reading. Derrida, as Rodolphe Gasché has shown, also comes to a similar conclusion in his creation of such things as the "quasi-transcendental" concepts where a limit concept is placed "under erasure," or as Warminski would say, "forgotten" in a procedure not all that unlike Lacan's crossed out ~~The~~ Woman. See Gasché, *Inventions of Difference,* 20. Describing this reconnecting activity as "gathering," Gasché puts it very clearly: "To reject all gathering, because it can turn into self-identical individuality, totality, or System is to close the doors of reflection and philosophical interpretation. [. . .] To abandon all gathering because inevitably it would have effects of totalization is only the other side, the speculative inver-

sion, indeed, of the effort that turns the manifold into a homogenous whole. Such renunciation of all gathering surrenders the still-open possibilities, the yet-invisible future of thinking," Gasché, 20. Hence "High" deconstruction is *not* identity politics' infinite play of metonymic slippage but a rigorous attempt to theorize the impossible *from within its own system of possibility.* As I go on to argue, then, both psychoanalysis and deconstruction set themselves the same task but where they differ is in the way each "submits to the phallic function," as Lacan would say. See later.

30. Peter Hallward, "Translator's Introduction," *Ethics: An Essay on the Understanding of Evil*, trans. and intro. Peter Hallward (London: Verso, 2001), xxx.

31. See Zupančič's discussion of the Benjamin Constant controversy and Kant's response, "On the Supposed Right to Lie Because of Philanthropic Concerns," in her chapter, "The Lie." Alenka Zupančič, *Ethics of the Real: Kant, Lacan* (London: Verso, 2000), 43–63.

32. See Jacques Derrida, "For the Love of Lacan," in *Resistances: Of Psychoanalysis*, ed. Werner Hamacher and David E. Wellbery (Stanford: Stanford UP, 1998), 39–69.

33. The Lacanian master signifier, the phallus, is one of the Symbolic forms of the missing signifier for woman's desire. See Lacan's explication of the "paternal metaphor," the substitutive procedure through which the Name of the Father stands in for the unrepresentable "desire of the mOther." Hence, rather than signifying full presence, as deconstruction imagines, it is rather the signifier that "signifies" lack. Jacques Lacan, *Écrits: A Selection*, trans. Bruce Fink in collaboration with Héloise Fink and Russell Grigg (New York: Norton, 2002), 190.

34. Hence again the preponderance of what Neil Hertz has called "lurid figures" that litter deconstructive texts like Wordsworthian beggars and other outcasts. See Neil Hertz, "More Lurid Figures," *Diacritics* 20.3 (1990): 2–27.

35. In *Encore*, Lacan describes the "contingency" of the phallus in these paradoxical terms: the phallus "doesn't stop not being written," 94.

36. It is for this reason that Badiou's ethics is not the pure fanaticism that comes from the systematic elimination of every last "limit." Badiou makes this clear in his discussion of how absolutizing a truth results in "Evil": "That truth does not have total power means, in the last analysis, that the subject-language, the production of a truth-process, does not have the power to name all the elements of the situation. At least one real element must exist, one multiple existing in the situation, which remains inaccessible to truthful nominations, and is exclusively reserved to opinion, to the language of the situation. At least one point that the truth cannot force," 85.

37. For an illuminating discussion of this shift, which is the shift from an "ethics of desire" to an "ethics of drive," see Zupančič's final chapter in *Ethics of the Real*, 170–248, especially 238–45.

38. *The Seminar of Jacques Lacan: Book VII. The Ethics of Psychoanalysis, 1959–1960*, ed. Jacques-Alain Miller, trans. with notes Dennis Porter (New York: Norton, 1992). "The moral law, the moral command, the presence of the moral agency in our activity, insofar as it is structured by the symbolic, is that through which the real is actualized—the real as such, the weight of the real," 20. Further references cited in the text as *Sem. VII*.

39. This false "fidelity" is accordingly expressed in the already mentioned refusal of deconstructive and psychoanalytic critics to actually *read* each other's work—a state of affairs Jacques Derrida himself points out and decries. See Derrida, *Resistances*, 60.

40. The graph is adapted from Copjec's interpretation of Lacan's graph of sexuation found in Sem. XX, *Encore*, 78. See Copjec, *Read My Desire*, 214.

41. Thus if deconstruction is a modern-day Kantianism, psychoanalysis can be thought of as equivalent to the Hegelian "overcoming" of Kant. But it must be reiterated that this overcoming is no aestheticization of the Kantian divide, as deconstruction imagines it to be. It is, rather, equivalent to the Hegelian recognition that what, from the finite perspective of Kant, seemed to be a strict division between phenomenal and noumenal worlds, is actually the product of a perspectival illusion seen from the phenomenal point of view. The opposition of phenomenal and noumenal realms, in other words, is an opposition generated from the phenomenal side (hence the need to "reconcile" phenomenal and noumenal realms is also a phenomenally generated need). Recall Žižek: in Hegel, "The actual synthesis of the Sensible and of the Intellectual is already effectuated in what was for Kant their splitting," *Tarrying with the Negative: Kant, Hegel, and the Critique of Ideology* (Durham: Duke UP, 1993), 39. The Hegelian *Aufhebung* in fact possesses the structure of the internally generated limit and not, although it appears very similar, the (aesthetic) internalization of an external limit.

42. An analogy of this structure with physical sexuality is revealing. (I say analogy, because although Lacan does indeed talk about "sex," it should be clear that he is describing not physical but psychic structures in his "formulas of sexuation"). Although men can only know what Lacan calls "phallic jouissance," women can "know" both phallic and nonphallic jouissance. We can make this clearer by means of a very intuitive analogy: male orgasm is entirely centered around the phallus, while women, as Freud was quick to discover, can have both phallic (i.e., clitoral) and nonphallic ways by which orgasm can be achieved. It is exactly the kind of structural impossibility I am describing that is experienced by any sexually active woman who, when asked tenderly after the act of love by her partner "Did you come?" is faced with a question whose answer is in a sense impossible. That is, had she experienced "phallic" jouissance (clitoral orgasm) the question is an easy either/or: yes or no. But because there is also another way of experiencing pleasure (what Freud was obliged, for lack of a better term, to call "vaginal orgasm") the terms of the question are revealed to be as false as the Kantian mathematical antinomy. She cannot answer the question under the conditions by which it is posed, since phallic jouissance does not admit of the possibility of "another jouissance." Hence, as Freud again was forced to admit, the answer to the question of woman's pleasure or desire is not only difficult to answer but actually "impossible." For within the binary terms of the system of either/or, the system of counting which is, after all, all that there "is," there is no signifier for woman's (nonphallic) jouissance. Again, however, it is this missing signifier that becomes (in the Hegelian twist that is becoming familiar to us now) nothing other than the blind spot, the condition of possibility, the internal limit that creates the law of the count. To Stransom's endlessly repeated, phallic "one more, one more" (and the sexual overtones of the last scene are unmistakeable, when James describes how "the descent of Mary Antrim opened his spirit with a great compunctious throb for the descent of Acton Hague"), James counters with the woman's (necessarily negative) articulation of a structural impossibility, "no more, no more."

43. The historical coincidence of psychoanalysis with surrealism in the early twentieth century is instructive, representing different disciplinary expressions of this same loss of belief in the aesthetic's promise of reconciliation.

44. Joan Copjec, "The Tomb of Perseverance: On *Antigone*," in *Giving Ground: The Politics of Propinquity*, ed. Joan Copjec and Michael Sorkin (London: Verso, 1999), 233–66, p. 253. Henceforth cited as *Giving Ground*.

45. The formulation is Lacan's in Seminar VII, 293. In his essay on Leonardo, Freud gives the following definition of sublimation: it is "the power to replace [the sexual instinct's] immediate aim by other aims which may be valued more highly and which are not sexual." "Leonardo Da Vinci and a Memory of His Childhood," in Peter Gay, ed. *The Freud Reader* (New York: Norton, 1989), 452.

46. The close relationship between Lacanian psychoanalysis and Romanticism, which has been frequently noted by Žižek and, more recently, by Justin Clemens, reappears here in this evocation of the way aesthetic representation stands in for an original loss. See Justin Clemens, *The Romanticism of Contemporary Theory: Institution, Aesthetics, Nihilism* (Aldershot: Ashgate, 2003). But although this cause/cure paradox finds one of its most powerful expressions in the Romantic tradition, it would not be hard to trace this idea further back through the literary tradition, to Milton of course, and his medieval predecessors. See especially Lacan's discussion of the medieval courtly love tradition and sublimation in *Seminar VII*, chapter 9, 139–54. The main difference between Lacanian/Freudian sublimation and the aesthetic recuperative fantasy that deconstruction critiques in Romanticism lies, as I have been arguing, in the logical and temporal paradoxes supplied by the psychoanalytic concept of the Real which enables a subject to become its own *cause*. This is a different proposition than that found in the Kleinian "reparative" concept of sublimation that underlies the critique of aesthetic recuperation. Aesthetic recuperation aims to restore a lost whole; Lacanian sublimation retroactively "creates" it. For a critique of Klein and the redemptive aesthetic, see Leo Bersani, "Death and Literary Authority: Marcel Proust and Melanie Klein," *The Culture of Redemption* (Cambridge: Harvard UP, 1990), 7–28.

47. De Man, "Phenomenality and Materiality in Kant," *Aesthetic Ideology*, ed. and intro. Andrzej Warminski, Theory and History of Literature 65 (Minneapolis: U of Minnesota P, 1996), 70–90, see especially, 80–82.

48. It is surely no coincidence that trauma studies is linked historically to De Man, as Ortwin De Graaf, Vivian Liska, and Katrien Vloeberghs have pointed out. They observe how Cathy Caruth, one of the founders of this discipline, was a former student of De Man's, whose doctoral dissertation possesses impeccable De Manian deconstructive credentials. See De Graef et al. "Introduction: The Instance of Trauma," *European Journal of English Studies* 7 (2003): 247–55, esp. 250–51. This seems to bear out my suggestion that materiality in the late De Man implies a concept that already possesses certain structural similarities to Lacan's "jouissance." This implicit "hidden kernel" of De Man's work also bears out my assertion regarding the relation of the discourses of deconstruction and psychoanalysis as corresponding to that of desire and drive: drive is, if you like, "pure" desire, just as, perhaps, psychoanalysis is simply "pure" deconstruction. For more on this relation between drive and desire, see Zupančič, 243. This is perhaps also the place to

acknowledge how, in his introduction to his edited collection of De Man's *Aesthetic Ideology*, Warminski employs a mathematical argument that is in some ways strikingly similar to my own to show how De Man's concept of materiality carries with it something of the ineluctable "thingness" psychoanalysis associates with the Real. See especially pages 30–32.

49. A slight clarification is perhaps necessary. To the extent that it remains within its foundational discovery (that every text possesses its own blind-spot or point of short-cirtcuit that permits a transfer to take place between two irreconcilable realities), deconstruction exhibits the form of double vision characteristic of perversion. Yet the moment deconstruction begins to "read" (as it always must), this discovery has to be "repressed" in order to generate its endless, self-replicating series of allegorical readings. How it chooses to *act*, in other words, is a choice in favor of hysteria, i.e., an ethics of desire.

50. James's extraordinary conversational gifts were well known in his literary circle and he was an avidly sought-after dinner guest for precisely that reason. In her letter of condolence to Theodora Bosanquet after James's death, Edith Wharton observed how, had James never written a single word, he would still always be remembered by his friends for his astonishing gift of speech. See Lyall Powers ed., *Henry James and Edith Wharton: Letters, 1900–1915* (London: Weidenfeld and Nicolson, 1990).

Works Cited

WORKS BY HENRY JAMES

James, Henry. *The Ambassadors*. Ed. S. P. Rosenbaum. New York: Norton, 1964.

——. *The Art of Criticism: Henry James on the Theory and Practice of Fiction*. Ed. William Veeder and Susan M. Griffin. Chicago: U of Chicago P, 1986.

——. *The Art of the Novel: Critical Prefaces*. Intro. Richard P. Blackmur. New York: Charles Scribner's Sons, 1962.

——. *Collected Stories*. 2 vols. (1866–91), (1892–1910). Sel. and intro. John Bayley. New York: Knopf, 1999.

——. *The Complete Notebooks of Henry James*. Ed. and intro. Leon Edel and Lyall Powers. New York: OUP, 1987.

——. *Essays on Art and Drama*. Ed. Peter Rawlings. Hants: Scholar P, 1996.

——. *Hawthorne*. Ed. John Morley. London: Macmillan, 1909.

——. *Henry James and Edith Wharton: Letters 1900–1915*. Ed. Lyall Powers. London: Weidenfeld and Nicolson, 1990.

——. *Italian Hours*. New York: Grove P, n.d.

——. *The Letters of Henry James*. 2 vols. Ed. Percy Lubbock. London: Macmillan, 1920.

——. *The Notebooks of Henry James*. Ed. F. O. Mathiessen and Kenneth Murdoch. New York: Oxford UP, 1947.

——. *The Portrait of a Lady*. Ed. Robert D. Bamberg. Norton Critical Edition. 2nd ed. New York: Norton, 1995.

——. *The Tales of Henry James*. 2 vols. Ed. Maqbool Aziz. Oxford: Clarendon, 1973.

——. *The Wings of the Dove*. Eds. J. Donald Crowley and Richard A. Hocks. New York: Norton, 1978.

GENERAL WORKS

Adorno, Theodore. *Negative Dialectics*. Trans. E. B. Ashton. New York: Continuum, 1973.

Armstrong, Paul B. *The Phenomenology of Henry James*. Chapel Hill: U of North Carolina P, 1983.

Badiou, Alain. *Ethics: An Essay on the Understanding of Evil.* Trans. and intro. Peter Hall-ward. London: Verso, 2001.

Berkson, Dorothy. "Why Does She Marry Osmond? The Education of Isabel Archer." *American Transcendental Quarterly* 60 (1986): 53–71.

Bersani, Leo. *The Culture of Redemption.* Cambridge: Harvard UP, 1990.

Bradbury, Nicola. "Nothing That Is Not There and the Nothing That Is": The Celebra-tion of Absence in *The Wings of the Dove. Henry James: Fiction as History.* Ed. Ian F. A. Bell. London: Vision, 1984, 82–97.

Brake, Laurel. *Walter Pater.* Writers and their Work. Plymouth: Northcote House, 1994.

Braudel, Fernand. *Capitalism and Material Life: 1400–1800.* Trans. Miriam Kochan. Lon-don: Weidenfeld and Nicolson, 1967.

Brennan, Teresa. *The Interpretation of the Flesh: Freud and Femininity.* London: Routledge, 1992.

Breuer, Josef, and Sigmund Freud. *Studies on Hysteria.* Trans. James and Alix Strachey. Ed. Angela Richards. London: Penguin, 1974.

Bronfen, Elizabeth. *The Knotted Subject: Hysteria and Its Discontents.* Princeton: Princeton UP, 1998.

Brooks, Peter. Introduction. *The Wings of the Dove.* Ed., intro. and notes Peter Brooks. Oxford: OUP, 1984, vii–xxiii.

————. *The Melodramatic Imagination: Balzac, Henry James, Melodrama, and the Mode of Excess.* New Haven: Yale UP, 1976.

Buelens, Gert. "Metaphor, Metonymy, and the Constitution of Identity in *The Wings of the Dove.*" *Canadian Review of American Studies* 31 (2001): 409–28.

Buell, Lawrence. "Introduction: In Pursuit of Ethics." *PMLA* 114.1 (1999): 7–19.

Butler, Judith, Ernesto Laclau, and Slavoj Žižek. *Contingency, Hegemony, Universality.* London: Verso, 2000.

Butler, Judith. *Gender Trouble: Feminism and the Subversion of Identity.* New York: Rout-ledge, 1990.

Cameron, Sharon. *Thinking in Henry James.* Chicago: U of Chicago P, 1989.

Chaitin, Gilbert. *Rhetoric and Culture in Lacan.* Cambridge: Cambridge UP, 1996.

Clemens, Justin. *The Romanticism of Contemporary Theory: Institution, Aesthetics, Nihilism.* Aldershot: Ashgate, 2003.

Copjec, Joan. "The Tomb of Perseverance: On *Antigone.*" *Giving Ground: The Politics of Propinquity.* Ed. Joan Copjec and Michael Sorkin. London: Verso, 1999, 233–66.

————. *Read My Desire: Lacan Against the Historicists.* London: Verso, 1994.

Copjec, Joan, ed. *Radical Evil.* London: Verso, 1996.

Cross, Mary. *Henry James: The Contingencies of Style*. New York: St. Martin's P, 1993.

De Graef, Ortwin, Vivian Liska, Katrien Vloeberghs. "Introduction: The Instance of Trauma." *European Journal of English Studies* 7 (2003): 247–55.

De Man, Paul. *Aesthetic Ideology*. Ed. and intro. Andrzej Warminski. Theory and History of Literature 65. Minneapolis: U of Minnesota P, 1996.

———. *Allegories of Reading: Figural Language in Rousseau, Nietzsche, Rilke, and Proust*. New Haven: Yale UP, 1979.

———. "The Epistemology of Metaphor." In Sheldon Sacks ed. *On Metaphor*. Chicago: U of Chicago P, 1978, 11–28.

———. *The Resistance to Theory*. Foreword Wlad Godzich. Minneapolis: U of Minnesota P, 1986.

———. "The Rhetoric of Temporality." *Blindness and Insight*. Minneapolis: U of Minnesota P, 1983, 187–228.

De Quincey, Thomas. *The Collected Writings of Thomas De Quincey*. 14 vols. Ed. David Masson. London: Blackwell, 1897.

Derrida, Jacques. "The Laws of Reflection: Nelson Mandela in Admiration." *For Nelson Mandela*. Ed. J. Derrida and M. Tlili. New York: Seaver Books, 1987.

———. "White Mythology: Metaphor in the Text of Philosophy." *Margins of Philosophy*. Trans. Robert Czerny et al. Toronto: U of Toronto P, 1977, 207–72.

———. *Limited Inc*. Evanston: Northwestern UP, 1988.

———. *Resistances: Of Psychoanalysis*. Ed. Werner Hamacher and David E. Wellbery. Stanford: Stanford UP, 1998.

De Sousa Santos, Maria. "Isabel's Freedom: Henry James's *The Portrait of a Lady*." *Henry James's* The Portrait of a Lady. Ed. and intro. Harold Bloom. New York: Chelsea, 1987, 117–29.

Devlin, Keith J. *Fundamentals of Contemporary Set Theory*. New York: Springer-Verlag, 1979.

Edel, Leon. *Henry James: The Untried Years, 1843–1870*. London: Hart-Davis, 1953.

Feldstein, Richard, Bruce Fink and Maire Janus, eds. *Reading Seminars I and II: Lacan's Return to Freud*. Albany: SUNY P, 1996.

Fink, Bruce. *The Lacanian Subject: Between Language and Jouissance*. Princeton: Princeton UP, 1995.

Freccero, John. "The Fig Tree and the Laurel: Petrarch's Poetics." *Literary Theory/Renaissance Texts*. Ed. P. Parker and David Quint. Baltimore: Johns Hopkins UP, 1986, 20–32.

Freedman, Jonathan. "James, Pater, and the Dreaming of Aestheticism." *Isabel Archer*. Ed. Harold Bloom. New York: Chelsea, 1992, 152–63.

———. *Professions of Taste: Henry James, British Aestheticism, and Commodity Culture*. Stanford: Stanford UP, 1990.

Freud, Sigmund. *Beyond the Pleasure Principle*. Trans. and ed. James Strachey. Intro. Gregory Zilborg. Biographical intro. Peter Gay. New York: Norton, 1961.

———. *Dora: An Analysis of a Case of Hysteria*. Ed. and intro. Philip Rieff. New York: Collier, 1963. Trade edition 1993.

———. *Totem and Taboo*. Trans. and ed. James Strachey. Intro. Peter Gay. New York: Norton, 1989.

———. "On Narcissism: An Introduction." Gay ed. 545–61.

———. *Leonardo Da Vinci: A Memoir of his Childhood*. Gay ed. 443–81.

Furet, François. *Penser la Révolution Française*. Paris: Gallimard, 1978.

Gasché, Rodolphe. *The Idea of Form: Rethinking Kant's Aesthetics*. Stanford: Stanford UP, 2003.

———. *Inventions of Difference: On Jacques Derrida*. Cambridge, Mass.: Harvard UP, 1994.

———. *The Tain of the Mirror: Derrida and the Philosophy of Reflection*. Cambridge, Mass.: Harvard UP, 1986.

Gay, Peter ed. *The Freud Reader*. New York: Norton, 1989.

Gilmore, Michael T. "The Commodity World of *The Portrait of a Lady*." *The New England Quarterly* 59.1 (1986): 51–74.

Girard, René. *Deceit, Desire and the Novel: Self and Other in Literary Structure*. Trans. Yvonne Freccero. Baltimore: Johns Hopkins UP, 1965.

Graham, W. *The One Pound Note in the History of Banking in Great Britain*. Edinburgh: James Thin, 1911.

Hallward, Peter. "Translator's Introduction." Badiou, vii–li.

Harasym, Sarah, ed. *Levinas and Lacan: The Missed Encounter*. Albany: SUNY P, 1998.

Hegel, G. W. F. *Aesthetics: Lectures on Fine Art*. 2 vols. Trans. T. M. Knox. Oxford: OUP, 1975.

———. *Phenomenology of Spirit*. Trans. A. V. Miller. Analysis and foreword J. N. Findlay. Oxford: OUP, 1977.

Hertz, Neil. "Lurid Figures." *Reading De Man Reading*. Ed. Lindsay Waters and Wlad Godzich. Minneapolis: U of Minnesota P, 1989, 82–104.

———. "More Lurid Figures." *Diacritics* 20.3 (1990): 2–27.

Heyns, Michiel. "'The Language of the House' in *The Wings of the Dove*." *Essays in Criticism* 27.4 (1989): 116–36.

Holland, Laurence B. *The Expense of Vision*. Princeton: Princeton UP, 1964.

Hutchinson, Stuart. "James's Medal: Options in *The Wings of the Dove*." *Essays in Criticism* 27 (1977): 315–35.

Ian, Marcia. "The Elaboration of Privacy in *The Wings of the Dove*." *ELH* 51 (1984): 107–36.

Izzo, Donatella. "*The Portrait of a Lady* and Modern Narrative." Trans. Cristina Bacchi-lega. *New Essays on The Portrait of a Lady*. Ed. Joel Porte. Cambridge: CUP, 1990, 33–48.

Janssen, Ronald. "The Power of Possession: Money and Marriage in *The Wings of the Dove*." Singh and Paniker, 160–67.

Kant, Immanuel. *Critique of Judgment*. Trans. and intro. J. H. Bernard. New York: Hafner P, 1951.

———. *Critique of Practical Reason*. Trans. T. K. Abbott. New York: Prometheus Books, 1996.

———. *Critique of Pure Reason*. Trans. Norman Kemp Smith. New York: St. Martin's P, 1965.

Kierkegaard, Søren. *Kierkegaard's Writings, IV: Either/Or Part II*. Ed. and trans. Howard V. Hong and Edna H. Hong. Princeton: Princeton UP, 1987.

———. *Kierkegaard's Writings, VI: Fear and Trembling/Repetition*. Ed. and trans. Edna H. Hong and Howard V. Hong. Princeton: Princeton UP, 1983.

Krook, Dorothea. *The Ordeal of Consciousness in Henry James*. Cambridge: CUP, 1962.

Lacan, Jacques. *Écrits: A Selection*. Trans. Bruce Fink. In collaboration with Héloise Fink and Russell Grigg. New York: Norton, 2002.

———. *The Four Fundamental Concepts of Psychoanalysis*. Ed. Jacques-Alain Miller. Trans. Alan Sheridan. New York: Norton, 1978.

———. "Kant with Sade." Trans. James B. Swenson, Jr. *October* 51 (1989): 55–77.

———. *The Seminar of Jacques Lacan: Book VII. The Ethics of Psychoanalysis, 1959–60*. Ed. Jacques-Alain Miller. Trans. with notes Dennis Porter. New York: Norton, 1992.

———. *The Seminar of Jacques Lacan, Book XX. Encore: On Feminine Sexuality, The Limits of Love and Knowledge, 1972–1973*. Ed. Jacques-Alain Miller. Trans. with notes Bruce Fink. New York: Norton, 1998.

Laclau, Ernesto. *Emancipation(s)*. London: Verso, 1996.

Lacoue-Labarthe, Philippe and Jean-Luc Nancy. *The Literary Absolute: The Theory of Literature in German Romanticism*. Trans. Philip Barnard and Cheryl Lester. Albany: SUNY P, 1988.

Lloyd, David. "Race Under Representation." *Oxford Literary Review* 13 (1991): 62–94.

Lukács, Georg. *The Theory of the Novel*. Trans. Anna Bostock. Cambridge: MIT, 1971.

Matthiessen, F. O. *Henry James: The Major Phase*. London: OUP, 1944.

Mitchell, Lee Clark. "The Sustaining Duplicities of *The Wings of the Dove*." *Texas Studies in Literature and Language* 29.2 (1987): 187–214.

Moody, A. D. "James's Portrait of an Ideal." Singh and Paniker, 21–40.

Newton, Adam Zachary. *Narrative Ethics*. Cambridge: Harvard UP, 1995.

Norton, Robert E. *The Beautiful Soul: Aesthetic Morality in the Eighteenth Century*. Ithaca: Cornell UP, 1995.

Odell, David. "The Way to Independence: A Journey in Set Theory." Unpublished paper.

Pater, Walter. *Imaginary Portraits*. London: Macmillan, 1910.

Paul, Robert. *Moses and Civilization: The Meaning Behind Freud's Myth*. New Haven: Yale UP, 1996.

Perosa, Sergio. "Literary Deaths in Venice." Pfister and Schaff. 115–28.

Pfister, Manfred, and Barbara Schaff eds. *Venetian Views, Venetian Blinds: English Fantasies of Venice*. Amsterdam: Rodopi, 1999.

Redfield, Marc. *Phantom Formations: Aesthetic Ideology and the* Bildungsroman. Ithaca: Cornell, 1996.

Reinhard, Kenneth. "The Jamesian Thing: *The Wings of the Dove* and the Ethics of Mourning." *Arizona Quarterly* 53.4 (1997): 115–46.

Rivkin, Julie. *False Positions: The Representational Logics of Henry James's Fiction*. Stanford: Stanford UP, 1996.

Rotman, Brian. *Signifying Nothing: The Semiotics of Zero*. Hampshire: Macmillan P, 1987.

Rowe, John Carlos. "The Symbolization of Milly Theale: Henry James's *The Wings of the Dove*." *ELH* 40 (1973): 131–64.

Sabiston, Elizabeth. "Isabel Archer: The Architecture of Consciousness and the International Theme." *The Henry James Review* 7 (1986): 29–47.

Salecl, Renata, ed. *Sexuation*. Sic 3. Durham: Duke UP, 2000.

Sangari, Kumkum. "*The Wings of the Dove*: 'Not Knowing, But Only Guessing.'" *The Henry James Review* 13 (1992): 292–305.

Schor, Naomi. "French Feminism Is a Universalism." *differences* 7.1 (1995): 15–47.

Siebers, Tobin. *The Subject and Other Subjects: On Ethical, Aesthetic, and Political Identity*. Ann Arbor: U of Michigan P, 1998.

Singer, Alan. *The Subject as Action: Transformation and Totality in Narrative Aesthetics*. Ann Arbor: U of Michigan P, 1993.

Singh, Amritjit and K. Ayyappa Paniker, eds. *The Magic Circle of Henry James: Essays in Honour of Darshan Singh Maini*. New York: Envoy P, 1989.

Smith, John H. *The Spirit and Its Letter: Traces of Rhetoric in Hegel's Philosophy of Bildung*. Ithaca: Cornell UP, 1988.

Soler, Colette. "Hysteria and Obsession." Feldstein et al. 248–82.

———. "The Curse on Sex." Salecl ed. 39–56.

———. "The Symbolic Order (I)." Feldstein et al. 39–46.

———. "The Symbolic Order (II)." Feldstein et al. 47–55.

———. "Transference." Feldstein et al. 56–60.

Stoddart, Scott F. "The 'Muddle' of Step-Parenting: Reconstructing Domestic Harmony in James and Forster." *Family Matters in the British and American Novel*. Ed. Andrea O'Reilly Herrera, Elizabeth Mahn Nollen, Sheila Reitzel Foor. Ohio: Bowling Green, 1997.

Stowe, William. "James's Elusive Wings." *The Cambridge Companion to Henry James*. Ed. Jonathan Freedman. Cambridge: CUP, 1998, 187–203.

Swales, Martin. *The German Bildungsroman from Wieland to Hesse*. Princeton: Princeton UP, 1978.

Todorov, Tzvetan. "The Structural Analysis of Literature: The Tales of Henry James." *Structuralism: An Introduction*. Ed. David Robey. Oxford: Clarendon, 1973, 73–103.

Verhaeghe, Paul. *Does The Woman Exist? From Freud's Hysteric to Lacan's Feminine*. Trans. Mark du Ry. London: Rebus, 1997, rev. ed. 1999.

Vopat, Carol. "Becoming a Lady: The Origins and Development of Isabel Archer's Ideal Self." *Literature and Psychology* 38 (1992): 38–56.

Warminski, Andrzej. "Reading Over Endless Histories: Henry James's 'Altar of the Dead.'" *Yale French Studies* 74 (1988): 261–84.

———. "Introduction: Allegories of Reference." Warminski ed. 1–33.

White, Hayden. *Metahistory: The Historical Imagination in Nineteenth-Century Europe*. Baltimore: Johns Hopkins UP, 1973.

White, Robert. "Love, Marriage, and Divorce: The Matter of Sexuality in *The Portrait of a Lady*." *The Henry James Review* 7 (1986): 59–71.

Yeazell, Ruth Bernard, ed. *The Death and Letters of Alice James: Selected Correspondence*. Berkeley: U of California P, 1981.

Zerilli, Linda G. "This Universalism Which Is Not One." *Diacritics* 28.2 (1998): 3–20.

Žižek, Slavoj. *The Fragile Absolute or, Why Is the Christian Legacy Worth Fighting For?* London: Verso, 2000.

———. *The Indivisible Remainder: An Essay on Schelling and Related Matters*. London: Verso, 1996.

———. *Tarrying with the Negative: Kant, Hegel, and the Critique of Ideology*. Durham: Duke UP, 1993.

———. *The Ticklish Subject: The Absent Center of Political Ontology*. London: Verso, 1999.

Zupančič, Alenka. *Ethics of the Real: Kant, Lacan*. London: Verso, 2000.

Index

Act: Isabel's, xiii, 2, 25, 122, 141; Milly's
   xiii, 85–86, 95, 141; Kate's, 91; in
   "Altar of the Dead," xiii, 124, 142; in
   Lacan, xi–xiv; passage à l'acte, xi,
   147n1
Adorno, Theodor, 20, 28, 32, 34
Aestheticism, 19, 21, 28, 71–72
Aesthetics: inseparability from ethics, xii,
   xiv; and hysteria, xvi; and ideology,
   xvi, 19–21, 32; and education, 1, 3;
   and vision, 3, 14, 21, 34, 39, 139–41,
   144; reconciliatory, 3–4, 13, 20–23,
   26, 28, 124, 135, 140, 162n43;
Agency, 12, 24
Allegory, 112–13, 117, 143, 163n49
Analogy, 50
Antigone, xv, 97, 100, 156n6
Apotheosis, xv, 62–64, 66, 69, 73–74, 77,
   84–86
Aristotle, 25
Armstrong, Paul, xvii, 15–17, 19
Art, 17, 38, 44, 58, 71, 73, 101, 130, 136

Badiou, Alain, 126–31, 131, 134,
   159n28, 160n36. *See also* Event
Beauty, xiv–xv, 15, 17–19, 34, 71, 79, 81,
   84, 144; beautiful soul, 20; Milly's, 77.
   See also Aesthetics; Kant; Desire
Berkson, Dorothy, 13–14
Bildung, 3, 18–19, 20–21
Bildungsroman, xiii–xiv, 1, 20–23, 27, 32,
   37
Blake, William, 137
Bosanquet, Theodora, 144, 163n50

Bradbury, Nicola, 63
Braudel, Fernand, 60
Brennan, Teresa, 94
Breuer, Josef, 45–47
Bronzino, Agnolo di Cosimo, 53, 62–63
Brooks, Peter, 43–46, 73
Buell, Lawrence, 2
Byron, Lord George Gordon, 144

Cameron, Sharon, 153n29
Cantor, Georg, 119, 157n12, 158n18
Capitalism. *See* Money
Castration, 132, 135, 138–39
Causality, xiv, 11, 24, 30–31
Chaitin, Gilbert, 71
Choice: primordial, xii–xiv, 30–31; of
   neurosis, xiii, xv; forced, xiii, 25–26,
   31, 95; ethical, xv–xvi, 134–35; sexual,
   xv; and freedom, 13–15, 26, 31;
   Isabel's, 18–19, 22, 24–25, 30–31;
   Kate's, 48–49, 95–96; Densher's, 89;
   axiom of, 119, 124
Clemens, Justin, 162n46
Community: ethical, 4, 32–33, 35, 37,
   99, 133
Contingency, 40, 101, 105, 111, 127,
   129–31, 134, 136, 160n35
Copjec, Joan, xvii, 2, 115–16, 121, 129,
   137–38
De Man, Paul, xiv–xv, 12, 19, 21, 38,
   112, 114; on Kant, 139–44
De Quincey, Thomas, 24, 127, 137,
   149n27

De Saussure, Fernand, 36
Death, 62–63, 66, 68, 86, 100–1, 136;
    between two deaths, 97, 123; repres-
    sion of, 100, 105; drive, xii, 97,
    137–40, 142–43
Deconstruction: and ethics, xv–xvi,
    99–145 *passim*; and repetition, xvi,
    131; neurotic structure of, xvi, 141.
    See also Event; Materiality
Demand, 138
Derrida, Jacques, 2, 131, 157n13
Desire: xii, 18, 20–22, 30–31, 33, 45,
    49, 51, 69, 71, 73, 84–86, 89–90,
    96–97, 142–43 155n47; triangular
    structure of, 67, 76; of woman, 66,
    68, 77, 154n41, 160n33, 155n51,
    161n42; and dissatisfaction, 69, 73;
    and prohibition, 69–70, 122; of
    mOther, 76, 96, 137, 156n55,
    160n33; and beauty, 79–80; ceding
    on, 89; support of, 91
Devlin, Keith, 120
Difference: sexual, xii, xv; and language,
    36; right to, 126–27, 133
Drive. *See* Death
Duty, 16, 20, 24, 28–29, 32, 49–51, 96

Emerson, Ralph Waldo, 24
Empty signifier, 35–37
Enjoyment. *See under* Lacan, *jouissance*
Ethics: of desire, xv, 94, 122, 135–36,
    163n49; of the drive, 122, 136; and
    the Symbolic, xii, 135, 141; of psycho-
    analysis, xii–xiii, 2, 136. *See also* Kant;
    Freedom; Impossibility
Event, 102, 125, 128–29, 134; decon-
    structive, 106–7, 109, 112–13, 133;
    psychoanalytic, 114, 130–31

Fantasy: 69, 71, 80, 86; structure of, xi,
    155n47; fundamental, xvi; aesthetic,
    22, 108, 132, 136
Father: primal, 75–77; Symbolic, 76. *See
    also* Lacan
Fetishism, 30
Fichte, Johann Gottlieb, 78, 117

Fink, Bruce, 142, 155–56n55
Foucault, Michel, 2
Freccero, John, 157n7
Freedman, Jonathan, 3–5, 14, 19, 21,
    34
Freedom: transcendental, xiv, 14, 23, 28;
    and determination, xiv–xv, 4, 10–11,
    16, 23, 25–26; and irony, 12; paradox
    of, 16; practical, 20. *See also* Choice;
    Limit
Freud, Sigmund: 45–47, 66, 85–86, 94,
    129, 138; choice of neurosis, xiii, xv;
    Totem and Taboo, xv, 43, 75; *Studies on
    Hysteria*, 46; *Beyond the Pleasure
    Principle*, 137; "On Narcissism,"
    153n28; *Dora*, 155n48; "Leonard Da
    Vinci" 162n45. *See also* Hysteria;
    Repression

Gasché, Rodolphe, xvii, 81, 150n33,
    154–55n45, 159n27, 159–60n29
Girard, René, 67, 153n31
Gödel, Kurt, 120
Good: ethical, 20–22, 33, 124; and evil,
    43, 52, 54

Hallward, Peter, 126
Hegel, G. W. F., 19, 61, 78–79, 99–101,
    106, 133, 136, 156n6, 161n41
Hegemony, 36, 127
Heidegger, Martin, 130
Holland, Laurence, 44–46, 72–73, 75,
    79, 84
Hume, David, 107
Hysteria, xv–xvi, 45–46, 48, 66, 90,
    94–96, 141–42; symptoms of, 45, 71,
    77, 129, 153n27, 154n41, 163n49

Ian, Marcia, 63
Idealism: 4, 12, 22
Identification, 58, 69
Identity, xv, 2, 22–23, 32, 37, 77, 85; and
    difference, 4, 34, 133; essential, 9; and
    metaphor, 19–21, 38; and death, 68;
    sexual, 85; symbolic, 97, 139; politics
    of, 126, 130, 159n29

Ideology: critique of, 2. *See also under* Aesthetics

Imaginary. *See under* Lacan

Imagination, 39–40, 78, 132, 143

Impossibility, xii, 32, 37, 41, 68–70, 114, 125, 128–29, 132, 134, 139–43, 161n42; of sexual relationship, 122, 134, 158n23

Inaccessible Cardinal, 120, 125, 129–30, 132–33, 158n21

Infinity, 107, 112–14, 117–20, 125, 127, 129, 132. *See also* Set theory

Intellectual intuition, 78, 84, 117

Intersubjectivity, 5, 34

Irony, 11–12

Izzo, Donatella, 13

James, Alice, 47, 151n9

James, Henry: *The Ambassadors*, 45, 153n26; *The Portrait of a Lady*, xiii–xiv, 1–41 *passim*, 52, 89, 94, 108, 122, 124, 141; *Wings of the Dove*, xii–xv, 5, 43–97 *passim*, 108, 122–24, 158–59n24; "The Altar of the Dead," xvi, 5, 99–145 *passim*; *The Golden Bowl*, 8; *What Maisie Knew*, 8; "The Beast in the Jungle," 8, 43; "The Turn of the Screw," 8, 43; "The Beldonald Holbein," 151n11

James, William, 5, 45, 110

Jouissance. *See under* Lacan

Judgment: ethical, xv, 33, 38, 100, 141–43. *See also* Kant

Kant, Immanuel: practical freedom, xiv, 28–29; Ideas of Reason, xiv, 5, 17, 28, 34, 39, 82, 116, 119, 143, 158n17; aesthetic judgment, xiv; 2, 33–35, 40, 78, 80–82, 154n43; cognitive judgment, 40, 78, 81, 116; Sensible and supersensible realms, 4–5, 11, 19, 21, 24, 32, 78–79, 84, 122, 140, 161n41; subject, 11, 24, 33; causality, 11, 24; moral law, 23, 28–33, 94, 127; sensus communis, 34; *Critique of Pure Reason*, 80–81, 115, 117, 126; *Critique of*

Practical Reason, 29; *Critique of Judgment*, 116, 141; sublime, 39–40, 119, 132, 142–43; transcendental illusion, 81–82, 109. *See also* Reason; De Man

Kierkegaard, Søren, xiii, 15, 25, 31, 149n28, 149n31

Knowledge: ground of, 10, 12; incompleteness of, 25, 32, 37, 68; unconscious, 69, 73, 85; deconstructive, 107, 109, 112, 114

Krook, Dorothea, 2

Lacan: xi, 86, 89, 97, 113–14, 140, 157n7, 159n29; *Ethics Seminar*, xii, 2, 138, 160n38; *Encore Seminar*, xii, xvi 2, 142, 160n35; on beauty, xv; imaginary, 67, 135, 140; paternal metaphor, 76, 154n40, 155–56n55, 160n33; *jouissance*, 90, 123, 138, 140–41, 161n42, 162n48; "Kant with Sade," 110; master signifier, 112, 129–31, 135, 142; Real xi, xii; xv–xvi, 114, 123, 125, 131–34, 136–45, 159n26, 160n38, 162n46; *tuché*, 114, 142; object (a), 125, 137–39

Laclau, Ernesto, 35–36

Lacoue-Labarthe, Philippe and Jean-Luc Nancy, 18

Law, John, 60

Levinas, Emmanuel, 2, 148n6

Limit: concept of, 35, 37, 84–85, 114–15, 123–24, 136, 160n36; and repression, xvi; necessity for, 80, 100, 107–8, 140; internal and external, 121–22, 131–33, 135, 139–41, 143; as guarantee of freedom, 122, 134. *See also* Representation, Set theory

Love, 48–49, 72, 130; and death, 64; and *jouissance*, 142. *See also* Money

Malraux, André, 144

Marriage: 13–14, 16, 25, 27, 30, 33, 48–49; aesthetic nature of 20, 22–23, 38

Master signifier. *See under* Lacan

Materiality: of language, 106–7, 133,
139–40, 163n48; material reading,
109–13; of vision, 144
Matthiessen, F. O., 46
Metaphor, 4, 7, 19, 21, 27, 33, 38,
54–55, 62, 70, 77, 80, 107, 110–14,
131, 135, 159n29
Metonymy, 38, 77, 95, 100, 107, 110,
113–14, 131, 138, 143, 159n29
Miller, J. Hillis, xvii, 148n6
Mimesis, 7, 11–12, 48, 63, 67
Mitchell, Lee Clark, 63, 153n23
Money; 58, 60, and love, 48–49, 51,
95–96; gold versus paper, 59–61; capi-
talism 59
Moody, A. D., 6
Morality, 17–18, 21, 35, 96
Mortality. See Death
Mourning, 47, 52, 73, 94, 101–2

Necessity, 11–12, 16, 23, 101, 111, 129,
136
Negation, 12, 27–29, 36–37, 76–77, 81,
84, 105, 107, 115, 129
Neruda, Pablo, 144
New Historicism, 99, 157n12
Norris, Christopher, 148n6
Norton, Grace, 1

Object (a). See under Lacan
Odell, David, xvii, 119–20, 124, 133,
158n16, 158n18, 158n19, 158n21

Pater, Walter, 3, 71, 151n11
Paul, Robert, 154.n39
Perversion, 109, 141, 163n49
Phallus, xvi, 123, 129, 141–42, 154n41,
155n48, 156n55, 160n33, 160n35,
161n42
Psychosis, 109, 141

Reason: antinomies of, 115–16, 121, 125,
134, 161n42
Redfield, Marc, 20
Reflection, 5, 7, 12, 52, 56
Reinhard, Kenneth, 63, 94–95

Relativism, 100, 126, 128
Repetition: xvi, 25, 31–32, 56, 75, 94,
109, 113–14; psychoanalytic concept
of, xiii–xiv
Representation: problem of, xv, 5–12, 32,
43, 46; limit of, 43–48, 53–54, 68,
70–71, 73, 77, 79–81, 84, 91, 95,
134, 143
Repression: 45, 71, 138; primary, xiii, 77;
of limit signifier, xvi, 141. See also
Death
Reversibility, 50–51, 62, 78
Revolution: French, 55, 60, 130;
American, 60; Chinese, 130
Rivkin, Julie, 58
Romanticism, 4, 137, 162n46
Rotman, Brian, 61, 152n21
Ruskin, John, 55, 71

Sabiston, Elizabeth, 6
Sacrifice, 21, 27, 33, 44, 49, 53, 72, 75,
85–86, 92, 94–97, 123; Christian, 76
Sade, Marquis de, 110
Santos, Irene Ramalho, 30
Schelling, Friedrich, 78, 117
Schiller, Friedrich, xiv, 17–18, 20–21,
28–29, 32, 126, 137
Schor, Naomi, 35
Self, 9–10, 12, 16, 21, 27, 107, 123
Set theory: 122; consistency of, 120,
158n21; empty set, 61, 118; power
set, 119; infinite sets, 112, 118. See
also Infinity; Inaccessible Cardinal;
Choice
Sexuation: structures of, xvi; formulas of,
122, 125, 135, 141–42, 161n42
Signifier. See under Lacan
Singer, Alan, 12, 150n32
Smith, John H., 10
Soler, Colette, 154n41
Sophocles, xv
St Augustine, 157n7
Subject: ethical, xii, xiv, 28; autonomous,
10; of desire, 56, 66, 70, 86, 143; des-
titution of, 123; of aesthetic judgment,
127; Lacanian, 139

Sublimation, 138, 155n47, 162n46
Superego, 110
Surrealism, 162n43
Swales, Martin, 20
Sympathy, 4, 21, 34
Synecdoche, 6, 21–22, 37–38, 50

Temple, Minny, 46–47
Todorov, Tzvetan, 45
Trauma, 30, 45, 47–48, 64, 95, 133, 140,
    162n48

Unconscious, xiv
Universality, xv, 18, 33–38, 78, 99–100,
    125, 128, 130
Unrepresentable. *See* Representation
Utilitarianism, 22–23

Verhaeghe, Paul, 85, 155n48

Veronese, Paolo Caliari, 72, 74–75, 77
Void, 43, 80, 117, 128, 130, 139

Warminski, Andrzej, xvi, 100, 105–15,
    117, 122, 134, 136, 141, 145
Wharton, Edith, 163n50
Whistler, James McNeill, 71
White, Hayden, 12
Will, 22, 25, 30, 51, 66, 85–86, 88,
    155n49; and voluntarism, 110. *See
    also* Freedom
Wordsworth, William, 137

Zerilli, Linda, 36
Zeugma, 107, 110–14, 117, 122,
    159n29
Zizek, Slavoj, 2, 60, 78–79, 142, 147n2,
    161n41
Zupancic, Alenka, 97, 127, 156n58